A GOLD MEDAL
IS A
WONDERFUL THING

367 DAILY MEDITATIONS OF PHILOSOPHY AND MOTIVATION, INSPIRED BY FILM

Matt Main

First published in 2022 by Compass-Publishing UK
ISBN: 978-1-913713-82-9

Printed and bound in Great Britain by CPI Group (UK) Ltd, Croydon, CR0 4YY

This book is made from Forest Stewardship Council® certified paper.

A CIP catalogue record for this book is available from the British Library

11.04.2024

To dear Helen

Happy reading!

Love   *signature*

To Ivan the Terrible.

CONTENTS

INTRODUCTION
A Little World on the ...

DAYS OF THE YEAR
January
February
March
April
May
June
July
August
September
October
November
December

THEMES, BY MONTH
Trees and Their ...
Time and the ...
Action and Inaction ...

GRATITUDES

Contents

INTRODUCTION 7

A further word on themes: 10

DAYS OF THE YEAR 13

January 15

February 47

March 77

April 108

May 139

June 171

July 202

August 234

September 265

October 295

November 328

December 359

THEMES, FILMS, ACTORS 391

Themes and their dates 392

Films and their dates 398

Actors and their dates 404

GRATITUDES 412

INTRODUCTION

Why do we watch films? Are they mere entertainment, or is there more to them than that? Does a film's influence last only while watching it and end with the credits, or can it reverberate within us long after the tape has stopped, promoting and inspiring change in our real lives?

Life is philosophy and philosophy is life. Inspiration, meaning and enjoyment can be drawn from any source. One could sit under a tree and receive a dose of all three; inspiration from the majesty and resilience of nature, a feeling of purpose in finding balance and harmony with one's surroundings, and enjoyment as one plays a game at guessing what type of bird will be the next to fly overhead.

By the same token, movies are as good a source of philosophy and motivation as anything else. When we look past the pure entertainment factor, films can shape and mould our interpretations of the world and our characters. They can be a tremendous source of inspiration and cause for reflection. Films exhibit the many dimensions and extremes of the human psyche. Because of their high entertainment factor, we may think that their impact is limited to the superficial, but it only takes a moment's thought to realise that films clearly have at least some impact on us, otherwise we wouldn't remember the scenes and the words. The truth is, they can have a big influence on our paradigms.

Films are interactive. They speak to the viewer, and the viewer speaks back. *Gladiator* asks the watcher; What is destiny? What is revenge? How does one face death? The watcher, perhaps unbeknownst to themselves, answers these questions. Because the questions are asked through the medium of the screen, in a non-confrontational manner, it allows the viewer the space to answer them in their own time.

Ultimately, movies are just another mirror, as all things are. Depending on our mood and depending on what is important to us, within movies we can find both outlet for our emotions and stimulation to keep searching. The truly great films are the ones that ask the deepest and most meaningful questions, leaving just enough breadcrumbs to help point us in the right direction.

This book is a celebration of the medium of film and the power it holds as a form of entertainment, art and education. It's aim; to inspire, motivate, ask questions and stimulate thought, reflection and consideration of one's own unique journey. There are 367 film quotes, one for each day of the year, including the leap day, February 29th, of course, plus a cheeky extra January 1st at the end. After each film quote, I have recorded my narrative; a meditation and an interpretation of the preceding quote. You will find some of the meditations are a direct address to the content of the quote, while other meditations are one or two abstract steps along from the literal meaning of the quote.

The film quotes used have been drawn from a range of films across genres and eras. Many of the quotes are my personal favourites, ones that I carry with me, impressed on my mind and always there to help me reflect or help me laugh. Other quotes have been dug up to extract the philosophical nugget contained within. I can say with absolute conviction that the narratives and inferences that I have drawn from each quote are only one of many that could be extracted. The inspiration and source for my interpretations of each quote have come through an exquisite and unique array of life experiences. You will notice that I like to use the words duality and paradox – that is a result of my observance of the seeming contradictory concepts that seem to be inherent to life, and certainly recovery groups. By the second or third use of Chinese Mandarin, you may be curious on the connection – I lived in Beijing for three years and have anecdotes and escapades enough to probably fill a book of its own. I was about to scribe another trend, but… you'll spot it.

As a suggestion, after reading the day's meditation, reread the movie quote and consider your own interpretation, which will, by definition, be as unique and nuanced as you are. Alternatively, why not read the movie quote but before reading my thought on it, first ruminate on your own interpretation, and then at your leisure, read mine. Use colour pens to annotate, mark and scribble your imprints and instincts upon the pages. Make the pages your looking glass.

The conventional way to read the book is to read and ruminate on a page a day for the day that you are in, however, at the back of the book there is an index of themes. At any point that you feel you want a hit of motivation or philosophy on a certain topic, such as love, detachment or self-worth, head to the Themes tab and look up the days that will give you a hint of what you seek. If a theme is not there, well, then you are going to have to be your own author. The answers are all within, anyway.

As well as a themes index, there is also one for films and actors, which makes looking up the soundbites for your favourites that little bit easier.

Best time of the day to read? Any time! That said, it can be enjoyable to read the day's meditation as part of your morning ritual which you can ponder on throughout the day. Even better, why not seek or look out for associated ideas, images and words that will build upon the day's meditation. Share the idea with a colleague or friend. A great incubator for ideas is conversation. Another benefit of early-doors reading is that a few of the meditations have a direct suggestion to carry out, and as sleep has a way of wiping the slate clean, your best chance of accomplishment might be as you arise, fully charged, full of vim and vigour, and ready to embrace a new day of life.

Whichever way you use this book... (even as a doorstop)... will be just perfect.

Remember – the universe loves you. You are enough. Be your authentic self and shine to the world.

With love and unity,

Matt

London, 2022

P.S. A fun challenge: see how many of the quotes you can mimic in the same voice as the original actor.

A further word on themes:

While reading the meditations throughout the year, you will probably notice some recurring motifs. These are some of them, and hopefully you will spot many more besides:

Choice – nothing or nobody can make any of us do, think or say something against our will. Emancipation of the soul starts and ends with that purifying self-knowledge. We literally rise and fall, live and die, of our own volition.

Opposites – every statement or presumption inherently carries with it its equal and opposite partner, e.g., *integrity is the key* – maybe integrity isn't the key at all, hence the use of *or not* and *(?)* dotted throughout the text as a tribute to the concept that even while making a point, I am simultaneously questioning that same point. When I speak of each of us being filled with love and light, because, naturally, we might want to accentuate and grow toward those qualities, don't forget, we each also carry a portion of their opposites. One of the many challenges of life lies in coming to terms with what Jung called the Shadow side.

Infinity – the universe is infinite. Space and time are infinite. This can potentially lend us perspective to everything (or nothing?) And yet as humans, we are very familiar with finiteness. For many, all too sadly, particularly in respect of food, freedom and peace.

God – God is everything, anything or nothing. Beings or powers as described by religion, science, the universe or nature, are just some of the possible ways that you can interpret the word *God* as used in this book. While impossible for me to catalogue every possible coverage of the word, when used, I am aiming at whatever it is that might be said to govern, or in that sense, simply exist, throughout space and time. Naturally, I retain my own nuanced belief of God, but I make no presumptions or attempt to do so for others.

Spirituality – the basic position of this book is that there is more to existence than mere matter, a good example being the body. While the body is surely a biological marvel and organism of immense complexity and functionality, there must be an underlying spirit or soul that animates the body, the same soul that evidences itself in our inherent disposition, tendencies and talents.

Unity – we are one species, one race, and if we can one day see it… truly one team. As an individual, a person can be and achieve whatever they want. But for lasting progress for humanity as a collective, unity and tolerance are indispensable.

Freedom – nobody can ever truly be their best self, fully manifest or fully self-actualise without a full measure of freedom. Freedom is one of the interchangeable units of measurement of glory along with love, light and truth. It is of paramount importance, now more than ever, that each of us remember that we are free. No atom, entity or being anywhere, in all space and time, can grant another their freedom. That is an oxymoron, a contradiction in terms. You are free or enslaved by your own determination.

Questions – question everything and let everything pose a question. Questions are a key tool each one of us possess to navigate our way. Like a submarine sonar pings a sound wave to feel its way, questions are our *ping* to find out more about our environment. This book will seek to help you put a little bit more quest in your questions and the book will ask you some questions. Play with questions. And consider this, what happens when we no longer need any questions?

Answers – people, the internet and our sensory organs will suggest answers to us every moment of our existence, but is it not only the answers within that have any meaning? Can any of us ever be told anything that we didn't already know?

DAYS OF THE YEAR

January 1st
THE OLYMPICS OF THE SOUL

"A gold medal is a wonderful thing. But if you're not enough without it, you'll never be enough with it."

COACH IRV BLITZER – COOL RUNNINGS

What are you chasing? The dream house? A Ferrari? The pin-up boyfriend or girlfriend? Maybe your goals and aspirations centre around a spiritual objective. Becoming *more* zen? Being able to meditate for ten minutes without scratching your nose? Figuring out why 42 is the answer to everything!?!

All worthy goals. Or not. You decide. Point is, you can be content now. You are enough. A wise man likes to share the St Francis of Assisi quote: "what you're looking for is where you're looking from." **You** are the goal, the desired end point, the pinnacle.

Until we realise that we are enough, no gold medals, mansions, Oscars, immaculately manicured social media pages, nirvana at a Tibetan retreat or ayahuasca-fuelled transcendence in the jungle of Peru, n-o-t-h-i-n-g is going to fill the hole in the soul.

Coach Irv, the beautiful John Candy, forgot this elemental truth. He became addicted to the *outward* success, and all that sliding around on the ice numbed his brain and made him forget who he is. He was determined not to let that happen to his four awesome protégés, and by how the film ended, he fulfilled his role perfectly.

By all means, keep striving. Life is enriched by our longing and stretching for worthwhile goals, but just remember, having or not having the perfect home, or any home for that matter, having a huge bank balance or being broke, having the dream hashtag high life or being considered a social media leper, none of those things change who **you** are. Sure, add the finishing touches of achievement and learning and prosperity, but never forget, you are enough.

January 2nd
WAY OF THE SPIRITUAL WARRIOR

"Perfect. They are all perfect."

KATSUMOTO – THE LAST SAMURAI (2003)

The Samurai were a noble caste of Japanese warriors who devoted themselves to the mastery of all that they put their minds and hands to. Perfection was not a mere abstract concept to them, it was the very idea that they lived their days in constant pursuit of. The moral code that the Samurai adhered to, *Bushido* 武士道, literally 'way of the warrior', demanded devotion to 7 virtues;

- » Justice   義
- » Courage   勇
- » Benevolence   仁
- » Respect   礼
- » Honesty   誠
- » Honour   名誉
- » Loyalty   忠義

These are beautiful attributes, and we might all benefit from adopting the Samurai mission statement of self-mastery, but we can't allow it to lure us into believing that perfection is elusive.

The thing about perfection is that it is a high-stakes game. Either nothing is perfect or else everything is perfect. Essentially one is left to choose between absolute pessimism or total optimism. Either no cherry blossom is perfect, or else, they all are.

Next time you see a tree, ask yourself, how would I improve this tree? Is it too tall? Too short? Not enough leaves? Wrong colour bark? What would make it *better*? Try the same experiment on anything. A person, a flower, a painting, a piece of music. You may just discover the same thing that Katsumoto finally did.

January 3rd
LISTEN FOR THE ECHOES

"Brothers! What we do in life... echoes in eternity."

MAXIMUS – GLADIATOR (2000)

For the believers in something after this life, these epic words by Maximus may hold special relevance. With a slight tweak, what would certainly be applicable to *all* of us would be: *what we do in life, echoes in... life!*

Choices have consequences. How often we hear people around us moaning and complaining. He made me do it. It was her fault. I wouldn't have said it if you hadn't made me so angry. You can find almost any excuse to abdicate your duty to the truth if you really want to, but it doesn't negate the fact that you are 100% responsible for your life. In the book *As A Man Thinketh*, James Allen writes, 'Men imagine that thought can be kept secret, but it cannot.' We have to claim ownership of our thoughts and actions. Only when we do will we rise to the level of freedom and contentment that is the birth-right of every human being.

Nelson Mandela walked out of captivity in 1990 after 27 years, 27 ripe years in which he would have been in his pomp – inspirationally, physically, politically – with forgiveness for his captors, "As I walked out the door toward the gate that would lead to my freedom, I knew if I didn't leave my bitterness and hatred behind, I'd still be in prison." He knew, as we must come to know, that responsibility for one's own life rests squarely and solely with self.

January 4th

THE CHOICE IS YOURS

"I guess it comes down to a simple choice, really. Get busy living, or get busy dying."

ANDY DUFRESNE – THE SHAWSHANK REDEMPTION

The next time you're feeling down, 'boohoo, my life sucks… I'm so sad… I don't want to live…,' close your mouth and pinch your nose. You'll quickly realise that your body (and soul) very much *do* want to live!

This clever observation has at least two layers of meaning. On the surface, it shows that the body will always fight for self-preservation. On a deeper level, it highlights that the dysfunction that we virtually all suffer from at different times is not physical or spiritual ailments but defective thinking.

In the film, Brooks and Red both faced a very similar crossroad, but only one chose to get busy living. If we've been in the doldrums, getting back to busy living can grow out of the simplest idea: seeing as I'm still here, I may as well give this game of life my best shot.

January 5th
A TOAST TO LIFE

"Health and friendship!"
"Life and love!"

BRIAN & DOUG – COCKTAIL (1988)

Pretty much sums it all up, doesn't it?

Make a list of things you have in your life that fall under these four categories for which you are grateful. Share it with people.

Let's not allow the scrolls of our heart to go unread by those nearest and dearest to us. Open up and feel the joy of expressing your love and appreciation to the relationships in your life. They say gratitude unspoken is like a gift bought and wrapped but not given. Give the gift. And then get back to showing it by your actions.

January 6th
DECISIONS, DECISIONS, DECISIONS...

"Do. Or do not. There is no try."

YODA – STAR WARS: EPISODE V – THE EMPIRE STRIKES BACK

Sometimes we bounce between two extremes; at one, the misguided belief that we have the ability to order the heavens, and at the other, the lack of confidence to orchestrate even our own life through decisions. The middle ground is contained within Yoda's simple message. Decide and do (or don't do.)

A practical example in which most of us are strong is a journey. Nobody says, "I'm taking the train from London to Edinburgh, but, you know, we'll see if we actually make it. We might have to rethink it at York. Who knows what could happen." That would be absurd. We plan the train journey, get on the train and allow it to take us. We may or not run in to an engine failure, fallen tree on the track or some other disruption, but we don't invent one and we don't allow it to deter us from the trip. And yet how often we do this exact thing in other areas of life.

The legendary teacher, Bob Proctor, argues that one reason for many people not living their best life is that they don't make decisions;

> *"You say you want the dream house, but you haven't made a decision to buy it!" he cries.*
> *"But I don't have the money," you say.*
> *"Why would you need the money(?!), you haven't made the decision!"*

Waiting for the right environment to make the decision is like expecting the weights to lift your arms... it's the wrong way round.

Have faith, have commitment, and follow through on what you say you're going to do or not do. Be decisive. By living this way, you create a strong self-image of action or deliberate non-action (both are fine), not one of I kinda-maybe-perhaps-would-sorta-like-to, if, you know, the conditions are right...

Look at areas where you're waiting and expecting others to do something for you that you can do for yourself. You have the ability to make decisions and work towards their accomplishment. It starts and ends with a decision.

January 7th

THE TWO POWERS

"What are we holding on to, Sam?"
"That there's some good in this world, Mr Frodo. And it's
worth fighting for."

FRODO & SAM – THE LORD OF THE RINGS: THE TWO TOWERS

How many doors on your street are white? How many cars are red? You probably don't have the foggiest idea because it's of no relevance to you. You aren't looking for them.

Goodness and humanity don't always have the most harmonious of relationships, any history book will remind one of that. Nevertheless, goodness does exist, and it is all around you.

Go out and look for nature thriving. Even in busy city centres there is always a tree or shrub never too far away. Look for the man playing enthusiastically with his children. Observe the old couple still madly in love, whose long years together have only crystallised and distilled the sweet affection of the younger days. Notice the people who do hold the door, do say thank you, do let other cars out when in gridlock. Goodness and kindness are everywhere. You don't need rose-tinted specs to see it, you just need to be willing.

You don't attract what you *want*, you attract what you *are*.

You don't see things as *they* are, you see them as *you* are.

January 8th
MY 'ME'

"Remember who you are."

MUSTAFA – THE LION KING (1994)

In a hyper-connected, high-octane, media-obsessed world, remembering one's true identity can be harder than ever. These days it seems every millennial wants to be an eco-warrior, influencer, pop-star, billionaire, pro athlete... and all hippy and zen to boot. It's not an easy balancing act.

Remember who you are, are soft but piercing words to all of us. Only you can define who you really are, and only you can really be you.

Ponder if you are living true to your own ideals, and the genuine dreams and wishes of your heart.

Walking your own path will be lonely at times, but the satisfaction is beautiful. Plus, every time you show others the true originality of your thinking, doing and being, your 'me', you automatically give others the inspiration to exhibit their authentic me.

January 9th
RIPPLES IN THE POND

"Good thoughts. Good words. Good deeds."

FREDDIE MERCURY – BOHEMIAN RHAPSODY

Freddie lived an incredible experience, jammed full of life. And yet throughout the indulgences, the glory and the madness, he never forgot the grounding principles that had been lovingly handed down from his parents.

We sometimes feel like our care or concern for somebody is not showing through. Countless parents believe that the lessons of tolerance, honesty or kindness that they've taught by word, and more importantly, example, to their offspring, didn't get through.

They did.

What we are and what we do shouts so loud that it's unmistakeable. We are always being an example to any person in our lives. Indeed, it's often at the precise moments we think we're having the least impact on others that we're actually having the most. So keep being kind, honest and brave. That flame is being seen and felt, and others are looking to you to light their torch.

January 10th
THE GLASS IS FULL

"Every man dies. Not every man truly lives."

WILLIAM WALLACE – BRAVEHEART (1995)

They say that on our death beds it's not the things we did do that haunt us, it's the things we didn't do. The words unuttered, the dreams never investigated, the love never expressed, the adventures we didn't race, chase and embrace.

Many people who have experienced near death experiences speak of being 'born again', 'awakened to a new sense of life' and other similar, fundamental attitude shifts following their almost-departure from the realm of the living. Easy for them, huh! Question is, for the vast majority of us who won't experience such a powerfully persuasive event, how do we learn to grasp the preciousness of life?

The paradigm shift necessary for many of us to really awaken to the full wonder of life isn't huge, it's just a 2mm nudge. What we're changing is the false sense of permanency and 'there'll always be a tomorrow-ness' that most of us have. That's because we're living in projection, not in the only place that there is and the only place that matters – the here and now.

Life is short (or is it long?) We're gone today and here tomorrow. Let's discover for ourselves what it means to truly live.

January 11th
THE GENIUS OF LOVE

"I've always believed in numbers and the equations and logics that lead to reason. ... And I have made the most important discovery of my career, the most important discovery of my life: It is only in the mysterious equations of love that any logic or reasons can be found."

JOHN NASH – A BEAUTIFUL MIND

Love is the question and the answer, the cause and the effect, the motivation and the destination, the means and the end.

Without it, all would be pointless.

Without it, we wouldn't be.

When you allow it, as Climie Fisher sang, love changes everything.

January 12th
FIND YOURSELF

"Wilso-o-o-o-o-o-o-o-o-n!!"

CHUCK NOLAND – CAST AWAY

At times in life, we may feel so inwardly detached and isolated from the world that we may as well be physically stranded on a tropical island. (No problems at all if you are hugging a volleyball while reading this! ☺)

Feeling such a way is perfectly fine and normal. The ebb and flow of life dictates that at times the waves seemingly pull us away from others and more in to ourselves. During other periods, we are pushed toward our fellow travellers and we enjoy the full spectrum of human relationship.

Solitude and isolation are not the same thing, although they may be hard to distinguish. Feeling isolated will lead to disempowerment and loss of hope. Solitude, however, is both necessary and invigorating. Albert Camus writes in *The Minotaur*; 'In order to understand the world, one has to turn away from it on occasion.' This is but to say, that at times, to get the bigger picture and know our part in it, we need to take a step back and disconnect, momentarily, to gain perspective.

Today, take a little time to yourself to reflect and contemplate on your life. Moving forward, try regularly to tap in to the energy, wisdom and creativity that lie within the still waters of the soul.

January 13th

AD ASTRA

"To infinity, and beyond!"

BUZZ LIGHTYEAR – TOY STORY

Well said, Buzz. Our shared motto for life.

All thoughts require the same amount of energy input. Calculating about building a next-generation rocket to take mankind further out in to the cosmos and wondering what one will have for dinner use up the same measure of thought material. Considering how one can help or serve another person and plotting to do harm to another, likewise, use up equal amounts of thought. What differs is the output. This should be self-evident through simple, personal investigation.

Give it a try. Spend a moment now thinking of something you dislike. Then take a moment thinking of a beautiful dream you've always had. Which one feels better? Which one leaves you excited, renewed and energised? Was it *harder* to think the pleasant thought?

So why would we ever spend even a second consciously choosing to focus on something negative? The answer is simple – we wouldn't. We entertain negative thinking because it's a lazy, learned pattern. A paradigm. We can change that paradigm.

Today, let's consciously choose our thoughts. As we learn to harness our minds to serve us, not vice versa, we will see our own lives blossom before our very eyes. We will go to infinity… and beyond.

January 14th
THE ONLY THING IS LOVE

"Each one of us here today will at one time in our lives look upon a loved one who is in need and ask the same question: We are willing to help, Lord, but what, if anything, is needed? For it is true we can seldom help those closest to us. Either we don't know what part of ourselves to give, or, more often than not, the part we have to give is not wanted. And so it is those we live with and should know who elude us. But we can still love them - we can love completely without complete understanding."

PASTOR NORMAN MACLEAN – A RIVER RUNS THROUGH IT

As the all-time favourite film quote of the author's mother, these deep words of pathos hold a special place.

In *The 7 Habits of Highly Effective People*, Stephen R. Covey speaks of the concept; *seek first to understand, then to be understood.* He relates a transformative personal experience of being on the subway in New York. A passenger's children were running amok, irritating him and fellow passengers. After a while, he asked the man if he could get a hold of his kids. The man came out of the trance he was in. He apologised. They had just come from the hospital where the children's mother had passed away. In an instance, Stephen's understanding of the true nature of things changed. It brought an immediate flood of compassion toward the man and his children. Words came. *Can you tell me about it? What can I do to help?'*

It transformed 'a man and his kids are driving me nuts' to 'a family has just suffered a deep loss. How can I be of service to a fellow human, if they desire it?'

But what if we don't understand the reason for certain behaviour? (Much of the time we won't.) Then we apply the beautiful words of the Pastor.

January 15th
THE UNIVERSE LOVES YOU

"If God does not love you, how could you have done the things you have done?"

NASIR – KINGDOM OF HEAVEN

Once upon a time there was a man making a long drive through Spain. It was late. Weary and fatigued, the man stopped at a petrol station to refuel the car and rest awhile. Picking up the petrol hose, he tried to fill the car. Nothing came out. He squeezed again. Nothing. Yet harder he squeezed. Why's nothing coming out?!

From the garage a worker beckoned him over. The man needed to put his card on deposit before he could use the fuel. He returned to the pump and lifted the same hose… oh, wait… he had been trying to fill the car with the wrong fuel! Astonished and looking to the heavens, the man said a prayer of gratitude to the Gods for their benevolence. They could have let the man use the wrong fuel, damage the car and possibly end up stranded for a little while. Nothing tragic. But they decided to help the man in spite of himself, and in the process the man's faith that the universe loves him deepened further.

Look back over your life. You've come through so much. Only you know exactly what you've been through. And that life journey that has brought you to this beautiful day has been your teacher and sculptor. Just as a master carpenter chips, saws and sands away at a magnificent, ornate table, so our lives are refined in the fires of pain and setback. And through everything, here we are.

The universe loves you. It wants you to be well. It is your biggest fan.

January 16th
EUREKA!

"Lightning's just struck my brain!"

SMEE – HOOK

When was the last time you had a Eureka! moment? If we're living in such a way that we allow our Muse to guide us, then we should be getting them frequently.

In Greek mythology, the Muses were nine goddesses that ruled over humanity's inspiration in literary, artistic and scientific expression. Daughters of Zeus and Mnemosyne, they were the creative power behind the pomp and glory of all ancient Greece's accomplishments.

Doctor Robert LeFever, a London-based psychologist and trauma-recovery specialist, has a three-fold personal mission statement, the third of which is of particular interest:

» Live with peace *despite* unresolved problems
» Cultivate mutually loving and beneficial relationships
» *Employ and enjoy spontaneity, creativity and enthusiasm*

As each and every snowflake is completely unique, so each of us have a unique talent to give to the world. We each have our own Muse, and as soon as we're willing, she will assist us in bringing our talents to the surface. Be it football, pencil, calculator, scissors, needle, hands, plectrum, trowel, mic, banner... whatever our tools are, let's use them and add our bit to the bubbling cauldron of creativity.

January 17th
PLAY WITH LIFE

"Let me tell you something you already know. The world ain't all sunshine and rainbows."

ROCKY – ROCKY BALBOA

What are you worth?

The universe knows you're priceless. But it doesn't matter what it thinks. What matters is what you think.

Work with life, not against it. Like the swing of a golf club or the riding of a wave, the secret is to work with the flow, harness it. As any newbie quickly learns on the driving range, trying to force the swing or dominate it usually results in a broken club. With an attitude of self-pity, resentment and antagonism, life will break us. With an attitude of gratitude, positivity and commitment to the good, it will elevate us to supreme joys. Play with life and make it your friend.

As Napoleon Hill wrote in *About Life*;

Life, you can't subdue me because I refuse to take your discipline too seriously. When you try to hurt me, I laugh – and the laughter knows no pain. I appreciate your joys wherever I find them.

Stake your claim on life. It will willingly oblige your every whim and desire. Set your standards, set your goals, and ride those waves.

January 18th
CRAZY GRATITUDE

"Isn't it wonderful!? I'm going to jail!"

GEORGE BAILEY – IT'S A WONDERFUL LIFE (1946)

What does it take to be positive in the face of difficulty, grateful in the face of loss, committed in the face of fear?

George found the answer.

Reminiscent, or rather, a precursor, of Alec Baldwin's character, Parker, in *Friends*, who was also ridiculously upbeat, George was blessed to gain a new perspective on life and what it means to be truly successful. From such a viewpoint, even jail can become an adventure.

To die would be an awfully big adventure!
To live would be an awfully big adventure!

PETER PAN

This is the attitude we can adopt. We're alive. That's enough. Our lives, like life in general, is one continual loop. Tide and season, growing and dying, ascending and falling. As the sun rises in Tokyo, it settles in New York. As one person is losing, another is finding. While some are welcoming a precious new soul in to the world, others are saying their goodbyes to another. This is life.

January 19th
ZIP IT

"Never rat on your friends, and always keep your mouth shut."

Jimmy Conway – Goodfellas

Gangster films can be tough, gritty and hard to digest at times. They can also be enthralling and extremely insightful. Robert De Niro's words of wisdom to the young Christopher Serrone may not have been the most eloquent in cinema history, but they do contain the kernel of two sound ideas:

» Be loyal to your friends
» Be circumspect in your words

Being loyal to the people we care about, of necessity, will call for sacrifice at times. Loyalty is the quality of knowing that at times in life the needs of someone close temporarily supersede one's personal needs. Without loyalty, we would all be units of one, drifting apart like flotsam and jetsam from the Titanic.

As for keeping schtum…

January 20th
NO FEAR

"I thought grown-ups weren't afraid of anything?"
"Quite the contrary. All grown-ups get scared, just like children."

MATILDA & MISS HONEY – MATILDA

The difference between childhood and adulthood is simply that in the latter,* we pretend we know what is going on.

In the self-help cult classic, *Feel The Fear And Do It Anyway,* Susan Jeffers talks about the gnawing fear that sits behind all of us, whispering away in our ears that we'll never succeed, never match up, never be good enough. This nameless fear causes us to shrink from the opportunities of life, but loathe ourselves the more for doing so. She outlines beautifully the antidote to these fears, which are summarised neatly in her title.

Some of our fears are natural, instinctive and healthy. Fear of getting run over by a bus keeps one's wits about them as they cross a road. But fear of failure keeps one from attempting to cross the highways of life. We forget that failure is not the opposite of success, failure is a part of success.

Today, consider honestly your fears. Do one thing that scares you. That could be smiling at a stranger, going to the cinema alone, asking your boss for a pay rise. Don't think, just do. You'll be rewarded with a little hit of serotonin (healthy buzz) and the inner glow of knowing you have courage (the act of doing something positive in the face of fear.) The more you put yourself out of your comfort zone, the more it becomes a habit. A good one. And we love good habits.

*The author does not make this claim!

January 21st
ABORT MISSION?

"Houston, we have a problem."

JIM LOVELL – APOLLO 13

As any business owner will vouch for, running a company is simply the art of solving problems. Your supplier has an issue, the printer breaks down, your website gets hacked, your star salesman leaves to join a competitor… to be a business leader means to be a problem-solver.

Life is no different. At times, you do get moments of tranquillity. All is well. Everybody loves you. Every day is a holiday and every night a honeymoon. But for much of life, it's more like a game of *Pac-Man*. The dots are the problems, the ghosts are the consequences of not dealing with those problems, and *Pac-Man* is you!

Staying still = entropy = problems catching up. The ghosts just keep coming, biting away, relentlessly. There's simply no choice but to keep one step ahead of the game. The way to do that is to *play* the game. Enjoy it. Use an attitude shift to change the dots from problems in to opportunities. Learning experiences. Growth accelerators. Printer broken? Let's go paperless! Website hacked? Let's develop the most secure system on the market! Star player has left? Let's learn to rely more on the team than on any individual. There is always an opportunity, and a solution.

Alternatively, you can continue to see them as problems and avoid them. If so, you better abort mission now.

January 22nd
WE SALUTE YOU

"Oh captain, my captain!"

JOHN KEATING – DEAD POET'S SOCIETY

Written in 1865 to honour the assassinated president, Abraham Lincoln, Walt Whitman mourned his fallen leader with this beautiful call. The sublime Robin Williams brought the words to life as he set the hearts and minds of his young charges free.

The film was art reflecting life, for Williams himself was a comet against the night sky. Roaring with heat and light, he scorched a trail that drew attention and wonder from all onlookers.

We too, heed the call. And who are our captains? Those who lift our spirits. Those who elevate us. The humble heroes all around us. Those in whom we see the better part of our humanity reflected.

You can be that captain to someone else. You *are* that captain to yourself.

January 23rd
BALANCE IS BEAUTIFUL

"I feel the need... the need for speed."

MAVERICK – TOP GUN

Speed fulfils our thirst for adventure. It makes us feel alive. If sitting peacefully under a tree meditating is food for the soul, then being rocketed along at tremendous velocity is the body equivalent. Theme parks, sports cars and sky diving are all highly popular for this reason. The sensory overload as one's mortal frame is pushed to limits of physical endurance can become highly addictive.

With the wave of mindfulness and spiritual seeking that is taking place across the world, we can sometimes swing from one extreme to the other. While some are only focused on physical and material benefits, others do a complete 180 degrees, renounce the outer and only care about the inner world.

The Chinese call this 物极必反 (wu ji bi fan) – anything done to extremes turns on itself, or, extremes touch. Take chocolate cake. A modest slice is delightful. A big slice is lovely but you feel it. A massive wedge turns a tad sickly and you kind of know you've overdone it. And when you scoff the whole thing, well, it's more like self-imposed torture than pleasure (think the Trunchbull and Bruce Bogtrotter.) When we let our passions and indulgences run to extremes, they can easily flip on themselves. Pleasure becomes pain and pain becomes pleasure.

This points us toward balance. Balance is the rare art of living in moderation. Doing it across a range of life activities? That takes poise and conscious effort. Work, study, family, friends, exercise, eating and wellness, hobbies, community, spirituality, religion. How many of us can say, I spend a little bit of quality time and attention across all the main areas of human concern?

Balance, as Bruce Almighty would say, is B – E – A – UUUUUTIFUL!!

January 24th
MIND THE MIND

"This is my house, and I have to defend it!"

KEVIN MCALLISTER – HOME ALONE

We live in a surveillance state. There are CCTV cameras everywhere monitoring our every movement. Our homes are alarmed. So are our cars, shops and banks. Our mobile phones and computers don't just require passwords anymore but biometric scans of body parts. Messaging platforms secure our conversations via military-grade cryptography.

We might ask ourselves, we spend all this time focusing massively on the protection of our material stuff, but what about the non-material?

Our minds and hearts contain priceless riches and treasures, far more of value than those held in our devices and bank vaults. The essence of who we are, the values, the hopes, the dreams, the commitment to being the best version of ourselves. Deep within our souls lie all of these. So while we devote time and attention to our physical property, let us spend at least as much time, if not more, on guarding the best of our essence. Let us defend against anything that would seek to deplete our spiritual and mental riches.

January 25th
MASTER?... OR SLAVE?

"The things you own end up owning you."

TYLER DURDEN – FIGHT CLUB

Everything we buy, everything we have, comes at a cost. It's deep and yet ever so simple. In the documentary, *The Minimalists*, the people of that movement declare that as they relinquish their grip on all the trimmings and trappings of modern life (that most of us cling to so dearly), a great freedom comes in its place. Tyler also expressed this principle;

> *It's only after we have lost everything that we are free to do anything.*

The great paradox of our times is that we want to have all the material gains and accomplishments... and yet we want to have the same freedom that *only* comes through complete detachment to material having and longing. And with each passing day that collective cognitive dissonance only grows.

Eventually, something will have to give.

January 26th
SORRY OLD CHAP

"We have a saying in Tibet: If a problem can be solved there is no use worrying about it. If it can't be solved, worrying will do no good."

DALAI LAMA – SEVEN YEARS IN TIBET

A paradigm is a mental operating programme. It is the automatic guidance code stored deep in our brain that directs the vast majority of our daily actions and behaviour.

A good example is a particularly peculiar paradigm that British people have. Which is that when a person has been inconvenienced they feel the need to say sorry to the other party (logic would suggest that if anyone ought say sorry it should be the person doing the inconveniencing.) It makes visitors to the UK laugh and scratch their heads in equal measure. But why this odd cultural phenomenon? Simple. It's a collective paradigm. The Brits' concept of what constitutes 'good manners' or how one should act, at one point went so far that it became the norm to say sorry for everything, even when one is on the wrong end of a minor kerfuffle. And once an idea becomes set in the mind, it transmutes to the sub-conscious and thus evolves to a fully formed paradigm.

The great news is paradigms can be added or replaced. We can learn to release the paradigm that instructs us to be fearful and anxious. We can state: "Today, I accept everything that is and happens, exactly as it is. I am calm. I am at peace. I am consciously choosing to think and act in a way that brings the best energy and seeks to inject a positive and proactive approach to situations."

Nothing you do is beyond the scope of bringing conscious observance to it and upgrading or replacing it at your leisure.

January 27th
WHAT'S YOUR TUNE?

"No-one play Chopin like you."
"I hope that's a compliment."

DOROTA AND WLADYSLAW – THE PIANIST (2002)

All concert pianists can play a beautiful piece of music with a high degree of technical artistry, but each also has their own unique signature. Some play methodically, others flow. Some are frantic, while others are supremely composed. Like the guys in *Cool Runnings* discovered, we've each got our own style and being true to it is very cool. Imitation is the sincerest form of flattery. The sincerest form of honesty? That is being oneself.

When we love what we do, we automatically become artists. The passion oozes out of us and our actions become unique because we're not performing a perfunctory routine, we're unleashing our visions and dreams. We're speaking not with our mouths or even our bodies, but with our souls.

Ponder the times you're at your happiest and most fulfilled. Being with family, being in nature, learning something new... Does creating feature in there?

You have something to give to the world. If you haven't already, reveal it. Start sharing it. And keep developing it. Your devotion to and commitment to expressing your talent is a sacred privilege. Honour it.

January 28th
BREAK THE RULES

"I'm not going to live by their rules anymore."

PHIL CONNORS – GROUNDHOG DAY

Relax. You're not about to read a suggestion to hotwire a car or rob a bank! That being said, it is something very serious to consider: Whose rules do you play by?

Your parents? The government's? Your peers? Society's?

The minute we're born we're handed down an instruction manual of how to *act*, the word 'act' being used very specifically and deliberately here (interestingly, the word act in Chinese is 表演 biao yan – literally meaning *surface performance*.) As though life is a furniture flat-pack, we're told; Just follow the funny stick man, don't lose any of those pesky little screws, and you should be OK.

Some of the framework of societal conditioning has its use. But much of it comes at the cost of individuality and self-expression. Millions of children are stifled and stigmatised because they don't fit neatly in to rigid boxes of what a 'good', 'intelligent', 'well-behaved' child looks like.

In such a society, becoming one's true, authentic self is not easy. Simple, yes. Easy, no. It takes courage.

You possess that courage.

January 29th
ACCEPT HELP

"Help is on the way, Dear!"

MRS DOUBTFIRE – MRS DOUBTFIRE

One powerful element of film dialogue that often gets ignored in favour of what is said, where it is said and how it is said, is the accent in which it is said. Anybody who read the quote above and didn't hear a soft, elderly Scottish lilt needs to go back and watch it again (to be fair, this line was fairly bellowed!)

Now, regarding help. We all need it. What, even the person who is intelligent, strong, gorgeous... truly invincible... even them?!

Yes, even them. Maybe especially them.

You see, we all require help. None of us are so far removed from the bonds of humanity that we stand aloft and aloof, self-sustained and totally independent. We all need each other. It is our interdependence that makes us so strong. Asking for help does not make one weak. Quite the contrary. It indicates strength and intelligence, as does the ability to receive help graciously. Two of the most beautiful sentences that can be uttered are:

Please help me.
Thank you for helping me.

Do things for yourself. Stretch yourself and develop your own capacities. But be brave enough to ask for help, too, when needed. When you do, the universe will come rushing over. Who knows, it might even be wearing a wig and speaking in a lovely brogue.

January 30th
BEGINNING TO UNDERSTAND

"Sometimes that is the way you have to do it: you go right back to the beginning."

1900 – THE LEGEND OF 1900

A young upstart asks, where should I start? and an old character makes the pithy response; 'at the beginning.' The wisdom in this is beguilingly simple. Oftentimes we've invested so much that to start again seems like a fate worse than death. Kind of like when you're on 98 playing *Snakes & Ladders* and you roll a 1 to hit the snake's head which takes you back down to 13. Tears and tantrums usually follow.

Just like a good story has to start at the beginning to make any sense (that said, directors do seem to be partial to the regressive storyline model these days,) we forget that the achievement of goals and aspirations has to start somewhere. We may roll our eyes when a wise old owl trots out 'Rome wasn't built in a day,' but just like proper tomato sauce and mozzarella are a must for authentic pizza, patience and persistence are two essential ingredients in any meaningful success. Have intensity and passion as you work toward goals, and balance it with a sure commitment that will ride the inevitable storms.

January 31st
THE PEARL IN GOODBYE

"I suppose in the end, the whole of life becomes an act of letting go, but what always hurts the most is not taking a moment to say goodbye."

PI PATEL – THE LIFE OF PI

Why do we struggle so much to let go of things? Is it because we're identifying the value and meaning of our being through people, places and things? Could it be fear of change? The problem with that, of course, is that everything changes. Change is a universal constant. It is law. The only thing that doesn't change is change.

The strangest part is, few things feel as good as letting go of something. Intuitively we know that most things must be let go of. We know that clinging to them in a death grip helps neither them nor us. To climb a ladder, you move toward and then grip each rung. But to keep moving you must release each rung.

If we can learn to embrace goodbyes then we may find that each one leaves us with a small lustrous pearl in our hand, another to be added to the adornment that is our life journey and the remnant of the places and faces we have welcomed and then let go of. And through all the wonderful goodbyes, we will find our hellos that never fade.

February 1st
ALL ROADS LEAD TO BEING

"For what it's worth: it's never too late or, in my case, too early to be whoever you want to be. There's no time limit, stop whenever you want. You can change or stay the same, there are no rules to this thing. We can make the best or the worst of it. I hope you make the best of it. And I hope you see things that startle you. I hope you feel things you never felt before. I hope you meet people with a different point of view. I hope you live a life you're proud of. If you find that you're not, I hope you have the courage to start all over again."

BENJAMIN BUTTON – THE CURIOUS CASE OF BENJAMIN BUTTON

If we can feel this message, we're close to being on to something.

Change or remain. Getter better or get sicker. Grow up or grow down. Be who you want to be, or keep living in fear. The choice is yours. The power lies within.

Perhaps what Benjamin was really trying to teach us was, ultimately, on the grand cosmic level, none of our choices really matter. We are all merely particles of energy floating through space and time. And yet, they completely matter!

Seeing as we're on this planet, here and now, and we think we understand the difference between love and hate, courage and fear, rising up and shrinking down, and if it's all the same anyway, why not choose the things that make us smile?

February 2nd
IGNORANCE IS BLISS

*"You know nothing. In fact, you know less than nothing!
If you even knew that you knew nothing, that would be
something, but you don't."*

BEN HARP – POINT BREAK (1991)

Neil deGrasse Tyson, the astrophysicist, likes to share a teaching aid whereby he draws a circle. The space inside the circle, he instructs, represents the knowledge a person has. The perimeter of the circle represents the border of what the person doesn't know. It is the place where what one knows meets what one doesn't know, and as it were, that person might be said to know that they don't know. And then everything outside of the circle is the unknown unknown.

The neat visual thought experiment is fully brought to life by him drawing another, larger circle. This circle, he elucidates, is the same person with more knowledge, hence the bigger circle. But wait. What has happened to the circumference of the circle that represents what they know they don't know? That, too, has expanded...

The truly wise person, despite, or perhaps because of, their stratospheric IQ, understands that what humanity knows in comparison to the immensity of infinite space and time is so small as to there being no suitable analogy one could make. Night and day, poles apart, are utterly futile attempts to illustrate the ratio between what mankind knows relative to the total of all that is.

The nearest star outside of our own solar system, Proxima Centauri, is one of innumerable stars in existence throughout the universe. Travelling aboard an ion propulsion rocket at a speed of 60,000 kilometres an hour, it would take humans....

.... over 70,000 years to get there. You didn't misread that. That is how long it would take to get to our **nearest** star of all the uncountable stars out there. Even if we could travel at 6 *million* kilometres per hour, it would still take ten lifetimes.

Science, maths and astronomy are wonderful. We've come so far. But let's put our knowledge into a little bit of perspective.

February 3rd
IS IT WORTH IT?

"Everything has a price. The great struggle in life is coming to grips with what that price is."

J PAUL GETTY – ALL THE MONEY IN THE WORLD

A phrase that seems to have lost its popularity in the 21st century is 'to know the price of everything and the value of nothing.' Which is a shame(?), because it has great depth. Truly, everything has a price. But living a life based only on weighing and measuring the price of things would be catastrophic, for man is not an accountant but an artist, and artists work not in pounds and pence but dreams and ideals.

We all know that we can't pay our rent or purchase a coffee using love, goodwill or a cheeky smile (not always true!) The structure of the world requires that we play the real-life game of Monopoly, hustling and bartering our way around the board in the hope of increasingly more salubrious surroundings. And yet, who among us doesn't rejoice in the raw gems of existence; sunshine on the skin, the sound of lapping waves on the shore, a warm hug, a hilarious joke. We seek refinement externally, forgetting that we already sit atop a velvet cushion that is called *being*.

February 4th
AN OCEAN OF REASONS TO BE THANKFUL

"I mean, I got everything I need right here with me. I got air in my lungs, a few blank sheets of paper. I mean, I love waking up in the morning not knowing what's gonna happen or, who I'm gonna meet, where I'm gonna wind up. Just the other night I was sleeping under a bridge and now here I am on the grandest ship in the world having champagne with you fine people."

JACK – TITANIC

How does one return to the wide-eyed exuberance of youth, where every little thing is a source of wonder and excitement?

If you're reading or listening to this, it means you have sight and/or hearing. Think about that a moment and give thanks.

If you're reading or listening to this, it means you have some desire to seek positivity, learning or connection outside of yourself. What a blessed attitude to have. Celebrate yourself.

If you're reading or listening to this, you've shown the ability to make choices. Rejoice in that inalienable right.

If you're reading or listening to this, it means you're breathing, which means you're alive, which means you are enjoying the greatest gift there is. Give thanks.

February 5th
KEEP DIGGING

"If you want to be a good archaeologist, you gotta get out of the library!"

INDIANA – INDIANA JONES AND THE KINGDOM OF THE CRYSTAL SKULL

Philosophy, like sport, rollercoasters and romance, are not pursuits to be theorised or debated over – they are to be *lived*!

At times, we may feel like a spectator, doomed to watch from the sidelines while others squeeze all the juice out of life. Being preoccupied with others' lives is a sure-fire way to sweaty palms and a dry throat. There is only one way to quench that thirst... and that is to get out of the library and make our own pursuits.

The urge to get up and get out starts and ends with one question. The question never loses its potency, never gets old;

What do I want?

Romance doesn't happen on dating apps... it happens out there with butterflies and wobbly legs to go for it.

Finds don't happen in history books... they happen out there in the field, in the desert, under the metal detector.

Dreams don't materialise in your bed... they happen out there in the stretching and striving.

We love libraries and we love books. And a good book and a good library should imbue us with the burning desire to live more richly.

February 6th
ONE MAN'S JUNK...

"Not all treasure is silver and gold, mate."

Jack Sparrow – Pirates of the Caribbean: The Curse of the
Black Pearl

On all the great treasure maps, X marks the spot of the buried goodies. It's a lot of fun seeking something we have our heart set on. The thrill of the chase makes us feel alive. Without knowing it, we superimpose the X on all kinds of places and things. Some foster the healthy pursuit of worthwhile goals, such as the desire to learn a new language, conquer a fear or start a new business. Other Xs are less healthy (and near impossible to obtain), like putting all our energy in to something we have little or no control over, such as a football team or love interest.

Grab a piece of paper and draw a big 'X' on it. Fold it up and put it in your pocket. You have found your treasure… it is you! Everything you've ever desired is inside yourself.

When we realise that we're enough, it changes everything. We may still want to go after outward pursuits, but it has become a no-lose game. We know that nothing exterior can ever define us. We're already enough. And with such an attitude, everything else becomes a bonus.

February 7th
TICK TOCK

"Time is a precious thing. Never waste it."

WILLY WONKA – WILLY WONKA AND THE CHOCOLATE FACTORY (1971)

Wise words from the confectionery king. However, often we need to lose a thing before we understand its value. The beauty of time is its duality. It is tangible and intangible. One might regret their life that has passed as having been wasted, and another might feel like elapsed time has been used well. The paradox is, it doesn't really matter. Whether you've built an empire, raised an army of wonderful little geniuses, invented the perfect photo filter, or conversely, if you feel like your existence has been a total waste... those are all simply egoic recall. The past no longer exists. A memory is only a mental construct in the present.

There is only ever the present.

Now.

Now.

Now.

Take in a deep breath. Feel the energy and sensation in the lungs and body. Release the air. Feel the muscles relax and the connection with your surroundings.

One of the core Hindu mantras is:

Sat. Chit. Ananda.

Existence. Consciousness. Bliss.

We exist. We can be conscious. We can breathe and be present in this moment. And that is pure joy.

February 8th
COMMODITIES MARKET

"The most valuable commodity I know of is information."

GORDON GEKKO – WALL STREET

If you wrote down everything you know, how much of it would be of use? And more importantly, of that which is useful, how much of that are you using?

Time, information, food, gold… different types of commodity, all have their use. But something only has value in so far as it forms a synergy with something else. Information is useless unless acted upon (or consciously not acted upon). Money doesn't have value if we allow it to enslave us by only seeking hedonistic pleasures. If time is spent worrying, then it has been spent poorly.

Question how you spend the resources of life. If you're not utilising one, why not? If you are, but you're abusing it (living off a diet of hamburgers or spending all of your income on trying to impress others), evaluate if there might be a different way.

February 9th
FAN THE FLAME

"What are you prepared to do?"

JIM MALONE – THE UNTOUCHABLES

The ability to do something is an equation:

Desire to do it (A) – Difficulty to accomplish (B) = Ability / Non-ability (C). C needs to be a positive number for you to be able to accomplish the task or goal. Now here's the big secret, of the two factors A and B, you can only affect one of them.

Some people don't bother brushing their teeth before bed. The task is eminently achievable, but their desire does not even meet the modest requirement.

On the other hand, some human beings accomplish ridiculously hard goals, fuelled by a blazing desire to do so. The sacrifice required to reach the finish line is irrelevant. The will has been set, and no force but death will stop the realisation of the goal.

The beauty of life is that it is merely a continual repeat and rephrasing of the same question: *What do you want?* And the unspoken follow-up question: *How badly do you want it?*

When you know what you want and you're prepared to do everything you can to get it, there can only be one outcome.

February 10th
REPAYING A DEBT

"Earn this."

CAPTAIN MILLER – SAVING PRIVATE RYAN

In the beautiful book, *The Miracle of Mindfulness* by Thich Naht Hahn, the master says, 'the miracle is to walk on earth.' Just being alive, having the wonder of existence, of breathing in air, of sight, sound, the presence of a tree, these alone can imbue any human with a profound joy, in as much as they are willing to embrace it.

In what was somewhat of an impossible command to follow, Captain Miller wished to instil a sense of gratitude in Private Ryan. Ryan would live because others had died.

We don't need to think of our life as being a debt to repay. That can only lead to failure. On the contrary, life is a gift. It asks nothing in return (as neither should people, although they often do). Life only gives.

You 'earn it' by being you. You maximise it by being your best you.

February 11th

FINAL SCENE?

"Oh, Danny, is this the end?"
"No, Sandy. It's only the beginning."

SANDY & DANNY – GREASE

As humans, we exist in a paradox. We have beginnings and endings everywhere.

The sun rises – a new day starts. The sun sets – the day closes.

We're born – our very first beginning. We die – our final curtain.

A football match kicks off – action commences. The final whistle blows – the game concludes.

Where is the paradox, you ask. Everywhere! Beginnings and endings exist because we chop up (often arbitrarily) an infinite blob of existence in to digestible, bite-sized chunks so that our brains don't explode. Take a day. Firstly, the sun only rises or sets because we are spinning around. It's not like the sun ceases to exist during the night, it's simply out of view. And even if we get hung up on it setting each night, (abandoning us, how dare it!) well, just wait a few hours and what do you know. It's back. But what about when our yellow dwarf (although a million times bigger than the earth, our Sun is a comparatively modest-sized, cold star) fizzles out in another few billion years? Well the cycle just continues…

Everything is one eternal loop. There is no beginning and no end. Everything is one.

February 12th
STAND FIRM

"A temptation resisted is a true measure of character."

LOUIS DEGA – PAPILLON (1973)

In the face of temptation, we find out where we are really at. We can talk a good game of principles, but it means nothing until those principles have been put to the test, and they don't come much bigger than temptation.

As Mike Tyson said of plans – everybody has one until they get punched in the face – so temptation probes us to know if we really have the courage of our convictions. In the time it takes to say 'oh, go on then,' can our inner compass be completely scrambled. Temptations come in every shape and size, too, of course, so none of us are able to employ a strategy of complete avoidance.

One defence mechanism against temptations, like with all types of challenges, is to have some degree of awareness and acceptance that they *will* inevitably come. The Stoic philosophers liked to drill home the idea that our attitude should be one of preparedness for every eventuality, meditating daily on the trials and temptations that are the lot of every human.

Today, let's have a wide lens view on the scenes of our life and the potential snares. Let's strive to show our best side when confronted, and if we do succumb, that's OK. We'll have to face the consequences. And then we have the choice to learn and move on, or repeat the cycle.

February 13th
SENSE IN THE NON(-)SENSE

"That doesn't make any sense."
"Not everything does. Not everything has to."

DOCTOR STRANGE & THE ANCIENT ONE – DOCTOR STRANGE

It is a curiosity of us humans that we seek to make sense out of everything. We seek to make sense of the chaos. Puzzle books, crosswords and Sudoku are highly popular for this very reason (albeit these are staged conundrums.)

The antidote to needing to understand everything is…

… accepting that we don't need to understand everything.

Today, when something baffles you that you would normally fight to find meaning in, perhaps see if you can simply surrender to it. Don't label it. Don't judge it. Just accept.

February 14th
TRUST ME

"All you got to do is trust me. That's all you got to do."

JACKSON MAINE – A STAR IS BORN (2018)

Trust. It's a big word. And we give it a lot of power. Trust vindicated gives one a sure footing. Trust broken, pulls the rug out from under one's feet. Usually in a film when a character says, 'trust me,' it's a cue for them to do something completely untrustworthy. Think of pretty much any mafia movie and the last words a victim hears before they get whacked... *trust me, you're all good, the boss isn't mad... we're not going to hurt you... thud!*

On screen and in song, trust is portrayed as a quality to be placed in another human being. Yet this is only a part of the matter. The middle. The bigger portions of trust must be directed at the two ends that go on either side of the trust placed in others – in oneself and the universe. Until we learn to trust ourselves, how can we possibly trust others? Trust of self is built through the glorious journey of self-discovery. Learning what oneself likes and doesn't like. Considering the experiences one has been through and the lessons garnered. Recollecting the tears shed, some of joy and some of sorrow. And with that trust, confidence, belief, call it what you will, in self, comes trust in the universe (God/nature/space and time). In the final analysis, we either believe that the universe is a cold and mean place, playing with our delicate sensibilities (and where does that lead?), or else we hold fast to the faith that we are all one, and beyond the limited scope any one of us holds at any given moment, there is an underlying, connecting thread of love, goodness and hope. As Gandalf said; "and that is an encouraging thought."

February 15th
WE ALL NEED SOME STARDUST

"I just want to be inspired."

DOROTHY BOYD – JERRY MAGUIRE

A day without inspiration is like a sandwich with no filling… very bland and incredibly hard to swallow. Inspiration is our cheese and pickle (butter and jam for those of you with a sweet tooth.) And this filling is best served in the morning when we open our eyes. A positive meme, a gaze at nature, the exciting thought of all there is out there to explore.

You know an inspired person when you meet one because they are inspiring. They have that twinkle in their eye. Every one of us can be inspired, and therefore become inspiring. In Chinese, one word for inspire is 鼓舞 guwu – literally, *to provoke a dance!*

There are many ways to be inspiring. One common thread is consistency. The most inspiring people are often those who hold true to something, whether that be working for a social cause, the desire to perfect their art form or simply refusing to let go of their joy de vivre no matter their struggles.

Be inspired and get inspiring.

February 16th
SET YOUR OWN PRICE

"You get what you settle for."

LOUISE SAWYER – THELMA & LOUISE

Too many of us settle for less than we're worth. We all deserve serenity, prosperity, mutually fulfilling relationships and satisfaction in work and personal pursuits. If we're not experiencing the abundance of life, perhaps we can take stock of areas that we might be neglecting, or limiting attitudes and beliefs that need our attention.

To claim all the goodies of life, we need to know our value. One way to build that self-worth is to spend time evaluating our life and our decisions. As we take a calm, balanced look at our choices and their consequences, we should be able to recognise choices we've made that left us far short of feeling good about ourselves. Equally, there have been some good decisions that led to growth. By contrasting the choices we've made in the past, it can build up a stronger desire to make more choices that empower and move us forward.

February 17th
MORE THAN JUST A PRETTY FACE

"I'm pretty sure there's a lot more to life than being really, really good looking. And I plan on finding out what that is."

DEREK ZOOLANDER – ZOOLANDER

Aesthetics are important. Vision is not just for functional ability to navigate the tasks of life, it's also to enjoy and appreciate the beauty of everything in the world. But surface level beauty devoid of soul is like fast food – easy to swallow but doesn't fill one up.

Beyond the surface, everything has true appeal, as wrote the Chinese sage:

Everything has beauty, but not everyone sees it.
万物皆有其美，唯慧眼能识之

We have but to open our heart to see it.

February 18th
LAST ACTION HERO

"Those who have the ability to take action have the responsibility to take action."

BEN GATES – NATIONAL TREASURE

Action is how we bring about good in our own lives and in the world around us. Sometimes, *deliberate* inaction is the best option for a given situation. Quite often, stillness and meditation are actions that can yield the best results. Whatever the scene before us, we can seek to move toward a life filled with constructive action. The alternative is entropy, defined in physics as the dissipation of energy within a system. Perfect entropy means complete inactivity. We can liken this to ourselves. The more we do, the more we have capacity to do, to shift through our spiritual and creative gears. The more we drift and let our passions and inner force for good to sit idle, the harder it becomes to shift out of neutral.

The beauty of every positive act, aside from its direct fruit, is that it also carries the reproductive seeds which fall into the fertile soil of others' minds. A hard-worker influences colleagues to work hard. A conscientious student cajoles one's fellows to also value learning. Most of all, an act of random kindness sets off a chain reaction of one human trying to help another. What could be more inspiring than to know our valiant attempts at noble action are a trumpet call for others to follow suit?

February 19th
CHOOSE WISELY

"Now is the time that we must choose between what is right and what is easy."

ALBUS DUMBLEDORE – HARRY POTTER AND THE GOBLET OF FIRE

A spiritual leader once said; "the greatest battles of life are fought out daily in the silent chambers of the soul." Who can relate?!

In the end, the only criticisms that matter, the only judgements that last, and likewise, the only words that can nobly lift the head, are those that come from the person looking at you in the mirror.

(Not the mirror in *Daddy's Home 2*!)

February 20th
FAMILIAR STRANGERS

"What a loss to spend that much time with someone, only to find out she's a stranger."

JOEL BARISH – ETERNAL SUNSHINE OF THE SPOTLESS MIND

Few changes seem to have the power to knock the wind out of our sails quite like an unexpected twist in a relationship with someone we thought we knew. Even the greatest Stoics amongst us have surely succumbed to the pain and bafflement that come with finding someone is not who we thought they were. A wise person masters the seeming paradox of loving and cherishing others, while accepting that *everyone* is human and *anyone* can let us down. By retaining a philosophical outlook, we can remember that this is the game of life. And what a jolly old game it is.

February 21st
IDENTITY FRAUD

"[A man] can convince anyone he's someone else, but never himself."

ROGER 'VERBAL' KINT – THE USUAL SUSPECTS

This makes one wonder, did Frank Abagnale in *Catch Me If You Can* really believe he was all those fantastic personas?! (…of course, Mr Abagnale is a real person, and perhaps he's answered this question in real life…)

Being one's true self is brave. It makes one open to attack. It divulges the real nature of who one is.

This above all, to thine own self be true,
And it must follow, as the night the day,
Thou canst not then be false to any man.

SHAKESPEARE

February 22nd
QUESTION EVERYTHING

"Asking questions may be more important than finding answers."

BRUNO FORESTIER – LE PETIT SOLDAT

We go through life seeking answers; *What's the meaning of life? How do I become successful? Why did that happen?* The questions are fine. The problem is they're pointing the wrong way. It is not us who ask life the questions, rather, it is life that questions us. The answers lie within each human being for that person only. No one of us can tell another what their purpose is, the reason for their suffering, how they might pursue happiness. The greatest adventure that we travel is the deep exploration in to the silent, infinite, glorious recesses of our own soul. There, if we are willing, we experience pure being. Beyond the questioning, beyond the contemplating, beyond the need for answers or words or meanings or debates… beyond everything, we are.

February 23rd
PLANT THE RIGHT SEEDS

"An idea is like a virus. Resilient. Highly contagious. And even the smallest seed of an idea can grow. It can grow to define or destroy you."

DOM COBB – INCEPTION

We suppose we can keep our thoughts secret, confined to the impenetrable vault of our mind, known only to ourselves. But in this we err. Our thoughts manifest in our outer material world. Knowing this can be highly transformative. As we look in our own mind at our paradigms, we see the foundation and framework that has shaped our lives. Like a connect-the-dots puzzle, as we make the connection between our thoughts and the things that happen in our lives, we see pictures emerging. We begin to acknowledge how the ideas we cherish the most have come to outline our character and our circumstances.

All it takes for an idea to grow is time and attention. If we plant an amazing idea today and take care to water it regularly, it won't be long before that idea takes shape and blooms. In this we learn that whether we grow weeds or waterlilies, reeds or roses, depends entirely upon which ones we water.

February 24th
24, 69, 32... HUT! HUT! HUT!

"According to Greek mythology, the Titans were greater even than the gods. They ruled their universe with absolute power. Well that football field out there tonight, that's our universe. Let's rule it like Titans!"

COACH BOONE – REMEMBER THE TITANS

A beautiful story of the work of a high school American football team in the early 70s. Set amidst the tensions of the racial struggle, a team of young athletes, led by an indomitable coach, Herman Boone, built a legacy that 50 years later is just as needed. People of different colour and culture came together. Through hard work, sacrifice, unity and equality, and most importantly, time, enough time to allow the magic of the process of mutual sharing and learning and falling out and making up again, to happen, they showed that the power of togetherness will always breed success.

The Titans' achievements on the field were enormous – they went unbeaten to win the State championship, but that paled in comparison to their spiritual victory. As Boone's number two, Coach Yost, said: "[they] taught this city how to trust the soul of a man rather than the look of him."

We, too, can cultivate our own environment of inclusiveness, tolerance and love. Our football field is our hearts and minds. We win our games by being willing to listen to, learn from and love our fellow humans all around us. There are no opponents, only teammates.

Huddle round.

February 25th
QUACK! QUACK! QUACK!

"Have you guys ever seen a flock of ducks flying in perfect formation? It's beautiful. Pretty awesome, the way they all stick together. Ducks never say die. Ever seen a duck fight? No way. Why? Because the other animals are afraid. They know that if they mess with one duck, they gotta deal with the whole flock. I'm proud to be a Duck, and I'd be proud to fly with any one of you. So how about it? Who's a Duck?"

COACH BOMBAY – THE MIGHTY DUCKS

Unity is the most precious quality that a team, family or business can have. A group can have all the resources and talents in the world, but without unity, disintegration will inevitably follow. And with it? A tribe that is united can weather almost any storm, make up for almost any deficiency, overcome virtually any catastrophe. It's a thread that weaves its way through sporting folklore. Teams that were dead and buried. The contest over. Until…!

Like a phoenix, rising from the ashes, the teams with absolute trust and confidence in each other, willing to run through walls for their teammates, willing to dig deep into their souls… time and again it's been shown that with such great unity, no situation is hopeless.

February 26th
MORE THAN JUST A THEORY

"It is clear that we are just an advanced breed of primates on a minor planet orbiting around a very average star, in the outer suburb of one among a hundred billion galaxies. But, ever since the dawn of civilization people have craved for an understanding of the underlying order of the world. There ought to be something very special about the boundary conditions of the universe. And what can be more special than that there is no boundary? And there should be no boundary to human endeavour. We are all different. However bad life may seem, there is always something you can do, and succeed at. While there is life, there is hope."

STEPHEN HAWKING – THE THEORY OF EVERYTHING (2014)

Maybe one day we will have all the answers. To Everything. But knowledge is not what defines us. Love is. Hope is. Our willingness to keep learning is.

You have a role to play. Nobody can cover for you. Your struggles and your journey are yours and yours alone to bear. You have the strength within.

Our delightful little home may be a minor planet... and our power source may be a very insignificant star... and we may be in the relative backwaters of the galaxy... but this is OUR home. Our shared task is to be wise stewards in the performance of our responsibility of taking care of this home. Our individual task, as Stephen Hawking showed, is to bravely face our destiny.

February 27th
IT COMES WHEN YOU LEAST EXPECT

"I knew what I needed to do and how to do it."

EDDIE MORRA – LIMITLESS

At one time or another, we all fumble around in the proverbial dark. We know there is something greater, something better, something more meaningful waiting for us, but we don't know how to get to it. Or maybe it's something less, something we're trying to offload… less stress, less busyness, less mind activity. It causes emotional pain. We feel a yearning and an aching. And the more we try and force a breakthrough the more it evades us.

And then one day… like magic, the path opens up. It all makes sense. Your calling calls you. You know what you have to do. And like Seabiscuit, you gallop forwards with intention.

February 28th
FEAR OF DEATH, OR DEATH OF FEAR?

"I ain't afraid to die anymore. I done it already."

HUGH GLASS – THE REVENANT

All the great philosophers give the subject of death a lot of attention. How strange. We don't much like the idea of death, do we?

Perhaps the great thinkers understand the inseparable connection between living and dying. Like all things in our finite mortal realm, there must be duality within the oneness. If there was no death, perhaps we wouldn't appreciate life? And if there was no life, this would be a moot point.

We can live free of the fear of death. That fear grips those who aren't living in the moment. It haunts those who haven't learned to forgive themselves and forgive others. It paralyses those who haven't come to love the great circle of life, and as a part of that, accept that death is owed its dues, too.

That is not us, though. We do not fear death. We know it must surely come, and when it does, it will find us ready. To die as we have lived. Graciously. Nobly. And with love, laughter and integrity.

February 29th

ALWAYS ON GUARD

"I was jealous. Your beauty. Your bravery. Your motherhood. You seem to surpass me in every way. But now I see there is no cause for envy. Your gifts are your downfall."

QUEEN ELIZABETH I – MARY QUEEN OF SCOTS (2018)

Ever had that experience where a food you once disliked suddenly became your favourite thing??....

Olives!!

The law of life states that anything can be flipped to its opposite. Weakness can become a strength. Love can turn to hate. Something once ridiculed can suddenly gain one's unbridled passion. Nothing is safe from this most peculiar of phenomenon. Many a great person, consumed by their victories, have lost their humility. From this we can learn to be ever vigilant. Let's not allow the positive qualities we've been endowed with and built up ourselves to become corrupted. Let's keep striving to be the best version of ourselves. Ever humble, ever learning.

March 1st
HAVE YOUR CAKE AND EAT IT

"Life is not the amount of breaths you take, it's the moments that take your breath away."

ALEX HITCHENS – HITCH

This calls our attention to a choice that comes up regularly: quality or quantity?

"Can't I have both?" you say.

Well, as it happens, yes, you can. By choosing to live in the present moment, you unlock the infinite potentialities that exist within every situation. You're no longer bound by the same repetitive cycles. You can make the current scene anything you want. It really is a blank canvas. That is the quality.

And the quantity is knowing that these moments never stop. Now. Now. Now. What an abundance you have. The only time they'll stop is when you pass on, and that won't bother you at all. You'll morph seamlessly into the next phase of your eternal evolution. Your spirit is immortal and it will continue its journey of enlightenment.

March 2nd

NICE SURPRISES

"The earth was made round so that we would not see too far down the road."

KAREN BLIXEN – OUT OF AFRICA

Have you ever fast forwarded to the end of a film or taken a sneaky peek at the last page of a book while still on chapter one? It's natural to be curious about what lies ahead, but it poses the idea, one that has been played out in books and films many times; if we could know the future, would we want to?

Somebody once said, "when the uncertainty of life is not accepted, it leads to fear, worry and a constant state of anxiety; but when uncertainty is accepted and embraced, it fosters enthusiasm and excitement." Would you want to know all of the story ahead of time? No way! Where would the fun be in that? It may seem counter-intuitive, but we thrive on not knowing what's coming and not having the answer to everything. It's in the state of uncertainty that everything becomes a possibility. As we venture in to the unknown, we're given the freedom to be whatever we desire.

March 3rd
VERITAS

"I want the truth!"
"You can't handle the truth!"

LIEUTENANT KAFFEE & COLONEL JESSUP – A FEW GOOD MEN

Can you?

March 4th
HOME SWEET HOME

"There's no place like home."

DOROTHY – THE WIZARD OF OZ (1939)

Home. Casa. Домой (domoy). Accuiel. 家 (jia). Whatever your tongue, home is home. It conjures up emotions and memories. For some it means freshly made cookies, indulgent bubble baths, the old sofa that's perfect for lazy days with popcorn and reruns. For others, it might mean noisy neighbours or sad stories. Home is another example of the beautiful duality we experience in life. Looking back, home can mean so many things. And looking forward, we can make it whatever we want and wherever we want.

Beyond the home of bricks and mortar, we also have a spiritual home. We get glimpses of it in moments of stillness and pure being. Awakening, we can know, this earth is our home. This universe is our home. This feeling, a sense more than anything, enlivens the connection we have one with another. We know we all come from the same spiritual home, and this shared heritage unites us.

March 5th
AN INSIDE JOB

"Everyone runs in her own way, or his own way. And where does the power come from, to see the race to its end?... From within."

ERIC LIDDELL – CHARIOTS OF FIRE

We're each running a race, but it's not a marathon, it's a time-trial. There are no competitors. The universe plays a few roles simultaneously; the fans cheering us on; the coach keeping the time; and the medic, for when we get a bit short of breath.

All any of us have to offer one another is the best version of ourselves. So often, what people need is not to be told what to do, but to be given the space to be what they are. All the support necessary is available, but the individual still holds the choice. They must look inside and find their truth. This is one part of the journey to self-actualisation – knowing, feeling, that one already possesses everything they will ever need.

March 6th

ROUND PEGS IN ROUND HOLES

"You're gonna need a bigger boat."

MARTIN BRODY – JAWS

Every job has an appropriate tool. Trying to paint a masterpiece with an axe or attempting to chop a tree with a paintbrush is like trying to catch a great white shark in a dinghy... it's not going to yield the desired result. One major skill in life is learning to identify what the right tool is for any given task. Selecting the most effective instrument provides a great start. With this in mind, we can view our lives with a sense of perspective and balance. Money is a wonderful tool that we employ to fulfil the material necessities of life, first and foremost, and then to enjoy and explore. Prayer, meditation and writing can be used as tools for our spiritual requirements. A healthy and balanced diet, good sleep and regular exercise are the elements for sound physiological conditions. No one tool can substitute for another. All the money in the world will not cover for spiritual starvation. Likewise, meditating under a tree all day might reveal the mysteries of the universe, but if we want to feed ourselves, we may need to get up and toil. Each tool can be employed in its intended way to gain the intended outcome. If we're not getting the results we want, perhaps a look to make sure we've got the right tool in our hand?

March 7th
THE BEST IS YET TO COME

"We'll always have Paris."

RICK BLAINE – CASABLANCA

As long as we remember that memories are a snapshot of the past, and can only be viewed and enjoyed in the present, there can be great joy in reflecting on happy bygones. Fond memories are surely a gift, (painful memories can be too, if we can learn to disarm and learn from them.) A fun holiday, the first time you met your soulmate, BBQs in the garden.

Feeling flat and low on gas is completely fine. It's OK to not be OK. Learning to sit with uncomfortable feelings is a necessary process along the path. But let's remember that the goal is to make this crazy thing called life enjoyable. Life is about joy. We're not here to be glum and trudge our way through. We're here to flourish and fly. Sometimes, a cherished memory can be just the pick-me-up we need to give us renewed energy and call our attention back to the present, with the strength to embrace the current situation and find our way forward.

March 8th
~~PROCRASTINATION~~ ACTION

"Spaaaaartaaaaans! What is your profession?!"
"A-WOO! A-WOO! A-WOO!"

KING LEONIDAS & HIS MEN – 300

King Leonidas was making a point. Don't call yourself a soldier when you're actually a potter or sculptor. It's not always easy to walk the walk. We've all fallen in to the trap of talking the talk, or maybe limping the limp… and we learn from the frustration of thinking, talking, wishing to be… rather than just being. Doing. At some point, one comes to the deep realisation that there is only action. Everything else is nonsense.

Words mean nothing. Action is the only thing. Doing.
That's the only thing.

ERNEST GAINES

One thing we need to banish from our lives if we are to become doers and not idle talkers is procrastination. It is the scourge of empowered people and the bed-fellow of underachievers. There is no easy antidote. The solution is in realising, feeling, that until you change your paradigms, you're never going to get the best out of yourself. When the pain of that fear surpasses the numbness of inaction, then things change. The dishes need doing – done. The friend that popped in to your mind – called. The book you've always wanted to write, first page – written.

Once you get on a roll with positive action, it becomes a habit. And as that ability to acknowledge an arising thought and take immediate action develops, your life takes off.

March 9th
BRAVE NEW WORLD

"Be wise, Judah. It's a Roman world. If you want to live in it, you must become part of it...I tell you, Judah, it's no accident that one small village on the Tiber was chosen to rule the world...It wasn't just our legions...No, it was fate that chose us to civilize the world - and we have. Our roads and our ships connect every corner of the earth, Roman law, architecture, literature are the glory of the human race."

MESSALA – BEN-HUR (1959)

Every human being alive, we each face the same question; to what degree do I maintain my autonomy to think for myself and take an objective view of the world? If we were all completely honest with ourselves, would we like the answer? We're so interconnected that to untangle oneself long enough to make an impartial view is quite difficult, but ever so necessary. Lots of advancements in science and technology may be beneficial for us, but it doesn't mean that they *all* are, or that we ought to subscribe to each new trend that arises.

March 10th
BUILD BETTER BONDS

"A boy's best friend is his mother."

NORMAN BATES – PSYCHO (1960)

The maternal bond runs through everything around us. Mother nature, mother earth. The feminine touch is the touch of kindness, love, softness, compassion and grace.

Not all human parents, though, live up to their responsibilities. Regardless of the kind of upbringing we've had, we can set a new path for our relationships with our children. If we've come at the end of a dysfunctional chain, we can break it. We can start a new pattern that emphasises the unconditional love and lessens the expectations and demands.

Parent-offspring relationships can be difficult, but they can also be an immense source of joy. Both parties can live up to the lovely Chinese proverb, 尊老爱幼 zun lao ai you – respect the elderly, love the young.

March 11th
SPEAK CLEARLY

"What we've got here is failure to communicate."

CAPTAIN – COOL HAND LUKE

Communication, when used properly, is a tool like none else. It can transform any situation and improve any relationship, even if that means clearly ending the relationship. Thus far, as humans, we haven't mastered the art of telepathy (if you have, please do let us know... telepathically, obviously.) Until we do, communication can mean talking.

There are many reasons why we don't communicate effectively, either because we don't know how to, or maybe, because we don't want to or are afraid to. Learning to express ourselves, particularly to those we love, becomes a wonderful learning curve. We're open, but can retain a little bit of mystique. We're forthright, but not insensitive. We're playful, but not childish. There's a lovely sweet spot somewhere in the middle of extremes. And because relationships are in a constant state of flux, so too are our feelings and stirrings, which spices things up further.

Let's keep working on our ability to communicate with the people in our life. The right people will value our honesty, vulnerability, humour and viewpoint.

March 12th
U-TURN

"I thought you said you came here to have a nervous breakdown?"
"About that, I've decided not to have one."

DR JASQUITH & CHARLOTTE VALE – NOW, VOYAGER

Outrageous! Who said someone can change their mind? Who said that someone can make a U-turn when they were about to do something they might later regret? Who said you can't go back on your word?

Not to be confused with the concept of resoluteness and dedication to a cause, which is vital if we are to pursue and achieve any kind of worthwhile goal, the ability to change for the *better* should always be welcome. We do not have to follow through with a choice to do ourselves or someone else harm. We do not have to make the same mistake yet again. We can break the cycle of the same old tired response that we trot out every time we face that certain stimulus. We can even "let someone down" to put our own self-care first (shock! horror!)

Nothing is set in stone. Each day we really do get to write a new script. We can scribble down the same old same old… again… or we can conjure up an entirely original, captivating blockbuster. The choice is ours.

March 13th
BUILD YOUR WORLD

"I used to be just like you. Then one morning when I was going up in the elevator, it struck me I wasn't having any fun. So I came right down and never went back. That was 35 years ago."

"Admirable. And you haven't done anything since, huh."

"Oh yes, yes, yes... Oh just the things I wanted to do... collected stamps, went to the zoo when I got the notion, took up the harmonica, and even found time to notice when spring came around."

GRANDPA VANDERHOFF & ANTHONY – YOU CAN'T TAKE IT WITH YOU

What would your life look like if you found a way to do the things you wanted to do, while still taking care of your responsibilities? Starting to doodle. Collecting shells. Focusing more at school. Participating in a charity. Learning to fly a plane. Connecting to a movement, religion or tribe.

How would you feel?

What would your relationships look like?

Would you be making the world a better place?

Your life is yours alone. It's up to you to squeeze as much juice out as possible. You may have been given a truck-load of deliciously fresh fruit; apples, oranges and mangoes; or you may only have been handed a few bruised peaches. You may have inherited a fancy juicer, or you may only have your bare hands. Whatever your outward situation, you can make the best of it. You don't have to let your fruit spoil. You can make invigorating, refreshing juice and share it with others.

Get squeezing.

March 14th
WE ALL KICK OURSELVES

"I'm sure that the way to say what I'd like to say will occur to me after you've gone."

FATHER O'MALLEY – GOING MY WAY

How many people would wish for the ability to say something smart in the moment? Singles can surely relate to that irritable feeling when you've met someone you like and fumbled over your words like a drunk person trying to find their keys. It's always as you walk away that all the clever jokes suddenly deluge the mind. Doh!

One of the countless things that binds us together as the human race is knowing that we all experience the same basic emotions and situations in life. It's this ability to relate to one another that enriches our interactions and reminds us that our similarities are far greater than our differences.

March 15th
GREATER LOVE HATH NO MAN

"It is a far, far better thing that I do, than I have ever done; it is a far, far better rest that I go to than I have ever known."

SYDNEY CARLTON – A TALE OF TWO CITIES (1935)

Everybody wants to live a long and happy life, yet when we see heroes in the films willingly giving up their lives to serve a higher cause, it stirs something within us. It reminds us that we are more than just our instinctual drives and base desires. The survival instinct, supremely powerful, incredibly, can yield to an even greater urge – the desire to be of service to a loved one or humanity.

We are human beings. And to be human is to have the innate ability to transcend the situation we find ourselves in at any given moment. The great characters of screen, some fictional, others portraying real persons, show us a way to be. They probe those unexamined corners of our hearts and minds, asking us; "What would you give for love? How strongly do you believe in your ideals?"

Each day we are in spiritual training, but the training is not for some abstract event that is always around the corner. The training each situation provides is for immediate application at the very same moment the training is being received. We get a chance to allow the spiritual training to seep deep down into our soul. And no sooner has one lesson been given than the next one is coming around to see what we've learned.

March 16th
PLAN-TASTIC!

"I love it when a plan comes together."

COLONEL 'HANNIBAL' SMITH – THE A-TEAM

Plans are like umbrellas; when you take one, you'll have the luxury of not necessarily needing to use it. But if you don't, you'll almost certainly wish you had.

It's like an unwritten rule. The more you plan, the less you'll seem to rely on your plans. Spontaneity is delightful, but oddly, it's often a well-conceived plan that acts as a conduit for some spontaneous off-piste adventure.

Learn to harness the ability to make plans first, and then go with the flow.

March 17th

THE WEIGHT OF A SOUL

"How many times do we live? How many times do we die? They say we all lose 21 grams... at the exact moment of our death. Everyone. And how much fits into 21 grams?"

PAUL RIVERS – 21 GRAMS

Some people believe that the only logical endgame for humanity is for our consciousness to be uploaded to the cloud or input within a robot. There is probably someone who has already called shotgun on R2D2!

But seriously, what is the ethereal stuff that makes a human, human? Surely it's not just the physical frame that we call the body, or even the voice or personality or beliefs or viewpoints?

Your soul is priceless. It is the complete package that is you. A part of the seamless oneness of the universe, but also entirely unique within the manifestation that is you. Nobody else can place the £∞ price-tag on you. Only **you** determine your worth. The universe *knows* you're priceless, but it will never force that knowledge upon you.

March 18th
EMBRACE LIFE

"You cannot find peace by avoiding life."

VIRGINIA WOOLF – THE HOURS

Some days we just want to retreat into our shells. Like a rudderless boat, we feel tossed about by the waves of life. At such times, detaching and retreating a little is fine. We're not robots, numb to the bumps of life, nor are we going to always have a positive attitude, energy to take action, or even the desire to do the next right thing, nor should we.

We. Are. Human.

This means we struggle and stress. We fall short. That is OK. No worries. When we come to accept ourselves and each other exactly as we are, we all have the freedom to grow (or not). We understand that the private wrestle we each have with our own soul – Who am I? What do I truly want? What do I stand for? – these things are answered in their own time in their own way.

And what of peace? Well, nobody can say definitively how peace comes to a person. Each of us must go within to reveal our piece of peace.

March 19th

THE REAL YOU

"It's better to be a fake somebody than a real nobody."

TOM RIPLEY – THE TALENTED MR RIPLEY

Go to your nearest park or into nature. Try to find the richest squirrel… or the most beautiful swan… or the most luminous parakeet… or the strongest tree…

- - - - - - - - - - - - - - -

If we are not careful, we can want to be a somebody so badly that we're prepared to be an anybody.

You are not anybody. You are you. Unique, special, replete with personality and qualities. Hold on to your true and innate identity.

March 20th

NOURISHMENT

"You wasted $150,000 on an education you coulda got for $1.50 in late fees at the public library."

Will Hunting – Good Will Hunting

The English word *education* derives from the Latin, *educare*, meaning to nourish, to bring up. It's easy to forget this and place emphasis on tick-box methods of learning that aim only to show an arbitrary level of outward accomplishment or the prestige of societal acknowledgement. The true purpose of learning is to learn! (Not merely to store information – that would be pointless these days, much more efficient to use a computer.) Education, as the original word means, is about developing as human beings. Discovering about this world and our part in it. Finding our individual purpose and meaning. This is real education. An easy way to bring this to life is if you stop and consider for a moment, what means more to you; the formal schooling you received, or the priceless lessons of life that have come through your experiences and willingness to develop from the inside out?

March 21ˢᵗ
TIME-OUT

"You know what drives me crazy? It's all these people talking about how great technology is, and how it saves all this time. But, what good is saved time, if nobody uses it? If it just turns into more busy work. You never hear somebody say, 'With the time I've saved by using my word processor, I'm gonna go to a Zen monastery and hang out.' I mean, you never hear that."

JESSE – BEFORE SUNRISE

As everything we do gets streamlined... quicker, more efficient, frictionless (one of the buzzwords of our times,) we're supposed to be *saving* time. But saving it for what, exactly? Are our phones, cars, apps and online-banking saving us more time to use them more, to save us more time to use them more, to save more time to.... ???

Time is the most glorious thing. When you pin it down and put it under the microscope, you discover that all you see is your own perplexed reflection looking back at you. Eventually, as one traces back through the dominoes of cause and effect, I do this because of that, I do that because of that, because of that... one reaches the beginning. Om. Nothing. Only the individual can discover what awaits in that hallowed place from whence all things spring forth.

March 22nd
PRICELESS

"What are our lives worth?"

JIM GARRISON – JFK

How does one even begin to contemplate this question. Are worth and value intrinsic? Must they be earned through performance or proven utility? It is a sad thought to consider those who take their own lives. Some people call it the cowards way out, which is to miss the point. To make such a fateful decision, presumably one has weighed and measured their own life and found that from whatever angle it is looked at, it has lost inherent value. In that moment, that precious soul, equal in weight and value to any other that has ever existed, have believed that to simply cease life would be the best option. They have not believed, or even just hoped, that there was a way to transcend their suffering, to change those things that they could, to find a new meaning, or seek whatever solution may have been available to the predicament, real or perceived, they were in.

The depth and breadth of all human experience is fathomless. As we consider the full spectrum of all humanity and our happenings, let us have compassion and empathy for all people. When we contemplate our own trials and tribulations, it should soften our perspective on every fellow traveller on the seas of life. Whenever we can, let us lift a shipmate, and allow others to lift us, too.

March 23rd
SUCCESS AT ANY COST?

"Uncle, you're basically a criminal now. But on the bright side, you're famous."

RICKY BAKER – HUNT FOR THE WILDERPEOPLE

What are you willing to do to get what you want? Will it be worth it?

On the quest to make £1m or get 1M followers or rack up one million air-miles travelling the world, the pertinent question is not so much the how, rather, the why, and what will it cost. What will the pursuit of this thing cause me to sacrifice in other areas? Will it have been worth it? Do my morals and scruples come higher or lower in the pecking order? What *are* my morals?

March 24th
PARLEZ VOUS FRANCAIS?

"I've always enjoyed studying a new tongue."
"One might say you have a natural ability."
"But practice makes perfect."

JAMES BOND & PROFESSOR INGA BERGSTROM – TOMORROW NEVER DIES

The study of tongues is a riveting adventure. Like some of Bond's other pastimes, it can be a lot of fun delving into the nuances of language or just learning to use cool phrases such as *je ne sais quoi* and *que sera sera*, or warm embraces used to endear and foster conviviality and connection, like *namaste* and *alhamdulilah*.

Every race, every land, every culture, brings its own vibrant colour to the tapestry that makes our world. Learning about people outside our own cultural paradigms is a fantastic place to widen our horizons and open our minds to the other ways of doing things. Why not learn a tiny thing today about a different culture? If you live in London, it could be wondering who exactly was Eros, the first Greek god and original matchmaker, with his statue in Piccadilly Circus. Or perhaps contemplating where chopsticks started and why. Maybe you might want to know more about some of the tribes of South Africa and the incredible level of democracy at their traditional gatherings, where every person in the village has a voice.

And before we explore other cultures, we might ask, what do I know about my own?

March 25th
THE HEAVIEST BURDEN

"It's a hell of a thing, killing a man. You take away all he's got... and all he's ever gonna have."

WILL MUNNY – UNFORGIVEN

Whether it's war movies, Westerns or just good old action flicks, killing is an ever-present on the big screen. But we'd do well to remind ourselves from time to time what that means, to take a life. The mental turmoil and cognitive dissonance that war veterans go through attests to what it means to end another human being's life. Natural disasters, disease and accidents will always happen. We can't stop that. But what would the world look like if we all sought to better understand and appreciate the value of a single human soul?

March 26th
ASK AND SEE

"You'd be surprised about what you can get, if you ask for it the right way."

JACK FOLEY – OUT OF SIGHT

How many times have you been afraid to ask for something? It might have been a burning question in geography class, year seven. It may have been the guy on the Tube, doodling something, which left you with curiosity as to his talent. Almost certainly there was at least one time you were itching to ask a guy or girl for their number or a date, and you didn't because of fear of rejection.

Join the club.

Another of the many fun processes that are open to us is the one of learning to ask. That's it. Simply ask. *How does that work? What's that mean? Do you mind if I have the last biscuit please? I would love to get your number, what do you say?!*

If you don't ask, you'll never know. Most of all, ask the universe. It wants you to be well. It wants you to be prosperous. It wants whatever you want.

Ask!

March 27th
LIGHTEN UP

"The two natural items to sustain life are sunlight and coconut milk."

ENRICO "RATSO" RIZZO – MIDNIGHT COWBOY

And what a superb combination those two are.

Sunlight is not just scientifically necessary to provide the heat and energy humans, animals, crops and nature need to grow, it also provides the necessary psychological boost that we thrive on. Even more than that, it represents a symbol of hope, of faith. Each morning the sun rises and illuminates the resplendent earth. Dawn ushers in the promise of a new day. Everything is possible. We don't need to be bound or weighed down by what has been. This is our day – and the light shines to show us the way.

(If it's raining where you are, count five benefits of the rain. ☂)

March 28th
DON'T MIMIC THE CYNIC

"You gotta look out for number one!"

BERNIE LAPLANTE – ACCIDENTAL HERO

Every choice comes with a pay-off. The person who smokes does so because they believe that the act of putting some rolled up tobacco leaves in their mouth and setting it on fire provides a benefit of some kind. Understood in this light, smoking makes sense. Getting angry makes sense. Being lazy makes sense. If the person didn't believe on any level (conscious or subconscious) that there was some benefit in a given choice, they simply wouldn't do it. To not see *any* reason to do the act, and still do it anyway, *that* would be true madness.

People aren't cynical or pessimistic because they're crazy. They're pessimistic because they've allowed a paradigm to take hold that gives them a pay off every time their negative viewpoint is vindicated. *"Bus is late – told you we'd miss the film. What did I say, she always lets you down. This is pointless, we'll never fix it."*

Let's not fall in to the trap of allowing negative thought patterns and choices to keep us in their grip because they, as absurd as it sounds, offer some sort of buzz. Let's break free and consciously choose to do the things that give us healthy rewards. We can start today by questioning choices we know are not optimal. Why am I choosing this? What reward do I get from choosing it?

March 29th
EVOLUTION

"Life finds a way."

DR IAN MALCOLM – JURASSIC PARK

Have you ever been walking down a street and noticed a random little shoot of foliage bursting through the pavement? An easily overlooked miracle, it represents the triumph of life through adversity. *Per aspera ad astra.*

Where there is life there is hope. Where there is hope there is reason to press on. We won't always have the answers. Remember, faith and belief are exactly that. Seeing or touching isn't belief, it's sensory evidence. But every leap forward in the evolution of humanity, every heroic act of love, every brave new step into the unknown, they are all life finding a way. Life showing that it has its own wisdom, far greater than any one individual constituent component, and yet each component carries the spark of that total divinity within.

Together, on this earth, we will find a way. That may mean the end of mankind, for now, but we'll be back.

March 30th
RED OR BLUE

*"I know you're out there. I can feel you now. I know
that you're afraid... you're afraid of us. You're afraid of
change. I don't know the future. I didn't come here to tell
you how this is going to end. I came here to tell you how
it's going to begin. I'm going to hang up this phone, and
then I'm going to show these people what you don't want
them to see. I'm going to show them a world without you.
A world without rules and controls, without borders or
boundaries. A world where anything is possible. Where
we go from there is a choice I leave to you."*

NEO – THE MATRIX

The Matrix is a phenomenal film on many levels. The
cinematography. The acting. The narrative. Neo's words to a
potential new recruit were the perfect way to close off. We're
all afraid. None of us have a crystal ball. Life isn't about us
choosing our outcomes, it's about us choosing our meanings, our
intentions. We can stay asleep; physically, mentally, spiritually.
Or we can wake up, accept the reality before us – our world, our
environment, our personal situation – and then work hard to
make the best of it. We can be a part of the solution.

March 31st
CAREFUL WHAT YOU WISH FOR

"There are two tragedies in life; One is not getting what you want, the other is getting it."

YURI ORLOV – LORD OF WAR

One peculiarity of life is when after a long time you eventually get what you want… only to find that it isn't very satisfying at all. It comes as such a shock to the system. I'm finally driving my dream car… why do I feel so flat?! I thought the perfect physique would make me feel a million bucks… but I still feel empty. I'm at this idyllic and peaceful meditation retreat, but my mind is still restless…. Aaarrrrgggh!!!

Sometimes getting what we want is harmful. Often, our wants are not necessary. But the paradox is, until we get what we want, we might never know that it isn't what we want. Or maybe it is what we want, but not the only thing that we want. Or perhaps it is exactly what we want, we're just not appreciating it. The possibilities are endless. What we can do is use gratitude to make what we have, what we want.

Gratitude is wanting what I have, not having whatever I want.

April 1st
QUESTIONS, NOT ANSWERS

"What do you want from me?!"
"What do you want for yourself?"

CAPTAIN ALGREN & KATSUMOTO – THE LAST SAMURAI

The answers are in the library in all the books. The answers are on the internet. The answers are being spoken each week in churches, synagogues and mosques. The answers are what we see through the end of the Hubble Space Telescope. The answers are… hang on… if the answers are all around us, why do we struggle? Why is there so much pain and suffering?

The answers *are* everywhere, but they only make sense once we discover the answers within ourselves. Life does not give answers – it asks the questions. It believes each one of us has the power to be and create whatever we wish. Until we take whatever things it is that are bothering us and turn them inwards, asking the question, what am I supposed to be learning here? Why does this elicit this reaction from me? What do I want? Until we elevate ourselves to a higher level of vibration and responding to the questions of life, we are prone to be stuck in the loop of reacting and fighting these situations.

April 2nd
LISTEN. THAT'S IT

"Whatever you wanna tell me, whatever you think might scare me, won't... and I will listen... I will be a good listener to you if that's what you want... and you know, you know... I won't judge you... I can do that sometimes, I know, but I won't... I can... listen to you and you shouldn't be scared of scaring me off or anything that you might think I'll think or on and on and just say it and I'll listen to you..."

OFFICER JIM KURRING – MAGNOLIA

Too often we speak when we should be listening. We think that the person before us needs a response, an answer, an idea, a suggestion, a condolence... when in fact, all they need is the presence of a sympathetic soul. To simply know that another human being is there, that they care, that they are listening and not judging.

This goes further. To be a good speaker, we must first learn to be a listener. To be a teacher, we must first be, and remain, the student. To become a master, we must humble ourselves as the apprentice. To receive, we must first give. As we gain wisdom and experience, we intuitively know which situation calls for which role.

April 3rd
THE GREATEST GIFT

"Whoever saves one life saves the world entire."

ITZHAK STERN – SCHINDLER'S LIST

In either creating or conserving, what higher glory is there in all the universe than to be the giver of life?

April 4th
ALL IN

"When you love someone, you've gotta trust them.
There's no other way. You've got to give them the key to
everything that's yours. Otherwise, what's the point?"

SAM 'ACE' ROTHSTEIN – CASINO

Releasing the handbrake in a relationship is at once the most exhilarating and most vulnerable thing a person can do. It opens one up to the supreme joys and fun and intimacy that are possible when two bodies become one heart and one mind. Yet the flip side of the coin always exists too… what if it goes wrong? As one ponders how best to navigate the exotic journey of love, all sort of bizarre tactics can be invented and deployed. However, to be anything other than fully trusting is like trying to make a skydive without ever getting off the runway. By getting airborne and strapping on a parachute, there is no guarantee that something might not still go wrong, but by staying on the ground it is simply impossible to experience the thrill of the jump. In relationships, the equivalent of a secondary chute is ensuring the maintenance of other healthy relationships (friendships, family bonds), and the equivalent of a thorough plane check is regular, honest and direct communication with one's partner. There are no certainties of a happy ever after, but we've got to believe, right? Otherwise, what's the point?

April 5th
GO AFTER IT

"I think the world is divided into those who go after what they want and those who don't. The passionate ones, the ones who go after what they want, they may not get what they want, but at least they remain vital, you know? So when they lie on their deathbeds, they have few regrets."

MAXINE LUND – BEING JOHN MALKOVICH

Which side are you on? Are you going to let life pass you by, or are you going to grab it and ride it? We only have this day, this moment. With each passing day, we don't know what our own lives will look like, let alone the world around us. This can give us even more motivation to set about squeezing as much out of our days as possible. We can be the ones who take the road less travelled. We can be a trailblazer, cutting and charting new courses.

As we know, change happens regardless. As C.S. Lewis said so well; "isn't it funny that day by day nothing changes, but when you look back, everything is different." Change is a given, growth is a choice.

Are you going after what you want?

No? Why not?

Yes? Are you remembering who you are and to be the best version of yourself as you do so?

April 6th
FOLLOW THE INNER COMPASS

"I don't know how I'm going to live with myself if I don't stay true to what I believe."

DESMOND T. DOSS – HACKSAW RIDGE

We can pretend to be someone other than ourselves all we like, but there will always come a day of reckoning. Building a fake persona in a bid to gain a benefit of some kind is like climbing to the top of a ladder only to realise that it's against the wrong wall. The success is not only hollow, but doubly saddening in the moment that we realise we've been lured in to the trap of ego. Being something we're not in the attempt to achieve something or persuade others to love, like or approve of us is a pointless exercise. It will work temporarily, only to come crashing down at some point, or it won't work in the first instance.

Today, be yourself. The real you. The quirks, the foibles, the snorty laugh, the care-free dancing in the street. The beliefs, passions and convictions. This is your life and your time. Your beliefs don't need to be validated by anyone. Your lifestyle doesn't need to be popular. Your thinking doesn't need to follow the crowd. Your portfolio of beliefs is your flag in the moment as you hold them. Even your own beliefs don't define you, but in any given moment they are a snapshot of the kaleidoscope of your soul. Change them as you please, but change them because you have evolved, grown and matured.

If I wanna be free, I gotta be me.

EARL NIGHTINGALE

Every person who is enlightened will rejoice and celebrate you for being your authentic self. Free the shackles of conformity and let the true you shine through.

April 7th
IMAGINE THAT

"Sometimes it's the people who no one imagines anything of who do the things that no one can imagine."

JOAN CLARKE – THE IMITATION GAME

Can you assess another person and tell their worth? If you judge it infinite, well done. If it's less than that, you might want to look again. The paradox of value (talent, worth,) has been proven time and time again. At surface level, we make judgements and assessments all the time. That football player is rubbish. That scientist has it all wrong. That leader is too weak. We can only ever make a judgement in a finite moment of time with a finite perspective, but a soul cannot be constrained in such a straight-jacket. At every turn, each one of us is able to create a whole new reality and a whole new manner of being. Albert Einstein was considered a failure well in to his late twenties… until he conjured up the principles of what would become the Theory of Relativity, which, naturally, made him a genius. Was he a genius only at the point that outward successes and social recognition said that he was? Or was he a genius all along?

When we judge anybody, we're being impaired by two huge impediments; 1. What we observe of a person versus the limitless depth of their soul (what we see amounts to less than 0.0000000000000000001% of their total being), and 2. It is only a momentary snapshot in time with extremely limited scope. It fails to consider the infinite possibilities of growth.

The real test is to see the homeless person and see the same divinity within them that you see in your wonderfully talented idol. The challenge is to see the drunken fool with your physical eyes but the amazing, revitalised human being with your spiritual eyes. The quest is to see yourself with compassion and know who you truly are. The gift is in coming to understand that whether one has the outward success of a Muhammad Ali or Leonardo da Vinci, or bumbles through life constantly misfiring and never finding the way to shine their best light, on a cosmic level of value, there is no difference between either. We are all of equal worth. We are all worthy.

April 8th
NO ROAD BLOCK ON THE 'YOU' HIGHWAY

"The only person standing in your way is you."

THOMAS LEROY – BLACK SWAN

Watch any motivational video online or a post from a motivator on social media and no doubt this idea won't be far away. It is a universal concept. But like all gems, which it is, its ubiquitous nature and seeming simplicity can be deceiving. The depth and power of the meaning not truly grasped. Once a person truly, deeply feels this truth, it changes everything. No more moaning. Whining. Complaining. But, but, but… just 100% accountability. *My* life is a result of *my* choices. Nothing more, nothing less. Make a list of everything in your life, tangible and intangible; clothes, home, possessions, friends, money, traits, accomplishments, thoughts, mistakes, wrongdoings… everything. Make a list. Which of those things did you not choose? Now consider the things that you desire. Make a list. Which of them cannot be achieved? Which of them do not subscribe to the law of the harvest, namely, if you put in the needed action, it will yield the desired result?

The infinite wisdom of creation ensures each of us hold the key to our own destiny. Circumstances may, at times, bear down upon us and limit our choices, yet there remains, always, a choice.

April 9th
TRUE REFLECTION

"That's the problem with mirrors. They always show you yourself."

Stetler – You Should Have Left

Seeing ourselves as we truly are can be scary. That's why someone invented filters. These days, some peoples' photos on social media resemble their real image but so little that the only real connection between the pic and the person is the clothes they're wearing. The reality of some spots or a double chin remedied at the touch of a button. Perhaps this new age mentality that everything can be airbrushed spills over in to other areas of life. Looking, pretending, *seeing* to live the dream. Spiritual void? No problem – a quick selfie on the yoga mat and bingo, what void? I'm Zen. I'm enlightened.

Look in the mirror, what do you see?
What you have done, or who you can be?

Mirrors are dualistic. They show us what really is and what we want to see. They show us what we really are – truth. They can also be used to show us what we may become – vision. There are other mirrors, too. Books, people, meditation and time also show us the reality of self. We can use them all to gain a fuller knowledge of ourselves. We can arrive at a place where the mirror of life reflects the peaceful, contented version of ourselves we always knew we are.

April 10th

ABRACADABRA!

"I think, with a little bit of magic in your life, you can do almost anything."

Ian Lightfoot – Onward

Without the magic where would we be? As humans, it's the art, the music, the love, the fun, the games, the creativity… all of these and much more that get our juices flowing. The magic is the juice of life. Without it, existence would just become robotic, transactional nonsense. Like a robot or piece of software, we would run our program; breathing, eating, sleeping… never deviating. Having life, but lifeless. It would be *The Terminator* meets *Groundhog Day.*

Magic is not only art and creativity and the fun stuff. It's the spiritual law that we can utilise. In the dictionary, magic can be defined as an unseen or supernatural force or energy that has the ability to influence or create. Today, let's use our minds to magic magic into existence. Through desire and adventure, let's be daring enough to allow our inner genius to create new thoughts, new patterns, new songs, new words, and then enjoy the fun and adventure that they bring.

April 11th
TAKE CARE OF BUSINESS

"Mankind should have been my business!"

JACOB MARLEY – A CHRISTMAS CAROL (1977)

Do you make serving and helping others your business? Do you strive to leave every fellow human you have an interaction with, a little bit better off for coming into contact with you?

We each have the power to be a force for good in the world. Imagine a person who is feeling so low that they are contemplating suicide. Maybe they're even at a train station getting ready to jump. But before they do, they make eye contact with someone else on the platform who gives them a simple smile. Just a smile, nothing more. The momentary flexing of a few dozen facial muscles. A silent "hello, I acknowledge you, you're not alone." The person smiling not even conscious of their little gift. And yet that tiniest of spark, tiniest divisible unit of love, could just be the moment that stimulates that sad soul to reignite the flame of hope. I don't have to do this. Things can change. I can find a way forward. I still have a contribution to make…

We completely underestimate the power for good that every single one of us possess. Which is bizarre, because we've all been lifted so many times by others. As we go about our business, let us not neglect our *other* business. Raising each other.

April 12th
ENOUGH

"I'm never gonna be good enough for you, am I?"

ELLE WOODS – LEGALLY BLONDE

All our lives we wrestle with the concept of being good enough. We want to shine, match up, conform, outdo, prove... all because we're missing the point. We are already complete. And from this place, we learn to say: "I am enough."

However, caveat; It's not enough to say, "I'm enough," when what we're really saying is "I'm enough, because later, I'll be more than enough." No, no, no. That is not enough. That is conditional enough... that is "I'm enough now, because really in my heart, I believe that through faith and action and abundance mentality (all correct principles, of course,) I will be even more enough at some future point."

Enough of that kind of enough!

What we're looking for is enough. Enough. Unconditional enough. Now enough. Pure enough.

I. Am. Enough.

We can never get enough of this kind of enough.

Enough said.

April 13th
IN THE BEGINNING

"My father's people say that at the birth of the sun and of his brother the moon, their mother died. So the sun gave to the earth her body, from which was to spring all life. And he drew forth from her breast the stars, and the stars he threw into the night sky to remind him of her soul."

HAWKEYE – THE LAST OF THE MOHICANS (1992)

Since the dawn of time, mankind has created myth, legend and fable to help explain the great mysteries of our earth, the waters and the depths below, and the starry night sky. We seek to understand our part in the immense tapestry of the universe. We sense a profound connection with the cosmos all around us, and we know that, surely, we are not a disconnected unit, but a connected cog, turning and clicking in harmony with the other celestial wheels.

April 14th
LOVE IS THE HEAVYWEIGHT CHAMPION

"There's only one thing impossible – that's to love and to part."

MR EMERSON – A ROOM WITH A VIEW (1985)

Love is both the most powerful and strangest force known to man. Its effects are felt long after the originating act. Its legend reverberates down through all the happenings of humankind. Its pull has no limits. Once you're struck by a bolt of it, it's game over. Like taking the red pill, there is no going back. Don't try to fight it. Resistance is futile. Surrender to its spell. Succumb to its power. Allow yourself to be swept away by it.

It isn't possible to love and part. You will wish that it was. You can transmute love, ignore it, muddle it, but you can never pull it out of you. I know by experience that the poets are right: love is eternal.

E.M. FORSTER

April 15th
A BETTER WAY

"Guns. So primitive."

- - - -

"In times of crisis, the wise build bridges while the foolish build barriers."

OKOYE / KING T'CHALLA – BLACK PANTHER

Where are we going as humanity? To the stars? To oblivion? Who can say. One thing is for sure, as our species goes through a range of challenges, ones that will define our future, now, more than ever before on this planet, we need to find ways to build bridges, to elevate ourselves in our thinking, our doing and our being.

Perhaps it is our nature to war and kill each other. Perhaps it is in our make-up to perpetually seek to subjugate and control other living entities. Perhaps it is in our genes, and to stifle that innate urge to destroy and conquer would cause other problems. But ask yourself this, in those moments that you feel calm, peaceful, connected, fully present in the moment, at any such time in your life that you have felt that way, have you ever, fully conscious and mindful, then shouted at or screamed at or punched or shot someone?

An interesting thought?

April 16th
WHO IS THE PUPPET-MASTER?

"Cue: The Sun"

CHRISTOF – THE TRUMAN SHOW

Who's in control? Tick (and add) as appropriate:

- » God
- » The Universe
- » My phone
- » Social media
- » A football team
- » My parents
- » My partner
- » Science
- » The government
- » My genes
- » Money
- » My fears
- » Paradigms
- » Fate

- » …. Nobody ….??

April 17th
VANITY IS VAIN

"Vanity and happiness are incompatible."

MARQUISE DE MERTEUIL – DANGEROUS LIAISONS (1988)

Lingering on one's own achievements, gifts and talents can only last so long before they begin to fester. Happiness comes as a by-product of giving something positive in to the world, not when we're bathing in self-adulation. The river would quickly run dry if it got too much into the habit of congratulating itself for some water well passed.

One way to keep our feet on the ground is to enumerate the ways in which we have been helped. From parents to mentors to books to the air we breathe to the fireman who rescued us... we've all been helped so many countless times by circumstances and things, and by people in the form of huge acts to tiny everyday ones. Every little moment of service has built us up to where we are today. Let's keep humble and hungry for more learning. As we do this and continue to serve others, happiness will surely accompany us.

April 18th
PURE SOUL

"Every human soul has seen, perhaps before their birth, pure forms such as justice, temperance, beauty and all the great moral qualities which we hold in honour. We are moved towards what is good by the faint memory of these forms, simple and calm and blessed, which we saw once in a pure, clear light, being pure ourselves."

IRIS MURDOCH – IRIS (2001)

Researchers in 2004 at the University of Exeter in England reported that new-born babies appear to show a preference for attractive people. When shown two pictures, one of what might be considered a very good-looking person and one of a person less so, the babies displayed a very noticeable predilection to gazing upon the more attractive person. If appreciation of beauty is in the eye of the beholder, but also fundamentally hard-wired into us, is it not so that honour, justice and kindness are also a part of our fundamental make-up? Do we not naturally gravitate toward these virtues, and hold ourselves accountable against them, more so than the man-made laws and societal framework that seeks to enforce arbitrary and synthetic rules?

Our goal is to return to our purity. It is our default state. We're striving for that state of being where we are at our best. The Peter Parker walking down the street helping old ladies, picking up spilt groceries, smiling at everyone and making a positive impact.

April 19th
SURPRISE SURPRISE

"Nothing here has worked out quite as I expected."
"Most things don't. But sometimes what happens instead is the good stuff."

EVELYN & MURIEL – THE BEST EXOTIC MARIGOLD HOTEL

When we let go of how we think things should turn out, relax, and let them unfold naturally, we're often surprised at how they turn out better than we could have imagined. The universe knows everything, and we have a choice to believe that everything will turn out exactly as it is meant to – cosmically perfect and perfectly cosmic – or we can keep flapping around trying to play the boss. It goes back to this fascination we have with control. We want to feel like we have some grasp on life, but when it comes to the crunch, the reality is we have no control. Paradoxically, letting go of the futile attempt to control allows us a feeling of peace and softens us to feel like we're in control, that is, in control of our thoughts and feelings, accepting that life is completely mad and virtually nothing that has happened in our life could have been predicted. For is it not the very unpredictable nature of life that makes it so much fun?

April 20th
OH TO BE FREE

"To be free. Such a thing would be greater than all the magic and all the treasures in the world."

GENIE – ALADDIN (1992)

In some ways, we're all trapped or handicapped by one thing or another. For some it's being raised in poverty or discrimination, lacking the opportunities to advance or progress. For others it may be parental pressure to toe the line and follow in the well-worn path of the generations before. For still others it could be religious or societal norms that restrict one from exploring themselves and their world. To look at a king, ruler, rich or famous person, and think that they have all the freedom in the world is to entirely misunderstand life. Living in Buckingham Palace may mean you sleep in a pretty comfy bed, travel rather well and eat considerably better than the average Joe, but it doesn't protect against envy, fear, the desire to control, or pain in personal relationships.

Let's remember this fundamental truth to soften and warm our view of all fellow humans. We're all on this rollercoaster we call life, together, and while at times it may seem like a chosen few are controlling the ride, they aren't. Let's strive to build relationships of freedom for ourselves and those around us. Of course, freedom can only be maintained arm in arm with principles of responsibility. Your right to act freely and express yourself must be done with the consideration to allow another the same, and for you and them to find the sweet spot where your two wills meet.

April 21st
NOW OR NEVER

"It's what you do right now that makes a difference."

SERGEANT JEFF STRUECKER – BLACK HAWK DOWN

Let's break this quote down:

You… it's what **YOU** do, not God, your mum, dad, sibling, spouse, friend, boss, teacher, idol, follower, influencer… does. **You.**

Do… Not thinking, not postulating, not plotting or perceiving or planning or perchancing… **doing.**

Now… today, this moment, this opportunity, this chance, this perfect window. Tomorrow never comes, for, by the time it does, it is today again. **Now.**

It's what YOU… DO… right NOW… that makes a difference.

April 22nd
(DON'T?) PROVE IT

"In this life, you don't have to prove nothin' to nobody but yourself."

FORTUNE – RUDY

Do we even have to prove anything to ourselves? It's an interesting concept. When we observe nature, it would seem that there is no concept of success in the animal kingdom (?) There is survival and there is death and there is simply being (being being synonymous with joy.) No wonderful David Attenborough documentary has yet reported a school of fish secretly building a new Atlantis, or a troop of monkeys constructing a rocket. Everything around us seems to live at a leisurely pace of fulfilling the requirements to sustain life, and then relaxing and enjoying pure existence. Has a lion proved himself worthy by catching the antelope? Does the bee have a quota of honey to make, and anything below causes it to go see the doc for depression? Next time you're in a park or field and get the chance to sit quietly, observe the trees. Their still, sturdy majesty can teach us a lot.

In life, are we trying to prove something, even to ourselves? Or do we simply have an opportunity to enjoy the gift of being alive?

April 23rd
GROW THE SOUL

"Great men are not born great, they grow great."

DON VITO CORLEONE – THE GODFATHER

Deep within each human is a spark of humanity, the flickering flame of white hot soul. The soul is pure, but in our finite physical world, it gets transmuted through the physical body and physical behaviour. This is the challenge of who we are and who we become. History is littered with egos that thought their physical birthright determined their greatness. Some great minds believe that their natural endowment of intelligence makes them masters of perceived lesser minds. The only path to true greatness is through the fire of the soul. One does this by transmuting the lessons of life, both the ups and downs, through the soul, to come back out in a higher, elevated way of being. The great ones amongst us are those who achieve the highest level of harmony, those whose vibrational frequency leaves every persons' vibration that they touch humming a little bit higher and lighter.

> ## April 24th
> ## PRESS PAUSE

"Life moves pretty fast. If you don't stop and look around once in a while, you could miss it."

FERRIS BUELLER – FERRIS BUELLER'S DAY OFF

Breathing is one of the oldest and best ways to take what is a frantic thing – life – and hit the pause button for a moment.

=

Actioning. Moving. Striving. Energising. Growing. Citius. Altius. Fortiusing. Being. Doing. Running. Climbing. Carpe dieming. Reaching for the stars…. Reaching for the chocolate bars.

All wonderful. Genuinely. But sometimes…. Sometimes it's pleasant to just take a time out… and sit… and do precisely zero.

Breathe in…. two… three… four.

Hold… two… three… four.

And release… two… three… four.

Enjoy the stillness. Enjoy the hum of silence. Bathe in the serenity.

April 25th
MANIFEST THE GLORY

"Our deepest fear is not that we are inadequate. Our deepest fear is that we are powerful beyond measure. It is our light, not our darkness, that most frightens us. We ask ourselves, who am I to be brilliant, gorgeous, talented and fabulous? Actually, who are you not to be? You are a child of God. Your playing small doesn't serve the world. We were born to make manifest the glory of God that is within us. It's not just in some of us; it's in everyone. And as we let our own light shine, we unconsciously give other people permission to do the same. As we are liberated from our own fear, our presence automatically liberates others."

TIMO CRUZ – COACH CARTER

🙏 🙏 🙏

We've all read or heard about the people who, confronted by an extraordinary situation, showed superhuman courage or strength. The policeman who hugged the man brandishing a knife in his face. The father who flipped a car upside down to rescue his family. The good Samaritan who ran into a burning building. These things are real. The light is inside all of us. Powered by love, the impossible becomes possible. For this to happen, we must release the shackles of fear and embrace the truth of our true identity and worth.

April 26th
FIND OUT

"To find something, anything, a great truth or a lost pair of glasses, you must first believe there will be some advantage in finding it."

JACK BURDEN – ALL THE KING'S MEN (2006)

This covers some discoveries, but not all. Indeed, some of the best modern inventions have come as an off-shoot of seeking to create or build something entirely different. Kids are intrigued to know that play-doh was meant to be used for cleaning chimneys! Life is very much like this. We have the best of intentions to go down one road, but life seems to keep taking us down these strange paths, like a rogue satnav. Flexibility and open-mindedness can be real assets when we encounter these unforeseen forks in the road. We can trust that the interconnected universe possibly knows something that we don't. In this sense, we can believe that there is some advantage in finding whatever it is that we will be led to find, but what that benefit will be is often only revealed in the moment we stumble upon it, and not infrequently, sometime much later.

April 27th
DREAM ON

"We walk away from our dreams afraid we may fail, or worse yet, afraid we may succeed."

WILLIAM FORRESTER – FINDING FORRESTER

Our dreams are the fuel that power us forward. They are oxygen to the soul. For us, everything has three creations; the first is the ever buzzing and humming infinite creative potentialities that sit dormant, covering, by definition, the creation of everything and anything throughout space and time; the next is the spiritual creation, crafted and given definition in thoughts, plans, longings and dreams; and the final stage is the physical manifestation, the culmination and embodiment of the creation in tangible form. We want to trust in the first and last stage but place our attention on the middle one. It is here we construct our world. We dream, dare, plot, plan… and then act on the impulses we are given. This takes the pure potentiality, transmutes it in to a defined, sculpted thing, and through faith and action, transforms it in to a result in the real world.

April 28th
WHO WRITES THE SCRIPT?

"When a defining moment comes along, you can do one of two things. Define the moment, or let the moment define you."

ROY MCAVOY – TIN CUP

This is your script. What's it to be? Is the pen in your hand? Or someone else's?

April 29th
THE QUESTION NO ONE ASKS

"You know the ancient Egyptians had a beautiful belief about death. When their souls got to the entrance to heaven, the guards asked two questions. Their answers determined whether they were able to enter or not. 'Have you found joy in your life?' 'Has your life brought joy to others?'"

CARTER CHAMBERS – THE BUCKET LIST

You know the scene. It's one of those training courses that work sends you to about... email etiquette... you fall asleep just reading the memo. Yawn. The only thing that stops you nodding off half way through the presentation is the private chuckles you have with yourself at the presenter's brilliant use of emoji. Finally, after enduring what seems like an eternity, it's the canapés and drinks. Yey! Salvation! You fill your plate and begin to mingle. A charming fellow intercepts you and starts small talk. "Where are you from?" "What do you do?" "Do you play sport?" "Red half or blue half of the city?" "Did you see *The Queen's Gambit*?".... and on, and on, and on... and eventually it may well get deeper and you may share with this perfect stranger your passions, your secret dreams, your fears... It's a lovely conversation, to be sure.

But!... the one question, the one question that holds ultimate depth, always goes completely unasked. And not just with strangers. With those closest to us in all the world. (Why?! How?!) When you follow all the dominoes back to the start (or the end – same difference), it's the question left standing...

> *"Are you happy?"*
> *("Have you found joy?"... "Are you living the life you desire?"... or any other variation)*

Are you happy? It's the only question that means anything and the only one nobody dare ask.

April 30th
PICK AND CHOOSE

"You need to learn how to select your thoughts just the same way you select your clothes every day. This is a power you can cultivate. If you want to control things in your life so bad, work on the mind. That's the only thing you should be trying to control."

RICHARD – EAT PRAY LOVE

No action can arise without there having first been a thought(?). That thought could be deep in the subconscious, it could have been buried and blurred, but a thought must precede an action, which is but to say that the flower must have come from the seed. Knowing this, we have an opportunity to experiment with newer, higher vibrational thoughts. What happens if I celebrated the weather every day, rain or shine? How do I feel when I send every human I pass on my daily travels a wordless *namasté* in my heart? Do daily tasks and chores of life become more bearable, even enjoyable, when I cultivate gratitude?

Can you imagine what it would be like to only entertain empowering, positive thoughts? What would our lives look like if we did?

May 1st
TRANSCENDENCE

"The gods have not made it easy to be a human being."
"No, they haven't. But I guess that's why it feels so
wonderful to beat the odds."

HAZARI & MAX – CITY OF JOY (1992)

Patrick Swayze was supremely proud of this film and couldn't understand why it didn't receive the same attention as his more well-known, mainstream hits, like *Dirty Dancing* and *Ghost*. When one considers the glory of the subject matter, you could understand his sentiments.

Based on the book by Dominique Lapierre and directed by Roland Joffé, it explores the depths of the human soul by charting the fates of residents in a Kolkata (Calcutta) slum, affectionately known by the inhabitants as *Anand Nagar – City of Joy*, and the American doctor who joins their community.

Imagine calling such a place – in which disease, deprivation and poverty are at heart-breaking levels – City of Joy. Imagine having the courage to willingly leave your cocoon of comfort and choose to suffer with the downtrodden and forgotten of society. Imagine having the humanity to welcome a stranger and make them one of your own.

Being a human isn't always easy. As the incredible people of this story show, the best way to deal with being human is by being human.

May 2nd
KEEP THE FAITH

"You think the only people who are people, are the people who look and think like you. But if you walk the footsteps of a stranger, you'll learn things you never knew you never knew."

POCAHONTAS – POCAHONTAS

The key bit of information is always the one bit we're missing.

One simple, rhetorical question that can help us honour and appreciate a fellow traveller is this:

What is the one thing that if I knew about this person's story would give me a much clearer understanding and increase of empathy toward them?

Faith says we all belong. Faith says we all matter. Faith says every way of being is equally valid.

May 3rd
THE MIRACLE OF PATIENCE

"Even miracles take a little time."

FAIRY GODMOTHER – CINDERELLA (1950)

I want it now!

Imagine if our bodies were designed differently such that automatic breathing on a moment-by-moment basis wasn't involuntary, gifted to us as it is, breath by breath, but rather we were given our oxygen in lump instalments, or maybe just one big tank at the beginning of our lives. In such a system, how many of us would be here? How many people might have used up their 80 years' worth of air in half the time? How many would have sold theirs? ...gasp.

Everything has a time and a season. When we trust in the universe it allows us to relax. Chill. There's no rush. But I want my success, now! I want my dream family, now! The best one of all – I want my peace and serenity, now! An oxymoron in practice, if ever there was one. Give time, time. Let the miracle happen. It *will* happen. It happens in step with cosmic timing, not ours.

May 4th
FAILURE NEVER FAILS TO TEACH

"The greatest teacher, failure is."

YODA – STAR WARS: EPISODE VIII – THE LAST JEDI

As chief Jedi and leader of the resistance against the dark forces, Yoda carried a huge weight of responsibility. George Lucas portrayed perfectly through the miniscule master the torn range of emotions that every teacher, and indeed, every human being, wrestles with. Failure. We're taught to hate it. Despise it. In a straight choice of being caught on the loo by the person of our dreams (embarrassment), or getting something wrong in front of others (failure), we choose the former every time. Failure shakes us to the core and suggests that we are not enough. It awakens and activates almost every fear it's possible to feel, conscious and sub-conscious. Is it a lack of education? Are we not taught that failure is the gateway to success? Are we not let in on the cosmic secret of duality? Namely, that failure is but one side of the coin, and that success literally cannot exist without failure, that behind every success there is a litany of failures. That, bizarrely, the great ones cherish their failures much more than their successes. Not that they disdain their glories, but rather that their glories are polished with the sweat, blood and pain of their mistakes and failures.

Yoda was at the helm of the resistance as it took crushing defeats to the Galactic Empire. He missed Anakin growing in dark menace under his eyes. His hubris possibly accounted for the undetected evil lurking in plain sight in the form of Senator Palpatine (Darth Sidious). What glorious failures. But in the pain of his choices, he learned. And there, at the end of all things, he entered in to the Force.

And so may we.

May 5th
MAKE MR REAPER YOUR FRIEND

"I knew a man who once said: 'Death smiles at us all. All a man can do is smile back.'"

MAXIMUS – GLADIATOR

He's smiling at all of us, right now. Mr Reaper. Smile back at him.

May 6th

EACH HAS THEIR ROLE TO PLAY

"It's a pity Bilbo didn't kill him (Gollum) when he had the chance."

"Pity? It is pity that stayed Bilbo's hand. Many that live deserve death. And some that die deserve life. Can you give it to them, Frodo? Do not be too eager to deal out death and judgement. Even the very wise cannot see all ends. My heart tells me that Gollum has some part to play, yet, for good or evil, before this is over. The pity of Bilbo may rule the fate of many."

FRODO & GANDALF – THE LORD OF THE RINGS: THE FELLOWSHIP
OF THE RING

Next time you're about to deliver a damning verdict… take an extra moment to ponder.

Next time you're about to tell someone some home truths… take an extra moment to ponder.

Next time you're about to parrot how dreadful a person has been and how harshly they should be punished… take an extra moment to ponder.

What Gandalf taught in this spiritual scene is wisdom, compassion and perspective that transcends space and time.

May 7th
WEAR WELL YOUR CLOAK

"I wish the ring had never come to me. I wish none of this had happened."
"So do all, who live to see such times, but that is not for them to decide. All we have to decide is what to do with the time that is given to us."

FRODO & GANDALF – THE LORD OF THE RINGS: THE FELLOWSHIP
OF THE RING

Some of us are born paupers, some of us princes. Some of us are born and grow to be supreme physical specimens, some of us are disabled or handicapped. Some of us live in peace and democracy, some of us live amidst war, famine, dictatorship and chaos. We do not choose nor control the cloak of responsibility that is placed upon our shoulders by the universe. We simply choose the attitude with which we wear that cloak. The hero, as in Mariah Carey's timeless classic, truly is within each of us. We each have the power and the love within to rise and claim the gift the universe bestows upon us, namely, our unique placement and position in the world. Pure acceptance means learning to wear our cloak lightly, with good grace. (Baddies get to wear theirs *dis*-gracefully... obvs.)

May 8th

LUCKY SON OF A GUN

"You know what they say brother – luck is where opportunity meets preparation."

RUDY RAY MOORE – DOLEMITE IS MY NAME

There are a million and one quotes on the subject. Everyone wants to know the secret of her royal highness, Lady Luck. The simple crux of the matter is this:

The lucky don't need any explanation or consolation of how she operates. The unlucky won't accept any.

What is commonly called luck is merely a misleading mental construct. To the hard-working, confident, well-prepared balls of energy that bounce through life, they don't see a lucky break as lucky at all. It is merely the operation of natural law. A beneficial effect to their industrious cause. To the negative, cynical, lazy portion of humanity, luck eludes them at every turn, with them, unbeknownst to self, repelling the fair lady through their own lack of alignment to receive the gifts that the universe is willing to bestow upon all who believe and *align their efforts and attitude to universal law.*

May 9th
CHECKMATE

"The good part, William, is that no matter whether our clients make money or lose money, Duke & Duke get the commissions."
"Sounds to me like you guys a couple of bookies."

RANDOLPH DUKE & BILLY – TRADING PLACES

There are some games of chess in which your opponent has you whatever piece you move. Smart people learn to avoid those types of game altogether. The rest keep on walking right in to them.

May 10th
INTEGRITY

"Telling the truth can be dangerous business. Honest and popular don't go hand in hand." (Sung)

CHUCK & LYLE – ISHTAR

Integrity. When we're stripped to the soul, the only thing left, hopefully, is our integrity. And love, of course. Whatever we're doing, wherever we're going, whoever we are with and whenever possible, let's strive to maintain our integrity.

Integrity: What I do when nobody else is watching. Why I do it when they are.

May 11th
TURN UP THE POSITIVITY DIAL

"It's just a flesh wound."

THE BLACK KNIGHT – MONTY PYTHON AND THE HOLY GRAIL

Classic Monty Python comedy, this quip actually contains a profound idea – positivity in the face of all odds. If one can have both arms chopped off and still feel invincible, well, most people would pay good money for brio like that. And how can we turn into Mister or Miss Positivity? By living, breathing, eating, sleeping the ideals of positivity. We read about the principles of positivity, we talk about them with others who share the same enthusiasm for becoming the best version of themselves, we meditate upon the concepts of high energy and can-do attitude, we do things that stretch ourselves and take us out of our comfort zone, we eat something loving, we do a good workout, we watch an uplifting film. There are a million and one ways to notch up our positivity dial. As we do, it becomes addictive. As we sustain these kinds of activities daily, eventually we find that we can no longer sustain a negative attitude, even if we wanted to. Moments of negativity become few and far between. When they do come upon us, we don't panic, feel guilty or sorry for ourselves, or apologise. We simply embrace the feelings. They pass, and soon we're back moving forwards, chin up, shoulders back, twinkle in the eye and ready to keep making a difference.

May 12th
BIG ACORNS, TINY OAKS

"Everything that made that giant tree is already contained inside this tiny little seed. All it needs is some time, a little bit of sunshine and rain, and voila! Now, you might not feel like you can do much now, but that's just because, well, you're not a tree yet. You just have to give yourself some time. You're still a seed."

FLIK – A BUG'S LIFE

We've all doubted ourselves at some point (if you haven't, please do tell us what that feels like.) Am I enough? Will I achieve my goals? Do I matter? Do I belong? Now let's imagine the acorn thinking the same thing. Why am I so small? Why can't I be mighty and tall like that guy? When will I have a big, strong trunk to be proud of? We would surely tell that little fella to relax. He will get there. All in good time.

Normally we say; tiny acorns, mighty oaks. But let's flip it on its head. Mighty acorns, tiny oaks. The might is in the growth, in the potentiality, in the humility, in the *becoming*. Being an acorn or being an oak, it's the same thing.

May 13th
GET OFF THE ROAD

"Roads? Where we're going, we don't need roads."

DOC BROWN – BACK TO THE FUTURE

When you have a vision so big, so audacious, so ridiculous, and you tell it to others, there is a good chance they won't understand. It is not your job to convince them with words. It is not your job to convince them with actions. (Yes, you did read that correctly.) Outward-facing life visions aside, the biggest and best vision you'll ever have is also the simplest – to fully inhabit yourself. To break off the shackles of what you think others think you should be. To move through the three phases of filtration (each which has its role and necessity) to arrive at the purity of the fourth and final one that Caroline McHugh speaks of in her TedX talk, *The Art of Being Yourself*;

Perception → Persona → Ego → Self

When we be self, wonders happen. The self is the infinite you. Not the you your limited you thinks is you. The you that cannot be defined, cannot be labelled, cannot be supressed, cannot be oversold, undersold, lost, found, bound... even by you. The you in the you-niverse. The you in the you-nited fabric of everything. The you in you-nique. The you that is so unspeakably resplendent that the heavens in their wisdom gifted the most glorious thing – a soul, your soul – to you! To exist as yet another manifestation of the ineffable wonder of being. And was your soul even formed, gifted, born? Or have you been around since before we knew what time is?

Time won't tell.

May 14th
KISS ME QUICK

"You had me at 'hello.'"

DOROTHY BOYD – JERRY MAGUIRE

Hands up if you've ever spent days, months or even years chasing after the guy or girl trying to make them see how awesome you are? What... it's only me?! Do we maybe enjoy the rejection? Being given the run-around? It's a curious one. Why do we invest our valuable time trying to persuade a person to like us? What is it in our psyche that gets a kick out of it? If at the end of the month your boss said, 'not paying you this month,' you wouldn't say, 'awww, you old rascal, I love you so much,' and then do another month of work, and repeat the same thing... 'two months of no pay? Oh, you really know how to get me excited, don't you!' In any other area of life, it would be absurd. We would cut ties and walk away. But when it comes to the object of our affections, we can act totally crazy. We don't try bashing square pegs in round holes, there are no holes there. Remember, if somebody likes you, they like you. If they don't, putting on a show like a strutting peacock is a complete waste of your time. Reserve it for someone who cares. This life that we're gifted is about learning to focus on the people, places and things that matter. The ones that say 'shut up and kiss me,' not the ones that say 'shut up' and 'kiss my a**e!'

May 15th
LIGHTER THAN THE NEWS

"Why so serious?"

THE JOKER – BATMAN: THE DARK KNIGHT

Unless your job is to read the news, lighten up.

May 16th

TAKE THE BEST GIFTS HOME

"The only thing that really matters... is how a man treats his family."

JOHNNY – CAPONE (2020)

We can be anything we want to the world. The joker. The nice guy/gal. Machiavelli. The butter-wouldn't-melt-in-the-mouth role or the always-on-hand-to-help character. The rapscallion. And whether our performances come under play acting or are a real expression of who we are, they aren't nearly as important as who we are in our home. Our family are the people that should see the real us and deserve the best us. Theories abound as to why we can act like Dr Doolittle meets Father Christmas outside the house and then the Grinch meets Ebenezer Scrooge inside it. It's irrelevant why, what matters is that we don't succumb to the trend. Give your good to others, but reserve your best for your kin.

May 17th
GRAVITY... IN NICE QUANTITIES

"Gravity is matter's response to loneliness."

ELLIE CHU – THE HALF OF IT

A beautiful idea.

We *are* matter and we *do* matter. To the keen observer, science often reveals spiritual truths hidden within the empirical ones. All things gravitate toward all other things. Sound like oneness much?

However, if you're going skydiving, please do still pack a parachute. Too much gravity and your relationship with other matter is going to get messy!

May 18th
REPEAT AFTER ME

"Repetition will bring hell down from on high."

CAPTAIN KRAUSE – GREYHOUND

Repetition will bring hell down from on high.

Repetition will bring hell down from on high.

Repetition will bring....

In the task of getting something from your conscious mind (your thoughts – transitory) in to your subconscious essence (your being – fixed but fluid), repetition is a vital tool. Daily affirmations are for the mind what a workout or brushing the teeth are to the body – transformative. It is also a good reminder that we become something through the becoming (what an outrageous idea.) Malcolm Gladwell postulated the highly acclaimed 10,000-hour rule in his book, *Outliers: The Story of Success*. In it, the basic premise is, practice something for 10,000 hours and you will be an expert at that thing. It has since been suggested that genetics, quality of practice, intention and other factors are just as important to the development of a skill or talent as simply the raw amount of time invested. However, debates on specifics aside, the elemental concept holds up fabulously, as it does in the law of attraction and our way of thinking – if you immerse yourself in something, it's going to become a part of your way of being. Quality is just as important as quantity, which is why we need to focus on the focused repetition of the things we intentionally want to become and inculcate into ourselves.

May 19th
ROARING TO GO

"Sometimes it's hard to roar for no reason."

IVAN – THE ONE AND ONLY IVAN

A lion roars to warn off intruders, protect its family, and simply to display its pride in its pride. It feeds on the energy that its role, its responsibility to protect its clan, and its place in the hierarchy, provides. We are much like lions. We want to roar and show off everything we're proud of. Sometimes, feeling bereft of reasons, we can lose our voice. We open our mouths to roar, but no sound comes out. Is the condition terminal? Certainly not. We may just need to look around at our savannah to recharge on motivation. It may be when hunger arises and we need to hunt a gazelle that power comes. It may be down at the watering hole that we find invigoration. If you're yearning to roar but feel like there is only a whimper coming forth, relax. Be calm and don't focus on the lack of voice. Sooner or later something in your kingdom will spark you in to action, and your bellow will be heard across the plains and through the valleys once more.

May 20th
CHANGE – A VIP FRIEND

"Change is scary for all of us. Sometimes you just have to take a leap of faith. Trust that kindness will always be there when you need it."

IVAN – THE ONE AND ONLY IVAN

Make a list of all the changes you've ever experienced. Include the ones you've consciously chosen and all the ones that environment has dictated. It's a short list, right? A mere 57 million things or so, and you're still so young. Change as a big, gruesome baddie…? Pah. So overhyped.

Change and letting go. Old pals. And they should be buddies of yours, too. After all, what's the worst either of them have done to you? As a fear, change, like all other fears, reveals itself as only a mirage and melts away when faced head on. But as a friend? Well, start embracing him and he's going to introduce you to his VIP circle; Adventure, Excitement, Energy, Enthusiasm, Acceptance, Serenity, Success. It's a very exclusive club. Failure, Heartache and Disappointment always seem to gate-crash, too. Although never invited, oddly, gatherings always turn out just fine in the end, *especially* with those guys in the mix. Meetings happen everywhere. Change sets them all up on the group chat. Get in touch with him so you don't miss out.

May 21st

POWERLESS

"In the real world, the power goes to where it always goes, to the people that already have it."

ART – PROJECT POWER

Maybe.

But what about the love? The peace? The unity? The kindness? Those who seek power *externally or over externals* will sometimes get a slither of it, a few will get a big chunk, but as has been seen down through the annals of time, power is a capricious mistress. You think you're the one giving her the orders... sooner or later you realise that is not quite her modus operandi. But love. Ah, love is loyal and faithful to the end, her embrace pure joy. Peace is a warm blanket that can be worn forever. Unity is a bond that can weather any storm. Power? To demand, direct, control or seize? Let those who would tame that sultry diva try their best. Not us. Our power comes from relinquishing power. Our power comes from the acknowledgement that the power comes from above, below and within. Our inner power is our power to be our best. Leading, loving and lighting this world. That's the power we want to be plugged into. Our power is the channelling of our qi to find harmony and oneness. In that sense, we embrace our inner power and, indeed, become all-powerful.

May 22nd
MENTAL COWBOY

"The more you think about stuff, the more you draw it to you."

BRAY JOHNSON – THE SECRET: DARE TO DREAM

A thought is like a lasso and you are the cowboy. When you want to round up bulls or draw in a wild stallion, you use your lasso to pull what you want toward you. Thoughts are no different. Use your thoughts with focus, intent and precision to draw the stuff you want in to your life. The more you use your mental lasso, the more proficient you become with it. No longer do you unintentionally sling it around cacti or make half-hearted throws in the general vicinity of the target. Cold, calculated precision only. Every day you get to boot up and perform another rodeo. Make your throws with the lasso count.

May 23rd
LEARNING FROM PAST MOVES

"I'm open to the possibility that whatever happens, even the bad stuff, can lead to better things."

BRAY JOHNSON – THE SECRET: DARE TO DREAM

Life is very much a game of chess. Each moment presents a new fork of choice, and with a new choice happening moment after moment after moment, the possible permutations are literally infinite. Another parallel with the 64-square game of mind is in the use of experience. Grandmasters, while undoubtedly possessing other cerebral skills, found their expertise at the game on remembering past experiences and then applying the learned principles in play. Leaving a pawn isolated puts it at risk. Allowing the king to be checked ruins the chance of castling. Overcautious defence can be as dangerous as kamikaze offense. We can do the same in life. We can recall how a certain pain or negative experience can be flipped in to something we can grow from. In this way, unlike a game of chess, where one can find themselves in a hopeless position, in the game of life, however bad a previous move, the next one can always be better. We allow the unique collage of experiences we've been bestowed with to give us a broader perspective. We know that everything can be turned for our good.

May 24th
IT IS WHAT IT IS

"What's happened, happened. Which is an expression of faith in the mechanics of the world. It's not an excuse to do nothing."

NEIL – TENET

"It is what it is." A classic. Five tiny words. Both a summary and a symbol of an elemental truth at simultaneously surface level and at the deepest possible philosophical level. Take anything that has ever happened in all space and time and this self-explanatory maxim applies. Coffee has been spilt on the carpet. It is what it is. You're sat on a beautiful beach watching a spectacular sunset. It is what it is. A loved one has passed away. It is what it is. You feel serene and content. It is what it is. You can't understand why people keep saying, "It is what it is,"… It is what it is. (Sorry! Not sorry!) Imagine you can reverse time and unspill the coffee… guess what, *It is what it is!* "Good," "bad," "amazing," "terrible," whatever labels, whatever definitions, whatever mental constructs, explaining it, not explaining it, categorising it, not categorising it, acknowledging it, not acknowledging it… nothing in all space and time can get away from the all-encompassing tenet – *It is what it is.*

Every single one of us gets to decide what we do with this. Not with the mental construct of the concept It is what it is (although that, too, of course, *Is what it is),* but with the actual non-cerebral reality of *It is what it is.* Do you want to watch TV and eat crap all day or not do that? Do you want to let that person go or fight to keep them? Do you want to let the pain get worse or go see a doctor? Do you want to moan and complain about the lack of light in the world or do you want to be the light? Do you want to read this book or not read this book? Do you want to make it happen or not make it happen? *It is what it is* is inextricably linked with choice. One can choose that pure acceptance of all that is does not preclude one from making choices. Or one can choose to feel or believe that It is what it is means some form of pre-determinism and allow their own decisive choices to atrophy, which is, of course, itself a choice (another paradox – everything is a choice – not choosing is choosing to not choose.) Both are fine. It is what it is.

May 25th
TIMESTAMP

---

*"It's not what time steals, it's what it leaves behind.
Things you can't forget."*

ANDY – THE OLD GUARD (2020)

Time, by its very nature, sooner or later removes most things from us. And therefore, whatever we do possess at this very moment, possess in every sense – thoughts, feelings, whims, material possessions, relationships, idiosyncrasies, wrinkles, memories, future – is our unique bundle of existence. So, at any moment, we can wish for something else, what time has stolen (or not given… yet,) or we can rejoice in what it is has given us (for now, at least.)

What has time left behind for you?

May 26th
FORGIVENESS

"Disappointment is an absolute certainty. Everyone lets everyone down at some point. How you come back from that, that's romance."

ROBERT FOSTER – MADE IN ITALY

We all must choose our boundaries and bottom lines. By definition, whatever is within or above that boundary or bottom line should be eligible for forgiveness *and* moving forward in the relationship. What happens outside or below, still requires forgiveness (or not, hold on to that anger/resentment), but not necessarily with a forward future.

"'Nothing is more rare in any man,' says Emerson, 'than an act of his own.' And it's quite true. Most people are other people. Their thoughts are someone else's opinions. Their lives a mimicry. Their passions a quotation. That's an Oscar Wilde quote."

YOUNG WOMAN – I'M THINKING OF ENDING THINGS

The refined ones amongst us will know that when buying a piece of rare art, a fine watch or a Ming vase, due diligence is paid to authentication. The subject must be proved to be what its owner is claiming it to be. How quaint an idea that we have an opportunity to authenticate ourselves. Are we an imitation? Or are we a 1 of 1 original? Perhaps it's impossible to be entirely original in some senses, as the edges of our being, the brilliance and the silliness, all overlap one another. Where do you end and I start? Perhaps it is more a question of intention. *Seeking* to be truly authentic. Questioning oneself. 'Am I being my authentic self? Am I at seeking to be the real me? What does authenticity mean to me?'

May 28th
NO WORRIES

"Hakuna Matata!"

TIMON AND PUMBAA – THE LION KING (1994)

Who can relate to that period of the film where Simba has been found by Timon and Pumbaa and the jolly duo rear and raise him in the ways of their sacred philosophy – *Hakuna Matata!*? A care-free lifestyle. Eating, lounging, bathing, playing… what a life. La dolce vita! Those are the days. In all our busyness, striving and stretching, responsibilities, let's keep our playful attitude. Humour, conviviality and youthful enthusiasm soften the mantles of responsibility that life thrusts upon us. Each of us will enjoy periods of play at different stages of life. Some have the happy-go-lucky times in childhood or adolescence, before career, marriage and mortgage kick in. Others do things in reverse to traditional convention, enjoying wild abandon in their 40s or 60s or 80s. There's no rulebook for this, no set order to when, where or how we kick back and go with the flow. Whatever our outward life situation is today, we can (re)discover the way to eliminating stress through finding fun and joy in life. This journey is about laughing and giggling and being silly. If you can maintain your childlike nature *and* achieve cool things… well, then you've really cracked the code.

May 29th
BETTER TO HAVE MET HER

"You make me want to be a better man."

MELVIN UDALL – AS GOOD AS IT GETS

Lots of things can inspire a person to be better. A demanding job, an uplifting book, a super-hard Sudoku. But none perhaps are as beautiful as a fellow human who inspires to be better, especially when it is a partner. The desire for self-development and self-improvement must emanate within to have potency, as no amount of pleading and pushing from others will ever compensate for a lack of desire by oneself to be their best. However, when a desire to be better is coupled with an intense love for another human and the wish to be able to offer one's best to that person, wonderful levels of humanity are possible. Through our love, we rise like hot air balloons, the hot air being the sacrifices, vulnerability, sharing and caring that carries us up to elevated views of life. Of course, like the old friend adage – to find a good friend, first be one – being inspired works the same way. We get in equal measure to what we give. When we are with a special person, it will feel natural and spontaneous to want to be better, which is perfect. A better us means a better world.

May 30th
A STREET-SMART BUDDHA

"Hey! I'm walking here! I'm walking here!"

ENRICO RIZZO – MIDNIGHT COWBOY

Many people don't like confrontation. They instinctively shy away from any situation that feels like disharmony, at times allowing themselves to be exposed or treated to behaviour that is not right. Other people are only too eager to square up to anything that gets in their way. They're the ones who glare at you when you smile and say hello. They hate it when you compliment them.

Entirely up to the individual where they fall on the spectrum. One can keep being walked all over, or one can keep picking fights with teddy bears. Learning to know that you have a voice, you deserve to stand up to treatment or situations that aren't right, while keeping your zen, can be a real journey. For some, the ideal is a kind of street-smart Buddha. On an even keel but with a hint of steel. *I'm striving to be zen, to be peaceful, high energy, full of good stuff, but don't let that make you think I'm not going to respect myself and my boundaries. If you try to zap my zen, I will act.*

May 31st
MASTER OF THE MOVEMENT

"Wax on, wax off."

Mr Miyagi – The Karate Kid (1984)

Kids these days might not get the chance to practice their karate while cleaning windows or washing cars. The only chores they get is to stay out of sight and keep the iPad on charge. Not us 80s - 90s kids huh. Who didn't try the crane and then hide the mangled lampshade behind the sofa?!

As with all seemingly mundane tasks, the magic lies in the simplicity. Bruce Lee said that he feared not the man who had practiced 10,000 different kicks one time. He feared the man who had practiced one kick 10,000 times. 小龙 (xiao long – the Little Dragon) understood that it was *that* man who is dangerous. The duality of the danger thus; dangerous because he had practiced and therefore subsumed the art of the kick, becoming one with the action; doubly dangerous via the self-evident, single-minded discipline it requires to devote oneself to such mastery.

Remember, your devotion to the positive things is your wax and old yellow car. You may not see the meaning now, but there's a gleaming reward awaiting at the end of it for you.

June 1st
YEARNING FOR LIFE

"I don't want to survive. I want to live."

SOLOMON NORTHUP – 12 YEARS A SLAVE

Every day for a month ask yourself these questions:

» Am I living the life I desire?
» Do I feel excited and invigorated each morning upon arising?
» Do I have a purpose?

If the answer is consistently no, then it's time to change something. We are not here to exist through the bare maintenance of taking on enough oxygen and food and sleep. We are here to embrace the imponderable joys of what it is to be human. The mountain-top vistas, the speechless wonder of a new-born tot, the sweet emotional rollercoaster of intimate relationships, the euphoria of using the creative juices. These are the juice of living. We will have to survive some periods of life, to be sure. Days on the calendar when we're low on battery and we can't seem to find our charger. During these we go in to emergency mode and it's about coming through and allowing ourselves to learn as much as we can from the feelings we experience. Should we one day find ourselves in a position where our freedom to live is impaired from the outside, then inevitably we will have to fight for that freedom. A man or woman without the freedom to follow the dictates of their heart is a parrot in a cage. It can be taught to imitate very well, but the greater part of its majesty is lost. We must always subscribe and support the right to life, liberty and the pursuit of happiness for all.

June 2nd

THE POWER OF A COMPLIMENT

"You is kind. You is smart. You is important."

AIBILEEN CLARK – THE HELP

Today, go out and pay as many sincere compliments as you can. Be genuine. Say it from the heart. Notice how you feel as a result. Lifting another lifts oneself. You cannot give out positive energy without it mysteriously boomeranging straight back to you. One of the many free serotonin-hits available. Every person deserves to feel good about themselves. Everyone deserves to be built up. When we get the opportunity to be a contributing influence to make someone smile, we can take it. Beautiful words of praise or admiration are usually cherished far more than diamonds, their lustre more than that of gold. The reason being that they are a salute from one soul to another, an acknowledgement of the divinity within. "You have a lovely smile. I love your sense of humour. You are so brilliant at singing. Your helping me has made all the difference. You've been tremendously patient with me." Spreading the love keeps the chain going in the game of compliment tag. Do it enough, and it's impossible that lots of tags won't keep finding their way back to you.

June 3rd
EVOLUTION

*"Wally, don't you see that comfort can be dangerous.
I mean, you like to be comfortable, and I like to be
comfortable, too, but comfort can lull you into a
dangerous tranquillity."*

ANDRE – MY DINNER WITH ANDRE

Comfort is lovely, and we love it because, well, it's comfortable. A hot shower is more naturally amenable to the senses than an icy cold one. An evening of channel-flicking asks less than a stimulating and thought-provoking book. Taking an air-conditioned, back-massaging, radio-playing car to go five minutes to the shop is much more appealing than a brisk twenty-minute walk, taking in everything along the way, smiling and connecting with nature.

Comfort is a luxury, and we keep it that way by not making it a default necessity. The irony is, a cold shower is a shock to the system at first, but take one regularly and before long you wonder how you ever got by without one. Discomfort turns to comfort.

When you can, see if you can take the slightly more uncomfortable option. You may find that you get quite comfortable being uncomfortable.

June 4th
DO THE UNNECESSARY

"Nothing is more necessary than the unnecessary."

UNCLE ELISEO – LA VITA E BELLA (1997)

Who decides what is necessary and what is unnecessary? Mother nature, perhaps.

Full expression of ourselves is the most necessary unnecessary aspect of life. If we stripped away all the unnecessary, what would be left? Life cannot be confined or shoehorned in to what is necessary only. Survey a field of sheep and you will surely see a gang of lambs cavorting around. On the savannah, one will see the same scene amongst cubs. Food, water and oxygen sustain life, but fun and frivolity enrich it. In our musings we find joy. You define your necessary unnecessaries. You don't need to explain them. It is the necessaries that we must live for. It is the unnecessaries that we want to live for.

June 5th

"If you speak my name, I vanish."

Dr. Lessing – La Vita E Bella

Silence, like idyllic moments and sunsets, needs no narration. Silence can be used dualistically – for both clearing out and for ushering in. Silence is louder than thunder, more persuasive than the strongest argument, more transformative than the greatest teachers. Silence is the antidote, the stimulus, the answer, the question, the power, the pain, the punisher. Silence consoles and it scolds. Silence is a friend and an enemy. Silence knows what you need and tells you so, if you're listening. Silence is golden. Silence is a song, a poem, a work of art. Silence is a trusted companion to the wise, an unbearable master to fools. Silence is the highest language. Silence tells you that you belong. Silence listens to you. Always. Silence is everything. And nothing. Silence is.

June 6th
DON'T FORGET YOURSELF

"Good people end up in hell because they can't forgive themselves."

DR CHRIS NIELSEN – WHAT DREAMS MAY COME

Forgiving others can come with a difficulty level anywhere between defeating an Orc to conquering a Balrog. At times, forgiving ourselves is on a par with getting the ring of power in to the fires of Mount Doom (why didn't the eagles just drop it in?!) We want our own mistakes to be cut as outtakes and scrapped in the studio bin, but somehow they keep finding themselves displayed on the big screen of our minds. We're the one in the comfy seat watching ourselves play out all-too-familiar scenes. We know all the lines. Until we take out that particular slide from the projector and lovingly confine it to the archives, we will continue to suffer the pangs of guilt and torment. Does forgiving ourselves for the harms we've caused others mean we're glib or insouciant about those wrongs? It need not mean that. Forgiveness for self is the understanding that on our path to oneness, to merging and blending harmoniously in to all that is, we must be right with ourselves. As is often true, the doctor can be the most stubborn patient, but this doctor must learn to take their medicine. And that medicine is accepting one's past, owning it and finding peace with it. If we can do that, then we'll find our way back to the Shire, amongst lush sights and warm friends.

June 7th
WIN WILL IT STOP

"Sometimes when you win, you lose."

ANNIE COLLINS-NIELSEN – WHAT DREAMS MAY COME

The ancient Greeks called it a Pyrrhic victory. It's when you win the battle but lose all your mind, money or morals along the way. It's this societal idea that seems to do the rounds – "I must win!" What, even if you lose your soul? Don't care... I must win! You don't mind ending up all alone as you show your loved one once again how right you are (as always). Don't care! I must win! Ill and need to rest? Nope, I've got to turn up and win. Win! Win! Win! That's all that matters. All this amazing winning we're doing on this planet. Isn't it wonderful. Winning is an interesting concept. By definition, for someone or something to win, someone or something has to lose. What about the win-win scenarios? Well sure, but that has to mean true win-wins. It can't be myopic, temporary or superficial wins – it must mean real wins for everyone, for the whole. Win at all costs is the mentality that has caused millions to die over a hundred yards of mud and companies to do anything to maintain profits. We're not here to win, we're here to begin. Begin what? To reveal and revel in the limitless love and enlightenment in us and that surrounds us.

June 8th
MAMMA MAYA

"Thought is real. Physical is the illusion."

ALBERT LEWIS – WHAT DREAMS MAY COME

Maya – the Hindu idea of the illusion of the permanency of the physical world around us. The magic show that never stops. Your beeping phone, a bus ride, the familiar sight of your home and surroundings. It's very convincing. We take comfort in the very consistent impressions that minute by minute seem to hold steady. The material world really does dazzle. But zoomed out and viewed from a galactic perspective, the physical happenings we experience are mere twinkles in time. Mirages. They dupe the blunted senses into thinking that everything stops at the level of what they can see. The irony in that being, everything one sees was at one time not there and will sooner or later no longer be there.

June 9th
SEE THE HUMAN

"You treat a disease, you win, you lose. You treat a person, I guarantee you, you'll win, no matter what the outcome."

DR HUNTER ADAMS – PATCH ADAMS

It can't be a coincidence that time and again Robin Williams played roles where he was the spirit guide to show others the cobbled and sometimes forgotten path that leads to humanity. Whether we're in a hospital, a home (wig or no wig) or a school, we all deserve to be treated like a human being. Now, more than ever, we need to remember that humanity. You are not a number, a figure, a statistic, a tick, a cross, a one or a zero, an M or an F, a Black, Asian, Caucasian or Other, an able-bodied or disabled, a have or a have-not, a rich or poor, young or old, technophile or technophobe. You are a human being. *Human*, meaning you are part of the beautiful, amazing, simple, complex, frustratingly brilliant, selfish, selfless, stubborn, adaptive, talented race that is the Homo Sapiens. And *Being*, meaning, well, being. You exist. You are an entity. An undefinable definable, valued, priceless blob of matter and mind and magical soul. Add those two ingredients together and you get = *human being*.

June 10th

ALL ROADS LEAD TO HOME

"All of life is a coming home. Salesmen, secretaries,
coal miners, beekeepers, sword swallowers, all of us. All
the restless hearts of the world, all trying to find a way
home…. Home. The dictionary defines it as both a place
of origin and a goal or destination."

DR HUNTER ADAMS – PATCH ADAMS

Behind every action there is an intention. And behind every intention there is a longing. A longing for love and a longing for home. Those who have experienced quite extreme physical circumstances; famine, prison, homelessness, know that the only thing that exists is love and kindness. On a moment-by-moment basis, those who aren't experiencing such extreme conditions forget it. They think life is about spreadsheets and the weather and checking the scores and getting past the next level on Candy Crush. Those things are all the fun of the game. *Maya*. Behind them all, behind the maya, we're trying to get home.

You know where home is.

June 11th
CUT TO THE TRUTH

"But if you had regular hands, you'd be like everyone else."

RED-HAIRED WOMAN IN TV SHOW AUDIENCE – EDWARD SCISSORHANDS

Do you want to be like everyone else? Or do you want to be you?

Trying to be like everyone else is lose-lose;

1. It's impossible.
2. It's boring.

Trying to be you is win-win;

1. It's easy.
2. It's cool.

June 12th
KINGDOM COME

"The natural state of mankind is, and I know this is a controversial idea, is freedom. Is freedom. And the proof is the length to which a man, woman or child will go to regain it once taken. He will break loose his chains. He will decimate his enemies. He will try and try and try, against all odds, against all prejudices, to get home."

JOHN QUINCY ADAMS – AMISTAD

Freedom = *free-dom* = the Kingdom of being free. Inner freedom of the mind and soul and outer freedom of the body and business. Both priceless. One worth fighting for. One worth surrendering for.

Make the decree: I am free.

June 13th

UNIVERSAL STUDIO

"So it turns out there's life on other planets. Boy, this is really going to change the Miss Universe contest."

JAY LENO – CONTACT

If you were visited by an alien, if you didn't run a mile, and after you caught your breath, what would you ask the other-worldly being? Where are you from? What are you called? What's your home like? Do you have family? Maybe the same things matter to all beings everywhere throughout the universe. Or perhaps home and family and belonging are peculiar to this planet. Scientists are pushing the boundaries of discovery on what we know about the cosmos. Quasars, neutron stars, black holes and event horizons, dark matter, and now dark energy (ooooooh in Minions voice), the wonders of space keep satisfying our never-ending curiosity to probe and explore the universe and our limitations. The beautiful duality of the discoveries is that they open our mind to the mind-boggling numbers, sizes, speeds, distances and energies that exist, and those in turn call us to remember the profound joy that we have in our existence here on our relatively infinitesimal fleck of rock. We've been gifted this hospitable home that has been good to us. While we may not quite yet be guardians of the galaxy, we each individually are custodians of our humble allotment wherever we've been placed on this lush, amazing oasis called Planet Earth.

June 14th
PROOF

"Your dad, did you love him."
"Yes, very much."
"Prove it."

PALMER & ELEANOR – CONTACT

Faith very much falls within the category of words that could be described as emotionally charged. It can elicit strong reaction within the hearer. For many who are or have been involved or exposed to religion, it will very likely have specific nuances and connotations. In other contexts, like self-help books or sports team dressing rooms, it almost certainly exists, but quite possibly under different names. Faith is the basic mechanism by which any organism both survives and thrives. It is the unobserved cause behind every observed effect. It is not a question of whether one has faith, only a question of what that faith is placed upon. Faith is always, always leading us on a path. Where to, we decide.

Faith can be a beautiful word. It can mean that you empower with positive charge anything you deem forward-facing and inspirational. It can point at anything you want to be or achieve. It can lift your spirits and act as a verbal touchstone to remind you that believing is seeing.

June 15th
DON'T WASTE YOUR BREATH

"If you've got something to say about me, say it to my face, not behind my back."

MALCOLM McDOWELL – THE PLAYER

Say what you mean and mean what you say.

When we are in our power, we speak our truth directly to people with tact and sensitivity. We consider another person's feelings, while considering our own need to voice something. The two get balanced. Feel the need to moan or criticise someone? Go home, look in a mirror, and moan to yourself about why you feel the need to moan about someone else. You are an agent of power. There is never a good reason to bitch on someone, and it never makes you feel good about yourself. If something needs to be said, say it to their face with maturity and honesty.

Which means when we do talk about people behind their back… it is to say how great they are. How we've learned something from them. How they impressed us with their attitude or humanity. Building people up becomes second nature. As we look for, find and voice the good in others, we start to see it in ourselves. Honest self-appraisal doesn't mean only recognising our faults and shortcomings. It also means acknowledging our talents and abilities. When we see ourselves as teammates rather than opponents we realise we can pass the ball. We don't fear others' achievements. We celebrate them. They act as fuel for our own strivings.

June 16th
DON'T BE AFRAID TO LOSE

"How many times have you lost everything, Jack?"

BOBBY DURAN – HAVANA

living – dying

winning – losing

remembering – forgetting

rising up – falling down

getting stronger – getting weaker

becoming – unbecoming

learning – unlearning

coming – going

What does it take to lose all our fears about losing something? What happens when the fear is gone? What becomes of us when we are refined in the fire and come out again, released, renewed and reborn?

June 17th

HEAVENLY GLORY

"Don't think, feel! It's like a finger pointing away to the moon. Do not concentrate on the finger or you will miss all of the heavenly glory."

LEE – ENTER THE DRAGON

Road signs, words, gestures – they are not end things in their own right. They are the finger pointing to the heavens. They direct one to something far deeper – a place, a meaning, a feeling. The glory is there to feel, if we can move past focusing on the form. Feel the amazing things that are all around. Close your eyes. Feel the love and energy that is flowing all around you. Acknowledge the limitless goodness and abundance. Feel it. Don't try to understand or compute it. Connect to it with your soul. Become one with the flow. Be water. Partake of the heavenly glory.

June 18th
BONKERS & BRILLIANT

"You're insane, but you might also be brilliant."

GEORGE SHAPIRO – MAN ON THE MOON

It's when we're thirsty that we go to the well and look down in to the darkness to draw up life-giving water. Similarly, it's when we're on the edges of our limits, that's when we get glimpses of the brilliance within. Sometimes we almost wish we could engineer extreme necessity because we know it stimulates the survival and thrive-all instinct within. It's when we're acting insane that we can be at our most authentic. Sanity, when it means being on a sound mental equilibrium, is lovely. But sanity meaning that we conform to convention and routine… nah, let's be a bit insane. Let's turn things on their head and experiment. If nobody had ever tried to do the weird stuff, we wouldn't have abstract art, jazz or peanut butter and jam sandwiches. We all have the explorer within us – the intrepid traveller that can carve out our own path.

June 19th
SUNSET

"How do you know when you're finished with a painting?"
"How do you know when you're finished making love?"

INTERVIEWER & JACKSON POLLOCK – POLLOCK

How do you know you're alive?

How do you know you didn't imagine that kiss?

How do you know you really did just see that pig fly past your window?

How do you know you love that special person?

How do you know what an apple tastes like?

We deal in such cold, calculative terms. Everything is based on knowledge, yet the only things that matter are feelings. Maya Angelou really got it spot on:

> *People will forget what you said,*
> *People will forget what you did,*
> *but,*
> *People will never forget how you made them feel.*

You may or may not remember how long the flight was. You may or may not remember how much the hotel cost. You may or may not remember the name of the resort. You may or may not remember what you had for dinner on the first night… But you will *always* remember the magic of standing on the beach, the setting sun kissing the glimmering aqua, dolphins cavorting on the horizon, peachy clouds lazily observing, as you gazed in to each other's eyes and felt true and perfect unison.

刻骨铭心 *ke gu ming xin*
Carved in the bones, etched in the heart

We know because we know. In a world where more and more bits of *data* are being filed on search engines, let's never forget, the only *engravings* are in our hearts.

June 20th
WATCH WHERE YOU'RE STANDING

"Take Louis 'The Lug' McGurk. Died tragically at 25."
"What happened?"
"Somebody stepped on his fingers?"
"And that killed him?!"
"He was hanging from a window ledge of the Edison Hotel at the time."

ANGELO, ANTHONY & ALDO – OSCAR (1991)

Context is everything. Which is why we can feel so good even when things seem so bad. Tell a guy he just lost his job and he'll frown, but tell him straight after that he's won the lottery and he'll leap and whoop. Inform someone that it's rained where you are for ten days straight and they'll apologise to you... but follow it up with news that prior to that there had been a ten-year drought and they'll retract their condolences and celebrate with you. Everything is context. And what is the best, most amazing bit of context any of us can ever be reminded of?

That. We. Are. Alive.

That. We. Matter.

That. Every. Second. Is. A. Gift.

June 21st
A CUP OF SPECIAL STUFF

"The entire British Empire was built on cups of tea."

EDDY – LOCK, STOCK AND TWO SMOKING BARRELS

Like Michael and Bugs did in *Space Jam* with Michael's secret stuff, we each get to find what acts as our magic elixir. It might be a good cuppa, it could be a morning yoga or meditation ritual, perhaps it's a secret path in the woods or a special song. Whatever it is, find your inspiration and use it to boost you to be the person that makes you happy. You can do this in many different areas. Experiment with your food, sleep and conversation. Find the literal and metaphorical juices that get your juices flowing.

June 22nd
HOT CHOCOLATE

"Overrated [talking about love]. Biochemically no different than eating large quantities of chocolate."

JOHN MILTON – DEVIL'S ADVOCATE

Maybe this is why divorce rates and chocolate sales are both at an all-time high?!

Let's play devil's advocate for a moment. Let's pretend chocolate could substitute for meaningful relationships with other human beings, would we simply stock the cupboards and lock out the outside world? As we advance further and deeper in to a digital epoch, we are going to be asked this fundamental question in multiple areas. When we can take a pill that gives us all the nutrients and energy of three normal meals, will we take it? When we can be plugged in and supercharged in ten minutes to substitute what would take eight hours of natural sleep, will we do it? When we have created talking, breathing, thinking robots who have been programmed to love us no matter what, will we still have need for one another?

June 23rd
ENIGMA

"I'm not going to tell the story the way it happened. I'm going to tell it the way I remember it."

FINNEGAN BELL – GREAT EXPECTATIONS (1998)

Within this simple quote lies a world of deep meaning. Your story is your story. Only you know the meaning of it. Only you have the key to decode the message it contains. Facts are irrelevant. One person sees a 6, another sees a 9. Who is right? It doesn't matter. What matters is that you fall in love with your own story, your own movie. You can make it a comedy, an action flick, a tragedy, a horror, a romance... you can make it all of these.

Do we even recall actual events with perfect clarity and integrity of the 'facts'? It has been suggested that we don't. It would seem that we quite literally rewrite the history books within our own minds. And that's OK. Because it brings us back to the same place – we get to choose our story, our narrative. To an observer, your life may look like a tough battle, but to you it could be a fairy-tale. Some see a person living a life of splendour, but in that person's own mind, they are living a nightmare. Your memories are not static photographs, they are kaleidoscopes. You choose the meanings and the feelings. You write your own story, both forwards and backwards, in time.

June 24th
TRUE OR FALSE

"We are who we are. People don't change."

ESTELLA – GREAT EXPECTATIONS (1998)

A profound, immutable, elemental truth?

Or one of the greatest, most persistent lies that has ever been perpetuated?

(Or both?)

You decide.

June 25th

NO SUPERSTITIONS

"Caesar. Caesar! Beware of the Ides of March."
"One date's as good as another for a funeral."

SOOTHSAYER & JULIUS CAESAR – CLEOPATRA (1963)

Superstition is as old as man, and putting on lucky socks when you have your Super Saturday's down at the bowling alley is cool. But when it comes to making a positive choice, doing something kind, taking action or changing direction, if you think that there is a better time than now to do so, you're…. wrong(?)!

The irony of the concept 'Beware of the Ides of March,' is that there was no fear or superstition associated with the Ides of March in Roman times. The Ide of a month was simply a mid-month reference point. Shakespeare entirely fabricated it as an ominous day, which then became charged with myth and legend. Myths and legends are great fun. But let's only allow them to affect us positively – never to deter or frighten us from facing life boldly and bravely.

June 26th
ABIDE WITH ME

"The dude abides."

Dude – The Big Lebowski

In science, the First Law of Thermodynamics states that within a closed system, energy can be neither created nor destroyed. How does this relate to you? Well, you are that energy. You are atoms and molecules, sharing the same basic elements as an elephant, a sandwich, the ocean, a star, a comet… all of it. 70% of your body is water, which is hydrogen and oxygen. Quite simply, this means that not only do you exist, current tense, but that you have always existed, and will always exist, in the most literal scientific sense. If this doesn't make you feel like a million bucks, heaven only knows what will.

On that note, up and atom!

June 27th
DO(N'T) PLAY THE PROPHET(ESS)

"Cassandra in Greek legend, you recall, was condemned to know the future but to be disbelieved when she foretold it. Hence the agony of foreknowledge combined with the impotence to do anything about it."

KATHRYN RAILLY – 12 MONKEYS

Hence the maxim that the wise abide by; avoid giving unsolicited advice.

Why? Because, it's fundamentally unwanted, and what is unwanted is rejected. Life is not about what we need, it is about what we want. Everybody needs a healthy diet, but only some eat a balanced, wholesome blend of food. Everybody needs positivity and inspiration, but only some actively seek it. Everybody needs love, but only some act and live in harmony with the principles that engender it. You may see very clearly the harm or trap someone you love is about to walk right in to, but you're powerless to stop it. They have to go through that experience (if that's what they choose.) You worry about the only thing you can control – you. In the common parlance, you do you.

June 28th
LEGOLAND

"I'm gonna disintegrate you!"

YELLOWJACKET – ANT-MAN

Just like when we were kids and we took things apart – lego, radios, Mum's special vase (eek!) – only to put them back together again, similarly, sometimes we need to feel disjointed to understand how to feel jointed; to know disintegration before we can rejoice in integration once more; to learn the working of our own cogs and mechanisms before we can learn how to be of service helping others fix theirs. And this is a joyful journey. Painful and confusing, to be sure, but through it all we learn about ourselves. Through it all, we are.

June 29th
HE'S TAKING THE P***

"I wake up in the morning and piss excellence."

RICKY BOBBY – TALLADEGA NIGHTS: THE BALLAD OF RICKY BOBBY

Whatever he is drinking, where are they selling it?!

A word on self-confidence. It is something we can all foster. Confidence cannot be understood looking at another. That is perception. Self-confidence is about building up your own value and self-esteem. Reading, praying, meditating until you start to believe that you are worthy. That you have inherent and intrinsic worth, regardless of any outward behaviour, achievements, conformity or acknowledgement. It is deepened by empowering behaviour, achievements of your own definition, and taking action for what matters to you.

June 30th
DISCERNMENT

*"There are good people in this world, a lot of them. And
there are bad people. You have to tell the difference."*
"Fine. But how does one tell the difference?"
*"Well, it's super simple. I mean, you just have to... You
can intuit it, you can sense it. Sometimes, you can even
feel it."*

EDDIE BROCK & VENOM – VENOM

Hands up if you've been the *good* person before?

Hands up if you've been the *bad* person before?

Hands up if you've met a *good* person before?

Hands up if you've met a *bad* person before?

How do you know the difference?

We've all been given Spidey-senses when it comes to feeling, intuiting another person. Sometimes another person can completely dupe us, but that's quite rare. Usually we know. And we allow or subscribe to the interactions we have with that person as an active choice. Our task is to try and be the *good* version of ourselves. Our choice, is to gravitate and seek out the *good* others that we may be uplifted and inspired. And most importantly, our opportunity is to look for the good *in* others, ourselves and the world.

July 1st
I AM A CHILD OF ...?

"You are a son of God."
"Thank you. I've never been called a son of God before.
I've been called a son of a you-know-what plenty of times,
but I've never been called a son of God."

SISTER HELEN & MATTHEW – DEAD MAN WALKING

We've probably all been called all sorts of names before. Some might take more offence at being called a son of God than a son of a gun. Whatever your position in relation to religion or spirituality, one thing is for certain, you are a child of the universe. Whether you like it or not, believe it or not, you have celestial heritage. When you can start to feel that connection, that glory, everything becomes easy. You don't need to fight anything. You know your place. You are a part of the oneness, equal in value to everyone and everything.

The universe loves you.

July 2nd
DO NOT FEAR TO FIND YOURSELF

"If you want to stay in London, be tough… be tough! Live the life. But don't do it because you're looking for someone. Do it because you're looking for yourself."

EDITH – ENOLA HOLMES

Some people, as a part of their efforts on self-development, and on the path to renewal and awakening, investigate the workings of their inner minds and explore past behaviours and events in a quest to uncover their fears. This is somewhat counter-intuitive, for fears, by definition, are the last thing we seek to find. Children, the old adage goes, are best seen and not heard. Fears shouldn't be seen *or* heard. They're lovely just as they are, tucked away deep in the subconscious. Of course, the truth is that they're influencing and impacting our every move, but as long as we're not conscious of the fact, we're happy to maintain the status quo. Yet, when we arrive at a place where we know that the outer circumstances of life are, paradoxically, irrelevant, that the whole of our existence is being played out on the inside track, within our own hearts and minds, then we have become invincible. Live wherever, do whatever, be with whomever, those things will take care of themselves, beautifully. First, let's be right with ourselves, let's find ourselves, and all will be right with the world.

July 3rd
FLOW AND CRASH

"The world is what you make of it, friend. If it doesn't fit, you make alterations."

STELLA – SILVERADO

Some truths are more annoying than others. This is one of them. We prefer to vacillate between trying extremely hard to change the world and others, and of course, failing miserably, and then swing to the other extreme, back in our shells, muttering to ourselves 'it's no use, it's no use, none of them are listening, the world has gone to pot…'

Water doesn't change the bottle, the tea-pot, the soil, the sea, the body, the cloud… rather, it shapes and shifts itself to the situation or environment at hand. If it gets hot, it starts doing a jive and spreads itself out in the form of gas. When it gets cold, it consolidates and battens down the hatches in the form of ice. It knows how to adapt, how to flow, how to crash. We can be like water. Willing to learn and adapt to the terrain before us. Remember, adaptability is one of the greatest of all human qualities. Sometimes we just need a reminder of how we can be our best, whatever the situation. By being water, what we are really saying is, we are the masters of every environment, every situation, every opportunity, because we assess what is happening outside of us and then elevate the energy inside of us to the best frequency to work with and maximise the moment.

July 4th

LOVE IS A BOUNCY CASTLE

"I am in love with you. And I know that love is just a shout into the void, and that oblivion is inevitable, and that we're all doomed. And that one day all our labour will be returned to dust. And I know that the sun will swallow the only earth we will ever have. And I am in love with you."

AUGUSTUS WATERS – THE FAULT IN OUR STARS

Ah, romance. Has there ever been any logic in love? Maybe love is the highest logic, the simplest yet most brilliant algorithm. Love is like a bouncy castle. When you enter, all sense of gravity, structure, boundaries, mature behaviour and routine goes out the window. You bounce around giddy and gleeful. It's fun, exhilarating, invigorating. You get kicked in the head, you don't care. You come out bashed, bruised and dazed. It doesn't matter, you're straight back in. It comes the end of the day and the castle gets deflated, you're right back in the morning, pumping it up again. Love has always and will always make us do crazy things. And that's OK. It's not meant to make sense. Love is like sunlight. One is free to simply bathe and bask in it. You may get sunburnt, you may suffer sunstroke, you may overdo it, and yet it remains, fundamentally glorious.

As the sun warms the body, so love warms the soul.

July 5th
LOVED BY LOVE

"Everything wanna be loved. Us sing and dance and holla just wanting to be loved. Look at them trees. Notice how the trees do everything people do to get attention... except walk?"

SHUG AVERY – THE COLOR PURPLE

We all have a thirst. And that thirst is for love. We all want it. We all need it. In this we are universally equal. Many care for money, some don't. Many care for learning and knowledge, some don't. Many care for success, achievement and prestige, some don't. But back of all the outward huffing and puffing that a person does or doesn't make toward some supposed attainment, each and every single one of us want to be loved. It is not a choice. It is not optional. It is the very essence of our souls. To exist is to be engineered and designed with the sole form and function to *be* love (giving, receiving, being, basking in, in the highest sense are one and the same manifestations of love and cannot be distinguished as separate elements, although at the surface level we often make this separation.) When we're angry, lost, violent, hurting, do we still want love? Yes, in those moments as in our Zen ones, what we're craving is love. And, of course, as love is everything, only love can bring us home back to love.

July 6th
OPUS DEI

"On the page, it looked nothing. The beginning simple, almost comic. Just a pulse. Bassoons and basset horns, like a rusty squeezebox. And then suddenly, high above it, an oboe. A single note, hanging there, unwavering. Until a clarinet took over and sweetened it into a phrase of such delight! This was no composition by a performing monkey! This was a music I'd never heard. Filled with such longing, such unfulfillable longing, it had me trembling. It seemed to me that I was hearing the voice of God." (Speaking about Mozart's symphony)

ANTONIO SALIERI – AMADEUS

What makes you hear the voice, see the face, feel the hand, of God?

We are all a manifestation of the ineffable wonder that is existence. We love music, film, dance, poetry, photography, nature and flowers so. They are the heavenly glory. When we can still the mind, halt the thinking, and feel, feel it, we become one with it. As Alan Watts said; "when you really enjoy the music, it is because you have become one with it. You are not self-consciously thinking, 'ah, this is splendid music, I really am enjoying it,' which, ironically, indicates you've stopped enjoying it. No, when you are truly enjoying it is when you've become one with it. When immersed, music and hearer have merged. You *are* the music."

What Mozart did in creating the music is what we are all capable of doing in listening to it: letting go of the mind-obsessed handbrake and cruising on the soul highway, hood down, wind in the hair.

July 7th
DOUBLE STANDARDS

"In a star it's temperament, but in a chorus girl it's just bad taste."

AUTHOR OF PRETTY LADY – 42ND STREET (1933)

Double standards are like taxes – an unavoidable part of life. People in the public eye are some of the ones most often on the receiving end of our hypocrisy. We simultaneously laud and loathe, commend and condemn, deify and decry the very same qualities and behaviours in them that in any ordinary folk would go completely without comment, care or even consciousness. Why do we do it? Perhaps by inherent virtue of being in the media, we find ourselves generating strong positive or negative emotions toward a famous figure. Also, perhaps, because it is very easy to see another person as better or worse than us. We have this curious disposition to want to compare ourselves to each other, placing fellow humans in a pecking order either above or below ourselves. The hardest thing in the world can be to remember that truly we're all equal. Equal in value, equal in potentiality, equal in our right to be here. Let us learn that integrity is key. Let us seek to be fair in the esteem we hold of all people.

July 8th
THE TRUTH ABOUT SECRETS

"No more lies. No more secrets!"
"Secrets are my life."

SARAH & ALFRED – THE PRESTIGE

Secrets keep us sick.

The truth sets us free.

July 9th
BEING OR PRETENDING

"Every great magic trick consists of three parts or acts. The first part is called "The Pledge." The magician shows you something ordinary: a deck of cards, a bird or a man. He shows you this object. Perhaps he asks you to inspect it to see if it is indeed real, unaltered, normal. But, of course, it probably isn't. The second act is called "The Turn." The magician takes the ordinary something and makes it do something extraordinary. Now you're looking for the secret... but you won't find it, because of course you're not really looking. You don't really want to know. You want to be fooled. But you wouldn't clap yet. Because making something disappear isn't enough; you have to bring it back. That's why every magic trick has a third act, the hardest part, the part we call "The Prestige."

JOHN CUTTER – THE PRESTIGE

Do you really want to be happy, or are you just paying lip service?

Do you really want to drive the top-end car to feel the power and the performance, or are you just in love with the idea of being seen in it?

Do you really want to taste and savour the sumptuous cake, or are you merely wrapped up in the idea of eating it?

Do you really want to inhabit and live the real you? Or are you simply aiming for the idea of being you?

Too many of us, too much of the time, are energising the *idea* of being, doing, feeling, experiencing. It's the modern-day phenomenon of filming the concert while being at the concert. When quizzed why you paid top whack for tickets when you could have watched the video of someone else who paid simply to record it, you take deep offence... *It's my constitutional right to go to the concert so I can record the concert so I can energise the theoretical concept that I was at the concert and proudly show off to other people that I had filmed a concert...*

Don't live in the *idea* of living. Live!

July 10th
FUN OR PHILOSOPHY?

"My intention has only been to entertain, nothing more."

EISENHEIM – THE ILLUSIONIST (2006)

The madness of life means that sometimes we end up inferring deep meaning where none was meant and ignoring the message where one was intended. The fun is in figuring out which is which. Take sport. Simply a game? Or a deep, philosophical and metaphorical representation of the struggle of life? Why not both? The beauty is, only you can decide. Nobody can convince you that a bunch of people kicking a ball or passing a baton is meaningless, none can convince you that it is beyond life and death. You and you alone know what it means. The same applies to everything.

July 11th
DOUBLE DUTCH

"Never do or say anything that the person standing in front of you cannot understand."

ARTHUR RIMBAUD – I'M NOT THERE

A habit that many of us have is explaining our actions to others. We do it to keep the peace. We do it because of fear of judgement. We do it because we haven't reached a place where we can simply be. We also seek to show off our knowledge, even when we know that the person before us either doesn't get or doesn't care what we have to share.

One of the most beautiful breakthroughs we can make is the day we realise that nothing we say (or do) changes another person. It can influence, inspire, cajole, annoy and inflame them, but they and only they will make the decision to change or remain. In this area, we expend too much energy in games of emotional validation – *you tell me that I'm OK, I'm accepted, I'm on the right track, and I'll tell you the same thing.*

Today, let's try to raise our words to the level where we realise that we don't need to say anything to anybody. When we do speak, we speak out of being. We speak from curated self-knowledge that whispers *'nothing I can say to another human being can change them, but it can change me.'*

July 12th
REMEMBER THE MEANS AND THE END

"I didn't think you'd ever give up the book, I thought it was too important to you."
"It was, I was carrying and reading it everyday, got so caught up in protecting it, I forgot to live by what I'd learnt from it."
"And what's that?"
"To do more for others than you do for yourself."

SOLARA & ELI – THE BOOK OF ELI

What's more important, the means or the end? Do we eat only to fulfil the bodily requirements to have fuel (the end), squeezing out the joy of the consumption? (loss of the means) Or is it a joy and a destination within itself to consume the meal?

We see an imbalance of means and end occurring in so many areas of life. Religious people, who are so committed to living the rules as a way of gaining salvation, focus completely on the letter of the law (the means) while forgetting it is the spirit of the law which ultimately creates *heaven* (the end).

We see this in our education systems, where learning has been consumed by the means – tests and measurements and frameworks – to test and live up to the means, to confirm the validity of the means, to consolidate our belief in the means... with complete loss of the end; for a person to be introduced to the universe and themselves, to the principles of glory that self-evidently exist and may be observed and framed under banners we call geography, music, mathematics... and much more importantly, to be able to think for themselves and learn of love, health and service.

We see the imbalance in sport, where winning at all costs has swallowed the means, the end, everything! But particularly loss of the means – that sport in and of itself is about the thrill of performing, about the joy of artistic and kinaesthetic expression, about demonstrating the virtues of sportsmanship, of competing for the game's own sake.

Duality asks us to remember both sides of the coin. When we lose balance in the equation, forgetting either the means or the end, we lose so much of what is on offer, of what it was we were seeking in the first place.

July 13th
THE PHOENIX

"What we lost in the fire, we will find in the ashes."

GOODNIGHT ROBICHEAUX / SAM CHISOLM – THE MAGNIFICENT
SEVEN (2016)

This beautiful proverb has rich and varied meaning. It says, whatever you think of a situation or event, particularly one that you may have labelled as tragic, difficult or unwanted, it can bring an equal and opposite benefit, if you're willing to be patient and humble enough to see it. It says, nothing you can do is lost forever. On a cosmic level, everything that one does returns unto that person. This is universal law. What you are, what you do, what you say, is what you are, what you do, what you say. The profound simplicity of it is mind-boggling. Nothing can be lost. Literally. The proverb alludes to the circle of life, the great revolving wheel that encompasses all life, all energy, all matter, that never stops, never ends. We are all a part of it. When we consider this, it can bring immense joy. The proverb calls us to have hope. Everything is OK. We don't need to mourn or energise a loss, it is already on its way back. It was never lost to begin with.

July 14th

SWORD OF TRUTH

---

*"Do you know what writing a book against war is like?
It's like writing a book against Wednesdays. Wednesdays,
Blue, are a fact of life... and if you don't like them, you
could stay in bed, but you can't stop them... because
Wednesdays are coming and if today isn't actually a
Wednesday, it soon will be."*

DAPHNE MILNE – GOODBYE CHRISTOPHER ROBIN

Sometimes, once aboard the positivity train, it can be hard to acknowledge the unpleasant challenges of life. It's like a person who previously only ever saw the dog poo at the park, causing them to moan, complain and lament the dogs, the owners, the smell. And now they've turned uber-positive, they've swung to the other extreme. Dog poo? What poo? I can't see or smell any!

It is one thing to acknowledge and accept something, it is another entirely to empower, fight or resist it. As we study the world around us, we will observe certain behaviour and situations that happen. All of it constitutes what we cannot control. We have a choice to be aware and accept the world as it is. We also have the choice to accept ourselves as we are, but also take up the challenge to change ourselves. We won't stop wars. They are a fundamental occurrence of humanity. They have always happened and it would seem like they always will happen (? – maybe they won't, maybe we will collectively one day reach enlightenment.) Either way, our energy goes to mastering ourselves. Am I creating wars in my own life, my own head? Am I building bridges, or blowing them up? Am I accepting that Wednesday is coming around, but preparing to meet it well with my shield of integrity, cloak of humility and sword of truth?

July 15th
TOTAL RECALL

"I'm tired of remembering it that way. Aren't you tired, too, Mrs Travers? Now we all have our sad tales, but don't you want to finish the story? Let it all go and have a life that isn't dictated by the past?"

WALT DISNEY – SAVING MR. BANKS

100% dictated by the past – I have no identity*, no freedom. My past defines me. I am chained and shackled by who I think I am, by who I think you think I am, by who I think you think I think I am. (*Or a completely fixed identity, depending on how you look at it)

75% dictated by the past – I am weighed down by the past. It is like an extremely heavy rucksack that I carry constantly. Occasionally, I take it off for brief respite, but never for long.

50% dictated by the past – I have many moments that I spend in the present. They are glorious. I do carry a lot of the guilt, shame and weight of the past around with me, too. Past and present blur and blend, and I'm not always sure where one ends and the other begins.

25% dictated by the past – I live my life with power and purpose. I am intent on creating my life in this moment, however, I do sometimes think 'if only I had made that choice or that thing had happened, my life would be even better.'

0% dictated by the past – I live here and now. This is all that exists. I honour, embrace and love this moment. I am able to look back and recall the past. I cherish happy memories. I appreciate ones of difficult times. They inform and influence my choices today, but only constructively. I do not hang on to any of them. I do not regret the past. I do not dwell on it, I do not fear it, I do not resent it. I would not change it, even if I could, for that would mean that the present me is not me. I love myself. I love life. I love this beautiful earth. I love my fellow human beings. This day, this moment, I choose to be.

July 16th
LIGHT A CANDLE

"Porthos dreams of being a bear, and you want to shatter
those dreams by saying he's just a dog? What a horrible,
candle-snuffing word. That's like saying "He can't
climb that mountain, he's just a man," or "That's not a
diamond, it's just a rock."

SIR JAMES BARRIE – FINDING NEVERLAND

The wonders of our imagination. The loftiness of our ambitions. The power of our purpose. Within you there are no boundaries. No speed limits on how fast you can travel. No wealth restrictions on how much you can enjoy. No cosmic quota on how happy you can be. No words in the dictionary that can capture the levels of genius you can achieve. Never let another impose a limit on you. Never try to limit someone else. And never, ever, limit yourself.

In short, don't be a candle-snuffer.

July 17th
FOOTPRINTS

"She's on every page of your imagination. You'll always have her there. Always."

SIR JAMES BARRIE – FINDING NEVERLAND

As Mufasa appeared to Simba in the sky, so our loved ones appear on the page of a bed-time story, from the favourite old bench in the park, via a Queen song out of the duke-box in the pub. Truly, none of us ever die. Our footprints remain, visible to all those who love us.

July 18th

DROWN OUT THE NOISE

"Sometimes you really can't listen to what anybody else says. You just gotta listen inside."

Miss Riley – October Sky

Listening to what is inside takes courage, focus and practice:

Courage – to face the fear of judgement. We all have naysayers behind our ear, whispering nonsense. Courage is needed to ignore them.

Focus – to drown out distractions. Stimuli is bombarding us from every direction. Only the true seekers of self-truth will stay locked on to the message coming from within.

Practice – to recognise the soft, subtle sound of our own soul. It's a language written by self, for self, and one that only self can interpret. We won't master it in one day or one explosive moment of revelation. It takes dedication.

July 19th
THE PERFECTION OF NOW

"Whatever happens tomorrow, we've had today."

EMMA MORLEY – ONE DAY

Energise this moment. It is all we have. Our two friends, Hope and Dreams, call us with allure and wonder to gaze forward, but they are also a wee bit mischievous, for they can cause us to choose to let go of the hand of Now. Whomever else we are with, whoever else is a part of our journey, they are most welcome, but the one friend whose hand we cannot let go of, is Now.

And Now has a twin. Her name is Gratitude. When we stay present, enjoy and savour this moment, we can't help but feel thankful. What if the today is bringing pain, discomfort or suffering? Then we need acceptance and gratitude even more than on the good days. By accepting and embracing today for what it is, we honour it.

July 20th
MOTIVES

"Why do you want this so badly?"
"Because they said I couldn't have it."

JO & CARL – MEN OF HONOR

Motives are everything. A popular phrase is: Know your why. Your why is your power source. But an even better function than being your power generator is that it also acts as a mirror to who you are in the moment of reflection. Why did I feel the desire to tip that waiter so generously? Was it genuine appreciation for a great service? Or was I trying to show off? Why am I doing this job? Is it my deep passion? Am I doing it to pay the bills? Am I doing it because I'm too lazy or afraid to change? Introspection of our motives can become a fun one-player game. Why did I just do that? Why did I just say that? By reflecting on the motives behind what we say and do, we can come to a better understanding of ourselves. That in turn can assist us to be the person we want to be. Where we see that our motives don't align with the motives we wish to have, we change. Next time we eat out, irrespective of our company, we tip based on how we feel about the service we received (or not – keep showing off.) Meditating on our motives, we gift ourselves an amazing thing – self-honesty. Do I really want to pursue this thing because they said I can't have it, or do I want to pursue it because it's what I truly desire?

P.S. If your waiter or waitress are amazing, show your appreciation!

July 21st
FERTILISER

"Is the world just s**t?"

TREVOR MCKINNEY – PAY IT FORWARD

Sometimes we just feel rubbish. Sometimes crappy situations happen. And sadly, sometimes truly abhorrent and horrific things happen. They can't all be sugar-coated and they don't need to be. Just as the last thing the person getting irate needs is for someone to say, 'calm down,' so the last thing the sad or wronged person needs is 'don't worry, it's just a feeling, it will all be OK.' Duality dictates that there is suffering to partner bliss, confusion to partner clarity, pain to partner peace. At times, yes, the world is just s**t. We each travel our own journey to decide whether that s**t just stinks the place out, or whether it is the fertiliser behind all the beauty in the world.

July 22nd
MEASURE UP

"I think we can't go around measuring our goodness by what we don't do – by what we deny ourselves, what we resist and who we exclude. I think we've got to measure goodness by what we embrace, what we create and who we include."

PÈRE HENRI – CHOCOLAT

If you measure your day by your success at not killing someone, not robbing a bank, not crashing a car, then you're likely to have had a tip top day (sincerest apologies if you've achieved any of those today.) But what if you measured it by how many smiles you gave, how much you listened and gave someone space to be, how mindfully you worked, what service you contributed to the world, how would that change your evaluation?

Every day we are laying contributions at the altar of life. But what we oft forget is that every night while we sleep, life quietly returns that karma and energy back to us. Let us give good offerings.

July 23rd
CALL THAT A KNIFE?

"Mick, give him your wallet."
"What for?"
"He's got a knife."
"Hahaha. That's not a knife. (Unsheathes his own knife)
That's a knife."

SUE & MICK – CROCODILE DUNDEE

If you're going to do something, do it properly. All in. This applies equally to mundane daily tasks as it does to the big overarching goals of life. The most annoying thing in the world is finding flecks of hardened food debris stuck to the plate after it's been washed or *three** corners of the duvet tucked down. Do something properly and you do it once, do it half-heartedly and you never really do it.

*Unless you're doing the cute little inviting-corner-fold-over thing, in which case three corners tucked down is fine.

July 24th
LEADERSHIP = SERVICE

"That's what a leader's about; sacrifice. The times he's gotta sacrifice because he's gotta lead by example. Not by fear and not by self-pity."

Tony D'Amato – Any Given Sunday

Now more than ever this is relevant to us and our world. We need leaders who measure themselves by what they can give, not get. We need leaders who love the people they serve and desire their wellbeing. We need leaders who are honest. We need leaders that rely on love, learning and listening to connect with the people they serve. Leadership is fundamentally a misnomer. In the dictionary it should say: n. *leadership* /ˈliːdə(r)ʃɪp/ – redirects to *service*. For sure, to lead is a concept – people that possess power, knowledge, resources and position guide other people – but the instant leadership loses its inherent and intimate relationship to service, it becomes at best, self-serving, at worst, tyrannical. Wearing the cloak of humility, a leader in business seeks to provide the very best service possible, promoting a workplace and practices that are ethical. A parent seeks to provide an environment in which children can express themselves, develop and flourish. A politician seeks to labour mightily to uphold the people's right to life, liberty and the pursuit of happiness. This is leadership. If you are a leader, question your motives, evaluate your service. Don't be the villain of the story. Be the hero, and the glory will be yours forever.

July 25th
SYNERGISE

"Either we heal, now, as a team. Or we will die as individuals."

TONY D'AMATO – ANY GIVEN SUNDAY

Sir Alex Ferguson was the manager of Manchester United Football Club for 26 years. During his tenure, he oversaw unprecedented success and glory on the pitch. It is well known that amongst his many guiding principles, one of major pre-eminence was the one about no one player being above the team. Yes, his teams had stars, huge ones. But they survived and thrived only to the degree that they served the team. At his training ground office, Sir Alex hung the epic New York skyline art, *Lunch atop a Skyscraper*. Rather neatly, 11 men, the same number as make up a football team, dined in camaraderie, dangling perilously 250 metres above terra firma. Having trust in the man next to you in such a situation is not an optional luxury, it is a necessity. In more prosaic settings, we might not always feel the imperative necessity of unity. But like a football team or the construction workers that make our homes, skyscrapers and football stadiums, when we unite and synergise, we maximise what we're capable of.

July 26th
PLACE HONOUR IN THE PECKING ORDER

"Winning without dignity or grace is not winning."

JACKIE HARRISON – STEPMOM (1998)

There was once a man who took the courage to start his first business. He didn't have savings to fall on, but he did still have considerable living expenses and the responsibility of helping family. By a strange twist of fate, the man had access to an account containing substantial funds belonging to his previous employer. He knew that his old boss was an unethical man, and that the funds had essentially been stolen. He reasoned, therefore, that taking them and using them to support the beginning of a new, more honest and ethical business could be justified. He wrestled with the decision for days. In truth, there had only ever been one choice to him. He sent the money back to his former boss.

The tender shoots of that new business found root in honest soil, and the tree of honest toil continues to grow, flourish and bear fruit to this day.

On the path to obtaining what we want, we all make choices. One of those decisions is whether our morals and scruples come before or after the goals we have set. Some of us want it all, but will only go after it in a way that doesn't jeopardise personal principles. If it can't be done the right way, then forget about it. Others of us only want a fistful of dollars, and nothing will stop us, including quaint ideas of honour or laws, to grab it. We each get to choose how important our personal honour code is. Setting a code early on in the process of working toward a goal can be useful. It will be much, much easier to be swayed by the lure of success and power to forsake our values if we've not set out our spiritual stall early. If we do set out our spiritual and ethical bottom lines early, we'll be free to climb up and down as many ladders as we please, encompassed by the guiding principles of the heart that will keep us true.

July 27th
MAKE THE LEAP

"The world's full of lonely people afraid to make the first move."

TONY LIP – GREEN BOOK

Declaring one's feelings or picking up the phone to someone can be like Indy's leap of faith in *The Last Crusade* – simply terrifying. You are stranded on the ledge, alone, and you know the Holy Grail that is meaningful connection with another human being awaits on the other side, but you're certain that a perilous fall in to the abyss awaits, should you jump out. We can never know love if we are not willing to offer out the hand. What we forget is that regardless of who offers the hand first, it will only work if both reach out. So what are you afraid of? Rejection? Embarrassment that you offer the hand and it isn't returned? Pah. Don't allow fear to separate you from what's on offer. That's like allowing the preoccupation that others will judge you to stop you from trying the tough moves at the salsa club. It's like allowing the fear of failure to stop you from starting the business you've always desired. It's like allowing the rain to stop you from playing tennis. Some people play tennis in the snow, in sub-zero temperatures, bare-chested (some do the smart thing and play indoors.) So many of us in this world suffer from addiction, isolation and loneliness. There are no easy, once-and-for-all solutions. But if you're feeling lonely, and you feel like you can, why not reach out to someone and see what happens.

July 28th
HAPPINESS IS EVERYWHERE

"Do you know about money?"
"It can't buy happiness."

WILLIAM & JOE – MEET JOE BLACK

Everybody knows about money. Everybody thinks they know about happiness. Despite the countless quotes, stories and lessons on it, not everybody understands the relationship between the two. As a society, we've become obsessed with outward displays. We equate wealth with happiness. We equate an amazing physique with happiness. We equate climbing the ladder with happiness. The truth is, they have nothing to do with happiness. Shock alert: Neither does your health. Heresy! Think about it, how can it. Athletes are constantly carrying injuries and pain, doesn't stop them being happy. People that have a disability, doesn't stop them being happy. What we can come to realise is, there is a fundamental paradox inherent to our human existence, namely, while we naturally want things – a home, money, fame, health, success, adoration, and so on – none of those things directly bring happiness. They are merely appendages. Dressing. We think they matter, and at the surface level, they do. But at the deep elemental level, they are irrelevant. At that level, the cosmic level of pure being, we are enough regardless of any temporary state of having or doing. That is what Buddha discovered. Being a prince or being a pauper, it's the same thing. He was existing. Remember the Hindu mantra – *sat, chit, ananda* – *existence, consciousness, bliss.* If I exist (I do), if I can have some tiny spark of stillness, of awareness, of presence (I do), then I *am* bliss.

July 29th

TWINKLE

"What good would wings be if you couldn't feel the wind on your face?"

Susan – City of Angels

In the book, *King Solomon's Mines*, by Sir H. Rider Haggard, the main character, Allan Quatermain, and his companion, find themselves entombed in the eponymous mine. They are surrounded by the greatest horde of wealth ever amassed yet they are about to die, buried alive in diamonds and gold. The author uses majestic simplicity to summarise the situation; *"truly wealth, which men spend all their lives in acquiring, is a valueless thing at the last."* This isn't a theoretical analysis about hording wealth versus spending lavishly now, it's about realising that we are all given wings – those wings are an inherent and automatic gift that come through existence. As the protagonist discovered, our bank balances or our credit ratings do not delay death. Nothing does. If we don't savour what we have now, what's the point? Let's shift the focus of our life from bean counting to bean planting – planting wonderful acts that will sprout an ever-growing abundance of love. Let's extract the juice of experiencing the wind on our face. Of rising on warm currents of adventure, powered by the glorious sunbeams of friendship in the day, and the lure of discovery under the twinkling stars by night.

July 30th
BEDTIME STORIES

"When you read a book as a child, it becomes a part of your identity in a way that no other reading in your whole life does."

KATHLEEN KELLY – YOU'VE GOT MAIL

"Logic will get you from A to B. Imagination will take you everywhere," so said Albert Einstein. He was literally the master of imagination. He used the power of thought experiments to uncover the theories which have shaped our modern world, taken us into space and maybe one day to the stars. Basically, he used his imagination. We are what we read and feed our mind. Have a happy moment of reflection on the books of your youth. Children will always have a need to be nurtured by good books. If you can, gift the power of the written word to a young person and give them the opportunity to develop the mental faculties to imagine and create a better world.

July 31st
TRY

"Everything happens for the best. You'll never know if you don't try."

JAMES HAMMERTON – SLIDING DOORS

When was the last time you tried something and felt bad afterwards for the attempt? Even when we're rejected, fail or don't enjoy an experience, we can still find gratitude that we gave it a try. Really everything is about the experience. The IBM computer, Deep Blue, that beat the chess grandmaster, Garry Kasparov, in 1997, did so because it *learned* (was programmed with) millions of potential moves. We do the same thing through our life journey. We learn by experiencing, and if we keep a philosophical outlook, we learn from all experiences, the so called good and bad. A mullet hairstyle might look ridiculous now, but back in the 80s it was all the rage. A youngster could laugh watching an old *Top of the Pops* rerun seeing the rock n roll stars all sporting them back then, but how would they know what it felt like to have one unless they tried? The paradox is we think we can intellectually understand things without experiencing them, and we can, to a degree. You don't have to have been mugged to know you probably wouldn't enjoy the experience. But that's not quite the point, not quite understanding. The point is, you wouldn't know precisely how it *feels* unless it had happened to you. And the further point is, you wouldn't learn the lesson which that experience contains, unless it had happened to you. Everything happens for the best. And the twin to that is, everything happens to teach us something. Question is, are we paying attention. The moral is, try something… and then observe your feelings. Try something… and see what you can learn.

August 1st
ANIMALS GET IT

"I've heard you help people with horse problems?"
"Truth is, I help horses with people problems."

ANNIE & TOM – THE HORSE WHISPERER

Who are causing all the problems on this planet, because it sure ain't the horses, or the bugs, or the giraffes, or the fish. They do their thing and generally find an equilibrium with their surroundings. David Attenborough has shown through his unparalleled work for well over half a century that the natural world is magnificent and that it is the human species that jeopardises not just the enjoyment of the abundance of the earth for animals and plants, but the very existence of all organisms on the planet.

Many conservationists have shown how creatures of all types and sizes will accommodate and harmonise with humans. Rarely does any creature harm or kill another for the fun of it. One only needs to see the plethora of videos of big cats hugging and playing with humans, or monkeys, chicks and turtles acting like family. It breaks the stereotype and makes one realise that it is the human species that need to fall in line and take a leaf out of mother nature's book, not the other way around.

If we can raise our game to be equal to the calling we have – to be wise and considerate stewards of this incredible home – a glorious future lies before all of us.

August 2nd
TOO MUCH MEANING

"Life is not merely a series of meaningless accidents or coincidences, but rather, it's a tapestry of events that culminate in an exquisite, sublime plan."

DEAN KANSKY – SERENDIPITY

Everything you've ever done has been of value. Every path you've walked has left breadcrumbs, every effort you've made has left an imprint somewhere, every word you've spoken has created the dictionary you carry today. As Viktor Frankl said so gloriously at the end of *Man's Search For Meaning*, it is not the meaninglessness of our existences that so terrifies us, it is the utterly incomprehensible *meaningfulness* of all existence that completely baffles and bewilders us. It is the mind-boggling truth that all things, everywhere, fundamentally are glorious by their very existence. They are not given further validity or meaning by any words or mental constructs of the human mind (which is, of course, also fundamentally glorious by its inherent nature,) they just are glorious. We are glorious. And yet we are on a journey. And we can choose in this current moment what that means to us individually and decide what little bit of cloth we are going to weave into the tapestry.

August 3rd
BEING HAPPY IS THE ONLY RIGHT CHOICE

"When are you people going to learn? It's not about who's right or wrong."

SERENDIPITY – DOGMA

When we get side-tracked into focusing on who is right and who is wrong within a conversation, an action or a belief system, we inadvertently fall into the twin trap of egoic consumption and utter lack of mindfulness. We are consumed by ego. I must be right. My worth, my value, my total validation of myself relies on me being right. And we are utterly non-present to the perfect moment that sits before us, choosing rather to get wrapped up in rewinds and fast-forwards of what the implications are of us being either right or wrong.

It. Doesn't. Matter.

Our value is not determined by a mind-centric assessment. Our value is already pre-set and immutably defined by our boundless souls – that value is infinite. For a day or a week or as long as you like, try removing the right/wrong filter on your perceptions. Try different ones. How does this thing make me feel? Do I have any power to choose and change my feelings? What is the view from the opposite bank of the river? Can I choose to be happy today and ignore the call to place attention on *my* perception of who or what is right or wrong?

The old chestnut holds true – do you want to be right or do you want to be happy? The only wrong is in choosing not to be happy (…or not.)

August 4th
THE WAY

"The time to make up your mind about people is never."

COUNTESS OF TRENTHAM – GOSFORD PARK

Seeing only the perceived negative traits in a person is the worst crime known, second only to seeing only the perceived positive traits in a person. Often what we love in someone is the very thing someone else detests, and vice versa. How often we think we have someone nailed down in a straight-jacket of labels – good, bad, smart, reliable, arrogant, selfish, lovely, kind, lazy – and then they go and spoil it by shattering our fragile construct of who and what we think they are. How rude of them. It's like seeing a tree in its splendour in Summer, and then revisiting it in Winter and being devastated by its ghastly change. Your... your... your leaves? What happened? You're not the tree I used to know. How could you do this to me?!

In the 道德经 *Dao De Jing*, an ancient text by the Chinese philosopher Lao Zi 老子, the opening line reads:

道可道 非常道 *dao ke dao, fei chang dao*
The way that can be spoken of is not The Way.

The beauty of what this means is that what it means is not what it means – as in, the text is self-perpetuating quicksand, a circular concept (all concepts are). Nothing can be defined, labelled or nailed down. In the very moment that you pin something, anything, down – God, tree, love, doughnut, Mary Poppins – you have, by definition, missed the mark, missed the essence.

August 5th
I HAVE A DREAM

"For in dreams, we enter a world that is entirely our own."

ALBUS DUMBLEDORE – HARRY POTTER AND THE PRISONER OF AZKABAN

If you could live in your dreams, would you? If someone could promise you that they would keep you protected, fed and watered while you slept perpetually, so that you could stay in your mental construct of being, having and doing all the things you desire in your dreams, would you take it?

It makes one wonder, what is the difference between our dreams and reality? *Is* there any difference? When our dreams can be so vivid, so real, if we could be promised to be kept alive, why would we not want to stay in the bliss of our perfectly constructed dream state? There must be some lure, some promise of rising and chasing our dreams in the real world, otherwise, why would any of us get out of bed?

August 6th
UP IN SMOKE

"I suppose that's the way life goes on. You have something now and then it suddenly goes... Poof!"

PROFESSOR SLUGHORN – HARRY POTTER AND THE HALF-BLOOD PRINCE

What was the last thing that went poof in your life? Were you expecting it? Were you happy or sad that it went? Perhaps we can learn to enjoy when things go... poof!

Perhaps we can be prepared, mentally, to accept that all these things we cling on to can and do change in an instant. The lesson is to find grace and serenity regardless of what is coming or going. If you had a fortune yesterday and today you lost it, or if yesterday you were in a hole and today your hard work finally paid off and a huge windfall came your way, can you treat these twin imposters, triumph and disaster, just the same? Like the beautiful Rudyard Kipling line from his poem, *If*, that cajoles the players at Wimbledon on the way out to Centre Court, if we can meet the vicissitudes and capricious comings and goings of life with grace and humour, really, what can hurt us?

August 7th

TRUE FRIENDSHIP WILL WEATHER STORMS

"It takes a great deal of bravery to stand up to your enemies, but a great deal more to stand up to your friends."

ALBUS DUMBLEDORE – HARRY POTTER AND THE PHILOSOPHER'S STONE

Sometimes we can be soooooo close to someone, so in harmony, so on the same page about things, that it makes us squirm to say or do anything that indicates we aren't 100% in agreement or approval of them. Friendships and loving relationships are like books – for it to work, you have to be close enough for the story to flow, but not too close. If your nose is against the page, you've gone too far. You're so in focus that you're out of focus.

No matter how much you love, adore and respect someone, your standards, your truth and your feelings are valid and valued. If there is something that needs to be shared with a friend, put it out there. Think of it positively – *if our friendship is what I believe it is, what I hope it is, we should be able to have this conversation. We should be able to share and air our views and feelings and see how that plays out.*

And if at times you find a friend is downright out of line, love them enough to correct them.

August 8th
HUMAN

"I've always believed that a portrait captures a person far better than a photograph. It truly takes a human being to really see a human being."

LETICIA MUSGROVE – MONSTER'S BALL

And that is what we have the marvellous opportunity to do... to see the human being in each other. Ignore the watch or the handbag or the car or the title or the dirty fingers or the lisp or the monocle or the reputation or the ego... look past all that... and there, in purity, is the person. By person, we refer to the whole being, the whole entity, not only some tiny, surface-level aspect of the person. The person is the small print behind the contract, the back story that explains current events, the all-important *why* behind the present *how*. The person is *The Hobbit* to *The Lord of the Rings*. The person is what's really going on below the façade that is the body (which is of course not not the real person, it most definitely is, but it is only one element.) The person is the individual. We cannot lose that individual. When we look at another, we are not looking at a number or a stat, we are seeing a living, breathing soul. Carl Jung spoke of the individual with great insight and reverence. He understood that the individual must be held up. It is our individuality that holds the key to our beauty, our unity, and, indeed, our survival.

August 9th
A SWEET ESSENCE

"'Regard without ill-will despite an offense,' that's
Webster's definition of forgiveness."
"Why do I have to forgive?"
"So you can get on with your life."

DR DAVENPORT & ANTWONE – ANTWONE FISHER

Everything we experience leaves a trace within us. We can think of each one as depositing a little vial of essence that we carry. Our experiences with others are some of the strongest and most pungent of essences. When we have a difficult experience, and choose to hold on to anger and resentment against someone, we are carrying that essence around with us. It is not so much a vial as a large jar, and even though we think we've tightened the lid securely on, the smell still seems to escape and it is not pleasant. By not forgiving, we continue to choose to bear that smell and that weight. At any time, however, we can choose to release that jar and trade it in for a sweet smelling, light vial that carries the essence of wisdom and forgiveness.

Eau du Forgive.

August 10th
ENDURANCE

"At the end of the day, we can endure much more than we think we can."

FRIDA KAHLO – FRIDA

We are extremely resilient. If we weren't, we wouldn't be reading this. As Rocky said so well, it's not about how hard we hit, it's about how hard we can be hit and keep moving. Today you're moving. You're still here, still trying, still in the game. Yesterday is past. You can deal with these 24 hours before you. You can deal with this moment. We all want the idyllic life, but ponder on this; all of your growth, all of your breakthroughs, all of your level ups have come via suffering, sweat, blood and tears. That's not a coincidence, it's the very design of life. There is resistance. That's why we have engines in cars and aeroplanes – because air and gravity try to stop us from moving. But we don't let those two friends stop us from getting where we want to go. We work with the elements and each other. We synergise. It doesn't mean that suffering doesn't really hurt, it does, and it's healthy to talk about our trials and sufferings and endure them in union and fellowship one with each other.

August 11ᵗʰ
GOING... UP!

"So how is the elevator business treating you, Reuben?"
"Oh, it has its ups and downs."

LONGFELLOW & REUBEN – MR. DEEDS

Elevators are a good metaphor for life. Sometimes you're on the way up, sometimes on the way down. Sometimes you travel alone, sometimes there is company. You may like the fellow passengers, or you may not. You always have the choice to disembark and hop on the next one. Sometimes the lift is there waiting to take you, sometimes you are obliged to wait, and get a chance to exercise patience. The stairs provide a reminder that there are different ways to get to the same destination. Some lifts are noisy, some are quiet. Some are super fast, some are incredibly slow. Sometimes the elevator breaks down and you're stuck until someone comes along to help. Every floor that the lift opens on to presents a different scene. If you don't like it, you can get back in the lift and choose another floor.

From this parallel angle of the analogy, you and you alone choose the floor to get out on and what awaits when the doors open and you step out. Today, use your imagination to picture yourself getting in the elevator, travelling to your floor, and stepping out to the world you want to live in.

August 12th
ALCHEMISE THE BAD STUFF

"It's like all of the bad stuff that you went through that you hated along the way, the people who disappointed you, the things that didn't go the way you wanted, suddenly, you feel grateful to them, because those are the things that got you to here."

ADAM FORREST – THE PERFECT MAN

The *bad stuff* becomes the propellant, the catalyst, the fuel, the juice. Once we make the mental adjustment, in a slightly crazy, hopefully not *too* whacky kind-of-a-way, we can learn to relish the *bad stuff*. Bring it on. As the catapult has to pull the projectile back before it shoots it forward, so life seems to draw us farther away from our dreams before it fires us right at, through and beyond them.

August 13th
I AM THE LAW

"A lie keeps growing and growing until it's as plain as the nose on your face."

THE BLUE FAIRY – PINOCCHIO (1940)

We tell lies when we forget universal law. Universal law states that the truth sets us free. Universal law states that when we lie we are out of harmony with that same law. We say so-and-so *broke* the law (a law of the land,) which is fine at a semantical level. In the philosophical sense, however, we cannot *break* the law, the law just is. Think about it. It would be like saying, Jim broke the law of gravity. What does that mean? Sure, Jim can build a massive rocket and using 10 million pounds of projective force (thrust) blast himself off in to space, seemingly breaking gravity. But he didn't really break gravity did he. Gravity continued to exist and apply at all stages of his flight. Jim simply used forces, through his understanding and manipulation of physics and maths, to reach a desired goal, *paying the price necessary* to do so.

Now, returning to us and when we lie. At surface level, we think we have manipulated a situation to our advantage through the mechanism of the lie. What we fail to realise is that the law, this particular law being spiritual, namely, *truth is freedom*, remains immutable. In other words, when we lie, we think we are cheating the spiritual law, but the law cannot be broken. It is us that are breaking ourselves *against* the law. Just as Jim needed to use a phenomenal amount of fuel and energy to counteract gravity (remember, it wasn't broken or ceased to apply,) so we must pay a hefty spiritual price when we lie. It has ever been thus. Let us learn to glory in the truth, and we shall have no need to carry such heavy burdens and pay such unbearable prices.

August 14th
GIDDY UP

"Down to Gehenna or up to the Throne,
He travels the fastest who travels alone."

GENERAL ERINMORE – 1917

A direct quote from Rudyard Kipling's poem, *The Winners*, Colin Firth delivered the evocative lines with usual aplomb. Another one of the seeming paradoxes of life; people will be needed by your side to find joy and to help you get where you want to go, and yet you and you alone hold the key to reaching your destination. You will get there fastest when you realise that. That includes every destination… even (especially?) the spiritual. Chart your course of where you want to go and get there as slowly or as quickly as you please.

August 15th
A LOVING KICK UP THE BUM

"Get up, ya son of a bitch, 'cause Mickey loves ya!"

MICKEY GOLDMILL – ROCKY V

Sylvester Stallone's insight in to the human psyche is evident throughout the Rocky films, but none more so in understanding what deep down we all need and crave – love. A heavyweight boxer is a bad man. He is a man trained for the sole purpose of inflicting pain on other men who are trying to do the same thing to him. Usually the pep talk or kick-up-the-bum from coach revolves around no regrets, grab the glory, you are the best, believe… so the visceral *get up cos I love ya* that the scriptwriter deftly created was pure genius, a touch of grace and glory amidst the guts and the gore. And ultimately it couldn't be more accurate or more effective. There is no higher motivation than love. Love of self, love of loved ones, love of humanity and love of freedom can take us anywhere.

August 16th

HEAR THE CALL

"Some people were born to sit by a river. Some get struck by lightning. Some have an ear for music. Some are artists. Some swim. Some know buttons. Some know Shakespeare. Some are mothers. And some people, dance."

BENJAMIN BUTTON – THE CURIOUS CASE OF BENJAMIN BUTTON

What's your calling? Do you have one? As Mark Twain said, the two most important days of your life are the day you were born, and the day you find out why.

We've all experienced at least one of those two days, and we can make it our quest to experience the other. Who knows when and where it will come. If and when it does, it changes everything. And if it never comes? Then just keep dancing.

August 17th
UNIVERSE = GOD = LOVE

"God can be whatever you want him to be. You're getting tangled in semantics. Try not to get caught up in the God who wants you to be kosher, or the guy that wants you to study the Torah. Start with God as the infinite universe, and imagine that force may be trying desperately to guide you through the most challenging part of your life."

RABBI ROSENBERG – WISH I WAS HERE

The word God is charged with different concepts for different people. On the negative side, to many people the word consciously and subconsciously draws feelings that are not desirable. Controversy. Control. Politics. Manipulation. Brainwashing. Fairy tales and fantasy. And to others, God is the amazing and loving being or entity that is defined within a given religion or belief system, and every good thing that stems and flows from there. And there are many more variations of what God is, besides. And there is also the kind of middle ground alternative that the Rabbi poses – the universe. The interconnected universe, wherein, each single strand of consciousness, each vibrating atom, is an integral part of the whole (all matter vibrates, even that which we label *inanimate* or *dead*.) If we believe that there is wisdom and love held in the very fabric of space and time, it could lead us to believe and take comfort that we are needed and valued, and that the universal intelligence, infinite and omnipresent, is manifesting through everything around us and indeed ourselves. And we can believe, if we so choose, that the universe wants us well. It wants our happiness. In this spirit, we declare, the universe is God, love is God. And the universe and love are of course all around us and within us.

August 18th
LIFE IS LIKE A BOX OF CHOCOLATES

"I have learned how to live, how to be in the world and of the world, and not just to stand aside and watch. And I will never, never again run away from life. Or from love, either."

SABRINA FAIRCHILD – SABRINA (1954)

Life is a DIY project, not a spectator sport.

Life is a diving in head first beats hesitant toe-in, inch-by-inch, every time.

Life is a camping trip. Muddy boots and chilly winds and wet clothes and fires and marshmallows and magic and moments. Priceless moments.

Life is real and raw.

Life is the peaks and the troughs.

Life is learning that sometimes we mix those two up.

Life is the boring, the mundane, the tax returns.

Life is seeing something hilarious right as you take a sip of tea and blowing it out your nose.

Life is loving ourselves enough to let ourselves be loved.

Life is everything and nothing. Life is whatever we want it to be.

Life is love. And love is life.

August 19th
START AT TRUTH

"As the world becomes more and more confusing, we tend to focus on the things that are right there in front of us, while ignoring the massive forces that actually change and shape our lives."

KURT – VICE

Living in the moment, taking in what's before our eyes is no bad way to live. But living this way doesn't preclude taking an active interest in the bigger picture. We abide by the ethos of *live and let live* and *be the change you want to see*, but such beliefs do not mean we do not live in a world where other peoples' actions have an impact on us. They do. And it is therefore right and proper that we seek to find solutions to the larger issues that impact upon all of the human race. People often remark 'what can I, one little person, do to make a difference?' There is much each of us can do to be a force on the side for good in the world. One possible starting place is a thirst for the truth.

August 20th
WOUNDED

"Some wounds do not close; I have many such. One just walks around with them and sometimes one can feel them filling with blood."

QUEEN ANNE – THE FAVOURITE

Our battle wounds and scars are as unique as our voices and fingerprints. There is a little (big) story behind each. We can learn to wear our physical scars with ease and acceptance. They are a receipt from life. They embellish us and they testify – we are alive. No snowflakes or softies around here. What about our emotional or psychological injuries, are they all healthy to carry, or should we seek their eradication? It might be good to get the wound treated, cleaned and bandaged, those three being acknowledgement, facing the feelings and time. Scars are a given, but open wounds don't need to be left open forever.

August 21st
C'EST LA VIE, MON AMI

"C'est la vie, as the Romans say."

NICK VANDERPARK – ENVY (2004)

Every language has a way of saying, *that's life*. In France, they say *c'est la vie*, (apparently in Rome, too, according to Jack Black,) the Spanish say *que sera sera*, Thais say *mai pen rai*, and Filipinos have the lovely phrase *bahala na*, meaning, *come what may, it'll be alright*. Whatever life is bringing you today, *c'est la vie*. Life is unfolding and you are a part of its cosmic equation. It makes one smile to consider how stoic and robust we humans are. *C'est la vie* is a deep philosophical observation that can frame anything in its proper context. Whatever happens, that's life. The fun is in the interplay between ourselves and life. We can resent what life is, we can accept what life is, or we can celebrate what life is. For sure, we will inhabit all three states at different times. Whichever way, *c'est la vie*.

August 22nd
KNOW THYSELF

"The more you know who you are and what you want, the less you let things upset you."

BOB HARRIS – LOST IN TRANSLATION

The man or woman on a mission does not let anything deter them. They have laser-like focus on what matters. Outside noise becomes of much less importance than inner clarity. Everything hinges on the singular question:

What do I desire?

With the answer to that comes lucidity and precision of focus and energy. It's what makes salesmen, mothers and Winnie the Pooh so ruthless. An absolute clarity of what they want… (in the cases given; to make money, protect and nurture their offspring and, find the honey… obviously.)

August 23rd
NOT AUTHORISED

"I am opposed to authority. It is an egg of misery and oppression."

DR STEPHEN MATURIN – MASTER AND COMMANDER:
THE FAR SIDE OF THE WORLD

n. authority – the power or right to give orders, make decisions, and enforce obedience. (Oxford English Dictionary)

With the meaning of the word authority in mind, and focusing on the first and third descriptive elements above, is it any wonder that many people are fundamentally opposed to authority when we witness the ubiquitous abuse of it throughout the world. The simple truth is this:

The more that authority is needed to enforce something or ensure order, the less likely it is to achieve such ends. In other words, the more authority is needed, the less it is needed.

Perhaps what we ought to do is look back through the chain of dominoes and investigate why we feel the need to give orders or enforce obedience in the first place. Where does that come from? Where does this incessant urge to control and govern others come from? What would happen if we gave up all notions of power and control of others and instead focused on ourselves being the kind of person we would like others to be?

August 24th
DON'T SHOW ANYONE WHAT I WANT

"Sometimes we don't do things we want to do so that others won't know we want to do them."

IVY WALKER – THE VILLAGE

Isn't it the most bizarre way of thinking ever, to not do what we want because we don't want others to know? To really know the answer, we might need to explore what reasons we wouldn't want a person to know what we want. Would it be fair to say that they may all come under the banner of fear?

There's one biscuit left on the table. If I grab it, everyone is going to know I'm greedy and selfish. Nah, better let someone else eat it.

That looks so much fun. I wanna try... I'm so going to fall off and look an idiot though. Better not.

I really want peace and redemption. I need to apologise, and I'm willing to, but then they will be reminded that I did something wrong and will have that moral superiority over me. They'll know I care, that I'm suffering remorse. They'll likely respond negatively, anyway. Forget about it.

Three real examples of not doing what we want because of a very misguided fear that by doing so we weaken our position and make ourselves open to hurt, rejection, judgement or ridicule. Such thinking is absurd. Enjoy the biscuit. Climb on the bucking bronco. Apologise sincerely and deeply to the other party and show the veracity of your words by changed behaviour. Let's claim the life we want and give others the space and empowerment to do the same. Let's be brave enough to make ourselves vulnerable.

August 25th
PURE LOVE

"There are different types of love."

LUCIUS HUNT – THE VILLAGE

Love is a funny old thing. Take the exact same situation with the exact same person going through a tough time. You could give them some encouraging words of hope and support, which is an expression of love. Or you could be silent and simply be with them, allowing them to feel your spirit and acknowledge the wordless validation, which is equally a show of love. With love, whichever form it manifests itself in, the intention of the giver is paramount. You might not know exactly what a person needs, but you can give whatever it is you have to offer. Learning what kind of love to give, and when to give it, is an enjoyable and unique journey we each travel. We can spend a long time figuring out that much of our love will never be reciprocated. In our quiet moments, we can also realise how some of our love has been selfish, and therefore, in a way, not really love. Nevertheless, the idea of pure love is intoxicating. The idea that we can elevate ourselves to such a high level, one where we are capable of doing truly breath-taking things for others, will exist as long as we exist. That brilliant love is our souls' true north.

August 26th
JUSTICE LEAGUE

"Justice delivered without dispassion is always in danger of not being justice."

Oswaldo Mobray – The Hateful Eight

Achieving complete impartiality as a human being is nigh on impossible for the simple reason that we have each experienced a tailored blend of life experiences which cannot fail to influence our thinking and reasoning. What we can do is be aware that reaching a totally unbiased view is extremely difficult, and use mechanisms to counteract the inbuilt prejudice which we all possess. If you heard of a crime that had been committed, and you had no connection or interest in the perpetrator, how would your opinion of what constitutes true justice differ to a case in which you personally knew and cared for the perpetrator? How much disparity would there likely be in your rationale? On positive issues, say fair remuneration for solving a problem or winning a tournament, would your judgement shift if it was you who stood to receive a bigger prize?

Justice and integrity go hand in hand. They are principles which we strive to uphold, trying our best to elevate and preserve them, independent of our own biases and passions. Justice must emanate from the most neutral and dispassionate place possible for it to be true justice. We can each strive to uphold this concept of justice. We do it by using compassion, balance, perspective, and thought-experiments in our reasoning process. We are also called to remember that on this coin of justice, mercy is on the flip-side, and that to purchase the good of all, we must have both.

August 27th
RETURN TO SENDER

"Those who live by the sword shall die by the sword."

JESUS – THE PASSION OF THE CHRIST

Everything we do, we do unto ourselves. Helping another is helping oneself. Harming another is harming oneself. How different might our actions be if we kept this in our minds. Sometimes we perceive what we consider an imbalance of cosmic justice – the good guys suffering and the baddies getting away with everything. But does this truly bear scrutiny? If you went about smiling, complimenting people and being generous, would you not undoubtedly receive the same measure of goodness *in kind*? If, say, you decided to join the Mafia or a violent gang, would your chances of being severely beaten or murdered be the same as a librarian? When Jesus said these words to his disciple, Simon Peter, he was teaching a simple lesson (Peter had cut off the ear of a man who had come to arrest Jesus. Jesus restored the ear.) How you live is how you shall die. If you live by violence, you shall die by such. If you abide in love, you shall pass in love. Such wisdom transcends confinement to only the literal. Not all Mafiosos will literally perish by the sword, as not all librarians will pass peacefully one day atop a pile of books. The concept is physical, spiritual and metaphorical. How you live is how you are. What you send out always returns home to sender.

August 28th
SILENT COMPANIONSHIP

"I once travelled with a guide who was taking me to Faya. He didn't speak for nine hours. At the end of it he pointed at the horizon and said, 'Faya!'. That was a good day."

ALMÁSY – THE ENGLISH PATIENT

Being able to enjoy silence in the company of others is another chapter in the Jedi master handbook. The paradox of language is that while it is extremely useful, in lieu of the fact that not all of us have learned telepathy, yet it is also completely superfluous. Granted, superfluous is fine, not all conversation needs to fall under the category of necessary or important. Shooting the breeze comes with its own joys, we are social creatures, after all.

Knowing how to indulge in the sound of silence is a refined art. If it stands to reason that we are much, much more than the amazing but limited words we can verbalise, then it would also be plausible that passing silent quality time in the company of others can be every whit as stimulating and bonding as a riveting conversation. Whether casual and humourful chat, a deep and meaningful tête-a-tête, or a reconciliatory parley, learning the importance of the spaces between sounds is as important as a composer working the space between notes. Some of the highest pieces of music are those that best honour the stillness. Sometimes, the best piece of all is the one that takes out all the notes and allows you to fill in your own.

August 29th
PERMANENT

"The things we touch have no permanence. My master would say: there is nothing we can hold onto in this world. Only by letting go can we truly possess what is real."

MASTER LI MU BAI – CROUCHING TIGER, HIDDEN DRAGON

Has anyone ever counted the paradoxes in life? The duality and oneness of permanence and impermanence has to be one of them. Perhaps this explains why we enjoy reminiscing of bygone times – it creates a momentary clash within the mind and soul of seemingly conflicting concepts. Our current situation, whatever it may be, seems so static, so fixed, and yet all we need do is cast our mind's eye, or better still, our physical eye, over an old photo, a forgotten trip, a distant lover, and whoosh!... we are back in *that* moment, that feeling. We are fixated on permanence, when the nature of life is fundamental impermanence. And yet, and yet, the things we deem impermanent in the moment – our most joyous crescendos and our biggest faux pas – they stay with us... permanently. Eternal. Indelible. Etched into the very marble of our souls.

So, which is it?! Is there permanency or impermanency? Is life impermanent permanency, or permanent impermanency? Is anything real? Is anything not real?

Existence is a funny old thing.

August 30th
FEEL THE FEELING

"To repress one's feelings only makes them stronger."

YU SHU LIEN – CROUCHING TIGER, HIDDEN DRAGON

Shaking a fist at the sky for raining on wedding day or burying the car under three feet of snow does not undo the fact. Feelings are like the weather; ever-changing, temperamental, conducive to determining how the day goes. And like feelings, we can shape the meaning and hue of the weather by our attitude. If we embrace the day, rain or shine, hot or cold, cooperative or not, and mould it to our plans and goals, we build our own power. Similarly, feelings can be manipulated to create a stronger version of self. There is no need to deny or bury a feeling. It exists and rises to the surface for a purpose. When we understand this, when we overcome the fear of feelings, we are truly being.

August 31st
BREAK DOWN THE WALLS

"Don't be like me. Salvation doesn't lie within four walls. I'm too serious to be a dilettante and too much a dabbler to be a professional. Even the most miserable life is better than a sheltered existence in an organised society where everything is calculated and perfected."

STEINER – LA DOLCE VITA (1960)

Exploration and intrigue. Without these juices, we are dead. Life happens dualistically – inside our being, and *out there*. The thrill of living comes from figuring out the spiritual Rubik's Cube inside us, while following the treasure trail on the outside. Depriving ourselves from either source of joy will lead to decay.

September 1st
THE BLESSING THAT IS WATER

"Water's precious. Sometimes may be more precious than gold."

HOWARD – THE TREASURE OF THE SIERRA MADRE

The rovers and probes that are sent out in to the far reaches of our solar system to analyse and photograph other planets and their moons take a keen interest in many details and qualities of the celestial bodies they observe, but no findings elicit more joy and euphoria to mission control back at HQ than the holy grail of them all… liquid water. Water is the elixir of life. For humans, animals, plants and trees alike, absence of water means game over. We presume that for there to be complex and intelligent organic life forms out there, they, too, must rely on nature's best cocktail – hydrogen with a dash of oxygen. If we are ever to break the shackles of our cosy earth home, we will need ample water supplies on our new cosmic home or on interstellar petrol stations along the way. But before we get to that, let us practice great gratitude for the beautiful and abundant life-giving water on this planet. It has brought us this far. If we look after and value it, it will surely continue to return the favour.

September 2nd
ON THE EDGE

"It's fair to say I'm stepping out on a limb, but I am on the edge and that's where it happens."

MAXIMILLIAN COHEN – PI

The point where any two things meet is always at their own edges. The warm, gooey centre of things are, by definition, insulated and protected from the edge. That is the comfort zone. That is the steady and stable. But the change, the growth, the glory, that comes on the edge. The edge is where the magic happens. The centre of the bed is warm and comfortable, but it's by departing the mattress via the edge that we are propelled into a new day of living. It is by issuing forth from the door of our homes, the edge of our safe haven, that we enter the world and go about chasing our dreams. It is as we leave the port of Knowledge, the edge, to set sail on seas of Hope, seeking the undiscovered lands of Potential and Promise, that new worlds are opened unto us. The centre is our heart, our home. The edge is our adventure.

September 3rd
DON'T COMPOUND THE WRONG – RIGHT IT

"Someone said this at some point about why we stayed when we knew we were losing. Ten percent was to help the South Vietnamese. Twenty percent was to hold back the Commies. Seventy percent was to avoid the humiliation of an American defeat. Seventy percent of those boys just to avoid being humiliated [by losing the Vietnam War]. That stuck with me."

DANIEL ELLSBERG – THE POST

Poor choices beget poor choices. After a mistake, the hardest of all the options available is to acknowledge it, address it and strive to redress it. But that is how we roll. We don't bury our head deeper in the sand. We don't lie to cover the original lie or misdemeanour. A step in to the darkness is not remedied by taking a further step in to the darkness. It is remedied by stepping in to the light.

September 4th

WHAT HAPPENED?

"I thought you wanted me to do this, it just sounds like now you don't want me to do it."

"What do you mean, I wanted you to do this?"

"This is what you wanted for me."

"To be in this band?"

"To be in a band, to have a steady job, you know to be... you know."

"Of course, I wanted you to have a steady job so that you could take care of yourself and your life and you could start your club."

"Yeah, so I'm doing that, so I don't understand like why aren't we celebrating?"

"Why aren't you starting your club?"

"You said yourself no one wants to go that club. No one wants to go to a club called 'Chicken on a Stick.'"

"So change the name!"

"Well, no one likes jazz, not even you!"

"I do like jazz now because of you!"

SEBASTIAN & MIA – LA LA LAND

Nobody will make your dreams happen for you. Nobody. No.Bo. Dy. Get that straight. It is a literal impossibility for someone else to realise your dreams for you. Your dreams are fulfilled through your conscious and deliberate actions. Earned. They cannot be won, borrowed or given to you. Not by your lover, not the lottery company, not the takeover consortium, not your parents, not God. That would contravene immutable, universal law. If your *dream* can be handed to you or fulfilled by someone else, whatever it is, it is not your dream. Only you can claim your dreams, in the same way that only you can see out of your eyes or think your thoughts. Don't allow anything or anyone to derail you. Live up to love and ideals and goodness. They and steadfast commitment to the fulfilment of your dreams are not mutually exclusive. But remember, you have sole ability and responsibility to manifest your dreams.

September 5th

FLOAT LIKE A BUTTERFLY

"When I was a little girl, my teacher told me butterflies don't live a long time. They live, like, a month. And I was so upset, and I went home, and I told my mother, and she said: 'Yeah, but, you know, they have a nice life. They have a really, beautiful life.'"

DR ALICE HOWLAND – STILL ALICE

At what point did we become so transfixed on the perfunctory mandate – live to 90 years old and you've done it, you've beat the game, beaten the average? What poppycock. Absolute balderdash. Hogwash.

Answer this one question: would you rather live this one day, today, free, alive, full of love, laughter, fun and exploration, to die happily at the end of it, or would you trade that for another 50 years of living locked up, grey, bland and lifeless, albeit with the base means to sustain basic existence?

I don't know about you, but for some, that's not even a choice.

September 6th
ODE TO OLD

"I can't think of anything worse than growing old."

SARA – WILD STRAWBERRIES

Growing old does not necessarily have to carry a negative connotation. Vintage cars, mature wine, proverbs, classical music, antiques... it is the *old* in them that make them so magnificent. Youth carries no promise of becoming old, but old can suggest that a youth has been passed through and enjoyed. The term, grow old, is lovely in itself. To *grow* old. Growth means life, change, adventure, newness. Advancement of years doesn't have to mean excitement gets locked away in the cupboard. It can mean finally having the time to indulge the simple pleasures of life. It can mean emerging through the other side of caring about rules and what others think. It can mean new horizons and new vistas. It can mean anything you want it to mean.

Old is gold.

September 7th
GOOD VIBRATIONS

"Once you get in the right frame of mind, I think anything's possible. I think we so often get caught in this state of negativity and it's a poison like nothing else."

PAT SOLITANO JR – SILVER LININGS PLAYBOOK

All matter vibrates. Every single atom in existence is characterised by its vibration. Our attitude sets our being, both the seen physical and the unseen spiritual, at its equivalent vibrational frequency. When we use the term *get in the right frame of mind* in a real life context, it shows how we can grasp this simple concept. For example, a performer behind the curtain jittering and having a sudden moment of self-doubt might be told these words by a colleague – *come on, get in the right frame of mind, you can do this, that stage is yours.* Nothing has changed from one second to the next, except the mental vibrational frequency that the person has set. A negative mind-set can seem so alluring. It gives a unique payoff. But it's a payoff of destructive, self-fulfilling prophesy. The right frame of mind, equally, yields fruit after its own kind. And what is the right frame of mind? Knowing we matter. Remembering that all we can do is try. Believing we are worthy. Laughing with ourselves at the madness of it all.

September 8th

BLONDE, BLACK, BRUNETTE, REDHEAD... DIFFERENT WIGS, SAME PERSON

"All people ever see is Marilyn Monroe. As soon as they realise I'm not her, they run."

MARILYN MONROE – MY WEEK WITH MARILYN

There is that concept that does the rounds, the one that refers to masks as a form of deception, an image projected for others to see. Take off your mask, and show the world the real you. This is true on one level. But what if we flipped the concept around and looked at it from a philosophical side. What if we acknowledged that at times, we all wear different masks, and that doing so is completely normal. This is what entertainers do as standard. They get up and project a part of themselves to their audience. That energy is not not the real them, of course it's the *real* them. Else, where did it come from? And the non-performing, elusive, insecure, aloof, humble, kind...whatever... side of them, away from the spotlight, that is just as much the *real* them. Being one thing, and always being it, at all times of day or night, anywhere, with anyone, could be considered really awesome and maybe even admirable. It could also be considered incredibly boring and such a restriction, a restriction on experiencing and experimenting with all the things one might be. If we can learn to love and accept the many masks we each wear, which are all the real us, we might one day see the souls that sit resplendent beyond whichever mask it is we're wearing.

September 9th
LIMITLESS

"There are limits to what one can give."

LADY SARAH – THE FAVOURITE

The good news:

You are infinite. You are a part of the oneness of all things. You share that universal heritage, you can achieve anything, you are full of light and love and truth (and the shadow side of all those things, which you don't necessarily need to act on, however, simply be aware and open to,) abundance, health and wealth and inherent value.

Now for the bad news:

The infinite you is bound and handicapped by some really annoying finite things at surface level; your time, your resources, your body, the strength *in* your body, your intelligence, your perspective, your money (a reader with a true abundance mentality will simply refute this paragraph – good for you!)... even your morals(?!). But! This is no bad thing, for it leads back...

...to some more good news:

This duality, this seeming paradox constitutes a big part of the joyful journey of life, namely, learning to make choices. You get to choose where and how and with whom you spend your time, energy, money, love, intelligence, wisdom and so forth. While you are a part of the cosmic oneness, you are also given a veritable gift, which is your autonomy. You decide how best to spend your resources, you decide how best to vibrate and how best to emit your energy.

September 10th
PLANTING SEEDS

---

*"If you take tough decisions, people will hate you today,
but they will love you in generations."*

MARGARET THATCHER – THE IRON LADY

Doing the right thing, speaking the truth, embracing the hardship now rather than deferring it to the next generation, these things are never easy. But every good thing we enjoy today is the result of someone before us doing one or more of the things above. Today, let us be the ones that give others further down the line something to rejoice over.

September 11th
EVERYONE'S A STAR ON THE WALK OF FAME

"My audience loves me. And I love them. And they love me for lovin' them and I love them for lovin' me. And we love each other. And that's cause none of us got enough love in our childhoods. And that's showbiz, kid."

ROXIE HART – CHICAGO

Roxie's words remind one of the song *Hunger* by Florence + The Machine, in which Florence sings with poignancy and deep feeling of being on stage and giving to strangers. Whichever side of the connection – whether it's the athlete in the arena, the musician on stage, or the actor performing live or through the medium of the screen – entertainer and watcher are connected in the moment. Two sides of one coin. Neither could exist without the other. We're not all born to be on the big stage, but we're all born on our own stage, and in those magic moments of being entertained, the truly great ones raise us up on to the platform next to them. They make us a part of their show, as we make them a part of ours.

September 12th
SECRET TRIFLES

"When I was a boy, I started to hide things in the lining
of the garments. Things only I knew were there. Secrets."

REYNOLDS WOODCOCK – PHANTOM THREAD

There are different types of secrets. Secrets that carry pain or shame should be shared if possible, as the act of sharing with a kind and sympathetic ear will unburden the carrier. But secrets of a more innocent nature; where the goodie bag is hidden, the initials carved in the tree, mini personal triumphs, buried treasure, these are all fun little things to be indulged. In all our sharing and openness, it's not a bad thing to hold back a few trifles that can tickle us in our private moments. While we share the road of life with many brothers and sisters, and therefore most of our joys, luxuries, successes and laughs will be communal, we can reserve a few just for ourselves.

September 13th
THE LIFT OF LOVE

"Love denied blights the soul we owe to God."

WILLIAM SHAKESPEARE – SHAKESPEARE IN LOVE

None of us can force love, either outbound or inbound. We love whom we love, and the same from others to us. Alas, love can be ephemeral and it can be everlasting. It can make sense, and it can be completely baffling. But one thing is for certain, love must be present for our soul to be elevated to its highest degree. Love is the purifier that reconciles us to God, the universe and each other. We might translate *love denied blights the soul we owe to God* to; *love unfulfilled hinders our ability to present the best version of ourselves to life.*

September 14th
QUICKSAND OF SELF-KNOWLEDGE

*"I had thoughts about him I hardly knew what to do
with, and he read every one. Whatever I wanted, he gave
himself up to, and in that moment everything I knew to
be true about myself was gone. I was acting like another
woman, yet I was more myself than ever before."*

FRANCESCA JOHNSON – THE BRIDGES OF MADISON COUNTY

Self-knowledge can be like a familiar old living room. You know
every inch of the room, where the lamps throw their light, the
slightly crooked painting, the best position for getting really
comfy on the sofa. But one day you walk in and instead of the
carpet there is a mass of quicksand that sucks you in before you
know what's happening. Everything gets turned on its head.
Everything you thought you knew about your cosy retreat
vanishes in a puff of smoke. Similarly, so goes our journey of
self-knowledge, which by definition, runs parallel to our journey
of self-discovery. A thing is only a thing until it's not a thing.
We only know for sure how we would react to an altercation, or
divorce, or success, or fame, or illness, or Mondays, until… we
encounter them. And even then, as we encounter circumstances
and gain a working knowledge of ourselves, it's still not the end
of the story. Acting one way this time does not automatically
mean acting the same way next time. Self-knowledge is an ever-
moving target… that's what makes it so much fun. Sometimes
we feel alarmed and dismayed when we react to something in a
way we later regret, which is quite harsh on self, because we need
that situation to trigger our behaviour to give us the opportunity
to reflect and grow. Likewise, new territory will provide many
opportunities for us to prove to ourselves we are much more
capable and brave and talented than we may have thought. The
double-edged sword of self-knowledge is thus: while we veritably
want to know ourselves, which breeds confidence and security,
we need, and indeed, should want, to prove ourselves wrong as
often as we do right.

September 15th
CONNECT THE DOTS

"We are the choices that we have made."

FRANCESCA JOHNSON – THE BRIDGES OF MADISON COUNTY

If you took some of the biggest decisions you've made in your past, and you picked one of those, and went back and took a radically different turn, would you be the same person you are now?

The answer is clear…

… Of course not. We all know this. We all know that the only things we can absolutely control are our own thoughts, choices and attitudes, and those choices have brought us to where we are today.

Suggestion for the day: take those biggest decisions you've made in your life and consider how those choices have shaped your life. Piece together the links in the chain that have brought you to today. In your mind, empower the truth, which is that *you* made those choices. Empower the sovereignty that *you* exercised as a human being with a heart and a mind and a will, to make those choices. Empower the knowledge that *your* choices can lead *you* wherever *you* desire.

September 16th
MISSING INGREDIENTS

"Brains'll only get you so far and luck always runs out."

DETECTIVE SLOCUMB – THELMA & LOUISE

If intelligence and good fortune don't cover all bases, what does that leave as the final go-to? Hard work? Peace? Serenity? Acceptance?

Who will play your knight in shining armour?

What part of self is completely infallible and can be trusted to take oneself all the way to the end?

September 17th
MUMS KNOW BEST

"My idea has always been that if we could bring the mothers of the various nations together, then there would be no more war."

RUTH WILCOX – HOWARDS END

The 20th century was a tumultuous and eventful one. Many advancements and breakthroughs in science took place. Yet blighting all the supposed leaps of mankind were the backward steps of war and the tyranny of governments. Weapons were created holding the destructive power to eradicate the whole of human civilisation. Walls dividing people were built up then pulled down again. Now some people want newer and bigger ones to go back up. Technology progressed, humanity regressed. Citius, altius, fortius became lazier, fatter, greedier. And the collective cognitive dissonance grew. Many people living in opulence; many more living without the most basic necessities.

As a species, how long can we avoid our true calling? How long can we pretend that this is the best we can be?

We need the love of mothers. The selflessness, the empathy, the kindness, the sacrifice. This is how we raise our collective consciousness. This is how we become the best version of our species. War and greed and division and hate have never resolved anything, regardless of what anyone says about them being natural or normal or even healthy. Love and true understanding of who and what we are, these are the way. Maybe it's time to let the mothers make the important decisions.

September 18th
WICKED WIZARDS AND WITCHES

"Everybody has a wicked side, Rose."

BUDDY HILLYER – RAMBLING ROSE

Projecting and polarising come naturally to us humans. That's why we love a hero / villain story in movies. Superman is perfect and never puts a foot out of place, while Lex Luthor is simply pure evil. We don't like anything to spoil the fragile narrative that we hold in our mind toward either receptacles of our extreme views. A step along the path of maturity is learning that usually even the most wonderful people have their flaws, and that the most dastardly of people have some redeeming traits. The reality is that the majority of us mere mortals are somewhere much closer to the middle. In learning to deal with others and most importantly, ourselves, we can remember that we all regularly fall short of our best. Embracing the shortcomings in ourselves with love and patience allows us the space to change for the better, and for the right reasons.

September 19th
STRONG FOUNDATION

"I have allowed myself to lead this little life, when inside me there was so much more. And it's all gone unused. And now it never will be. Why do we get all this life if we don't ever use it? Why do we get all these feelings and dreams and hopes if we don't ever use them?"

SHIRLEY VALENTINE – SHIRLEY VALENTINE

Life is like a colouring picture – we either fall short of filling it up to the lines, or we over-indulge and go way over them. It's hard to get it just right. Building up the importance of seizing every moment and maximising every opportunity is fine, but not every moment is meant to be memorable or exhilarating. Many moments are the framework for the thrilling ones. We can and we are living our dreams, but let's not be fooled by social media with its smoke and mirrors that say we can exist in one perpetual state of partying and driving fast cars and quoting Confucius and spending lots of money and looking immaculate and changing the world and basically all of the lovely things (material and spiritual) without any of the humdrum, the tough, the routine and the grind that makes all of the amazing possible.

September 20th

MEANT TO BE

"I got one... one life, right? Mine. But sh... f***, I want somebody else's sometimes. Sometimes I just feel like I'm fighting for a life I just ain't got time to live. I want it to mean something."

RON WOODROOF – DALLAS BUYERS CLUB

Trying to catch the meaning of life can be harder than catching a Golden Snitch in a game of Quidditch. Often, one finds that meanings must be softly coaxed and uncovered from within, not demanded from without. There are many roads that can lead one to find grand, overarching meanings within their own life, but they are not signposted, and nothing externally can give directions. Many a person has unwittingly stumbled upon their meaning, with no preceding conscious intention or guiding knowledge. Others seem to have always known theirs. Whenever it happens, it might be said that our meanings find us. Furthermore, meanings can obviously change. A meaning can be a source of great joy today and great sorrow tomorrow (and vice versa). Some meanings will generate increasingly greater motivational energy as time passes. Other meanings will need to be abandoned before they sink the ship. Some questions that can stimulate our pursuit of meaning are:

What are my passions?
What do I value?
How can I make an impact?
Where, when and with whom do I feel most alive?

September 21st
WHO WANTS NORMAL?

"Regular life? What is that? It doesn't exist."

DR EVE SAKS – DALLAS BUYERS CLUB

Every culture has what might be considered a conventional life journey. Some central themes probably carry over across all cultures; birth, growing and learning, meeting a mate, children, a career, retirement, death. But within those landmarks lie an awful lot of space to fill up. And even those pillars aren't a given for everyone. The only two that are is birth and death, and soon even those might not be a certainty. The beauty of life is that some people choose a very methodical, planned journey that ticks all the societal boxes; university, marriage, 2.4 kids, mortgage, SUV, steady incremental climbing of the corporate ladder and very predictable package holidays. While their opposites don't study, stay single, don't settle down, don't have children, don't build a career, don't ever 'get their s*** together.' There is no right or wrong, no better or worse. Ultimately, we all have bits of our lives that follow convention and bits that don't.

September 22nd
BAD SMELLING STORY

"The only thing standing between you and your goal is the bulls**t story you keep telling yourself as to why you can't achieve it."

JORDAN BELFORT – THE WOLF OF WALL STREET

You   > - - - - > - - - - >   ?????   > - - - - > - - - - >   Your Goal

What is your BS story? Is it BS, or is it a legitimate reason? Only you know the truth. Only you know what your next step needs to be. Only you can know what you need to do. Action flows from the vision within and the only person who knows that vision is you. Motivation is required to help you keep the dedication and discipline needed. Seek that out. Find out what stands between you and your goal. Acknowledge it. Name it. Decide if you will let that thing come between you and the joy of your self-actualisation.

September 23rd
HANDLE WITH CARE

(During a torrential downpour)
"You better get back inside your tent or you're going to freeze."
"I don't feel anything." (Oblivious to the cold)

CAPTAIN BLOCKER & SERGEANT METZ – HOSTILES

Our bodies and souls are all sensitive organisms. They must be treated with care, lest rough handling damage them and impair their ability to function to their optimum level. The body, in its capacity as the instrument of the soul, can be strengthened to become quite robust and sturdy against the physical stresses and buffetings of life, that fortitude being considered a good thing. Our souls, too, enlarge and grow in response to the challenges they face. How we choose to respond to the questions of life will determine what becomes of our soul. Our souls transcend the limitations of the physical, yet they must be accessed through the physical conduit, that conduit being the body. Each of us is given sole responsibility of our soul. We can numb or deaden it through repeated abuse of our conscience, abandonment of morality and neglect of our spiritual needs. We can magnify and expand it through connection, love and sacrifice.

September 24th
EXPLORATION

"I gotta tell you, the life of the mind... There's no roadmap for that territory... And exploring it can be painful."

BARTON FINK – BARTON FINK

Just as going for a physical check-up with its prods and pulls and thermometers in funny places can be a little uncomfortable, probes of the mind can produce their own equivalent of reflex kicks and yelps. The topology of the mind is like that of the earth – varied. There are some smooth, even flats that extend far in to the horizon; and there are mountains and valleys, jungles and deserts. One can easily get lost in their explorations. Perhaps the task we each face is that of exploring our mind without becoming wrapped up with the identity of an explorer, meaning, the terrain an explorer comes across or happens to be traversing at any given moment is of secondary importance to their own inherent qualities and being. All of the earth has its beauty, but some parts are more hospitable than others, and therefore desirable for prolonged camp. Each part of the mind serves its purpose. May we each find that place within it that we can call home. May we each experience harmony between mind, body and soul.

September 25th
PRESENCE

"What do you love about climbing mountains?"
"The absolute simplicity. That's what I love. When you're
climbing, your mind is clear and free from all confusions.
You have focus. And suddenly the light becomes sharper,
the sounds are richer, and you're filled with the deep,
powerful presence of life. I've only felt that one other
time."
"When?"
"In your presence, Kundun."

DALAI LAMA & HEINRICH HARRER – SEVEN YEARS IN TIBET (1997)

The only thing more beautiful than stillness without… is stillness
within. Holy places and enlightened people are beacons to the
thirsty soul. They beckon: Come. Rest here a moment. Find
stillness. Indulge in pure presence.

September 26th
RESPONSE-ABILITY

"I'm responsible for you."
"You're responsible for yourself."

MATT & TOBIN – SAFE HOUSE

People who seek to be co-dependent will say things like, *you help me and I'll help you, you protect me and I'll protect you* (seen this anywhere recently?) If you are an adult, claim responsibility for yourself and yourself alone. The moment you give away responsibility for yourself or try to assume it for another person, you're in violation of universal law. All matter is inherently self-governing. It's a nuance of the human condition that we are even able to think that we can either appropriate or abdicate responsibility. Watch out for being someone who makes the error of believing that flawed, surface-level thinking can override immutable law.

Avoid confusing vital interdependence with sovereign responsibility.

September 27th
LIKIN' AND LOYALTY AIN'T FAMILY

"A man is supposed to take care of his family. You live in my house, fill your belly with my food, put your behind on my bed, because you're my son... Not because I like you... 'cause it's my duty to take care of you. I owe a responsibility to you. Now let's get this straight right here, now, before I go along any further... I ain't got to like you! Mr Rand don't give me my money come payday because he like me, he give it to me because he owe me. Now, I don't give you everything I got to give you... I give you your life! Me and your mama worked that out between us and liking your black ass wasn't part of the bargain! Now don't you go through life worrying about whether somebody like you or not! You best be makin' sure they're doin' right by you! You understand what I'm sayin'?"

TROY MAXSON – FENCES

There is a big difference between somebody liking you and somebody caring about you. A world of difference. They are often confused and used interchangeably. Many people will like you and enjoy who you are, but won't lose any sleep or make any contribution when you need help. When it comes to the people in your life, actions are the only currency. Fuzzy notions and projected loyalties lull some people in to placing value in relationships that have no foundation. Know who has your back.

> September 28th
> **PAIN EXPLAINS**

"There is no normal life that is free from pain."

FRED ROGERS – A BEAUTIFUL DAY IN THE NEIGHBOURHOOD

Pain may not be an invited guest, but nor should it be run from. The more we try to run from it, the more it gives pursuit, and brings friends too. Pain is not the enemy. Fear and loathing of it is. Pain is only a messenger. Easy acceptance of its presence holds the key. When we can make our raison d'être a positive, empowering pursuit, when we extract the juice from life through conscious living in the moment, when we ride the highway of joyful being, the fear of pain's visits subside and we accept it as the oft-times travelling companion it is. Astonishingly, one day we can reach a place where pain, along with disappointment and delay, are greeted with as equal hospitality as wellness, contentment and advancement.

September 29th
LOVE LETTER TO SELF

"I hope you know that you made today a very special day by just your being you. There's no one in the whole world like you, and I like you just the way you are."

FRED ROGERS – A BEAUTIFUL DAY IN THE NEIGHBOURHOOD

We all need love and validation. We all matter. If that isn't true, who, then, is qualified to determine the ones that don't matter?

Romeo & Juliet is a beautiful, timeless love story. But it isn't the most important. Nor is Molly and Sam, Danny and Sandy or Rick and Ilsa. That honour is reserved for you. Saying 'I love you' to someone else is one thing, but what about looking in the mirror and saying it to yourself. Can you say it and really mean it? If you can't, that's OK. Just know that you are deserving and worthy of love. You are loved by the universe, and there is a path to feeling that peace and love within.

September 30th
SAIL TOWARDS CALM

"There's gotta be something other than being a fisherman and kidnapping people."
"Maybe in America, Irish. Maybe in America."

CAPTAIN PHILLIPS & MUSE – CAPTAIN PHILLIPS

Necessity and opportunity are powerful masters. The former demands rigorous obedience, the latter can promise escape from it. We each paddle our own little boat, and with each stroke we take, we propel ourselves closer to either stormy waves or peaceful waters. Pirating becomes an alluring opportunity when we lose the stomach for putting in the hard work of fishing. In many ways, the two occupations do bear similarities. Both require working a boat. Both take patience and diligence. Both are dangerous. Today, each of us have awoken with needs and wants. Nature calls us to serve the needs, while conscience guides the attendance of our wants. We choose how to meet those naturally arising cues. We choose whether to fly the flag of freedom or the Jolly Roger. Circumstance merely provides the props. We must choose which colours to hoist.

October 1ˢᵗ
PARADOXES ARE THE BEST

"I'm talking about the classic paradox of time. Imagine, for example, I go back in time and meet my own grandfather. Long before he got married, before he had children. And we have an argument, and I kill him. Now if that happens, how am I ever going to be born? And if I can never be born, how can I go back in history and meet my very own grandfather?"

WARREN LASKY – THE FINAL COUNTDOWN

Paradoxes abound in life. The paradox of oneness and duality. The paradox of infinity. The paradox of silly versus serious…

Life *is* a paradox.

Oneness & duality = two supposedly opposing manifestations of one thing, e.g.; the observer and the observed – how could a thing be observed without an observer, and yet how could a thing cease to exist simply because it is not observed?

Infinity = Take space, if space is infinite, how does that work? How can anything be numbered or defined in such an endless existence? But alternatively, if there is finiteness to space, where does it stop, and what is on the other side of the end of it? Is nothingness something? Can *nothingness* even exist?

Silly or serious = Where does one draw the line? Is life a game, to be laughed all the way through? Would that be appropriate at a funeral or in a business meeting? But why wouldn't it be appropriate?

Life. Overwhelmingly meaningful? Or utterly meaningless?

Happiness. Found in focusing on self? Or in being completely selfless?

What paradoxes do you see?

October 2nd
PLAY YOUR PART

"As you go through life there will be no shortage of people who will tell you how to live. They'll have all the answers for you. Don't argue with them. Say "yes, that's a brilliant idea," and then do what you want."

DAVID DOBEL – ANYTHING ELSE

If there is any aphorism that ought to be given ubiquitous exposure, *live and let live* is as worthy as any. In these four small words lies both high philosophy and the simple, open secret to peace and satisfaction in life.

Live – Be, do, dare, dream, fly, flop, try, hop, read, breed, give, get, wander, ponder, become, un-become, run, crawl, brawl(?!), go, come back, stand up for, stand down for, sing, dance, prance, float, drift, feel, breathe… breathe… breathe… manifest…

…and…

Let live – Don't try to stop, hinder, impede, judge, condemn or criticise any living (or unliving) soul or creature from doing the same.

October 3rd
CLING TO HOPE

"Sometimes the things that may or may not be true are the things a man needs to believe in the most. That people are basically good; that honour, courage and virtue mean everything; that money and power mean nothing; that good always triumphs over evil."

HUB McCANN – SECONDHAND LIONS

Does good always triumph over evil? Who knows, but if it doesn't, if sometimes evil comes out on top, does that change our attitude? Do we lose commitment to the good if we think we might be on the losing team? If Evil Disunited's quarterback is killing us, do we jump ship and swap jerseys at half time?

One of the biggest threats to our own individual salvation is self-sabotage. Never being good enough. Perfectionism. Self-condemnation. Quit playing that game, it's a losing wicket. We can't watch the fluffy films, with their beautiful ideals and stories of redemption, then beat and break ourselves. Regardless of what you've done and what you think that means, you stand renewed in this moment. You are as worthy as any human being that has ever existed of finding your measure of peace and meaning. That does not mean that there are not outer consequences and situations that exist now based on your previous choices, or that harmful actions do not have consequences that include emotional pain and remorse. But it does mean that you can choose to cling to hope. You can give yourself the gift of self-love and self-acceptance.

October 4th
CHOICE IS NOICE

"Man has a choice and it's a choice that makes him a man."

CAL TRASK – EAST OF EDEN

Use your voice to make your choice.

Use your feet to pick your street.

Use your hands to mould your plans.

Use your heart to play your part.

Use your vision to fuel your mission.

Use your resources to be your forces, for good.

Use your now to create your Wow.

Use your love to make the stars above, rejoice.

Use your talents to add to the balance.

By your being, you are a part of the all-seeing, oneness.

Arise and choose. By your choices, thus you create your world.

October 5th
KEEP IT REAL

"Well, I've wrestled with reality for 35 years, Doctor, and I'm happy to state I finally won out over it."

ELWOOD P. DOWD – HARVEY (1950)

There are some ways to engage with reality that will lead to a progressive and peaceful life, and some that will likely lead to anger and chronic frustration;

√ Accepting and embracing reality lead to peace and calm. They don't eliminate all types of pain, but they present a balanced viewpoint that can lead to decisions and actions to maximise one's own situation and experiences.

√ At the other end of the spectrum is completely creating one's own reality. Living in a fantasy world (positive connotation). Such living might cause even more pain, but if such genius/delusion is indulged to the extreme, it might also be the anaesthetic. If you do go down this road, make sure to be consistent.

X One guaranteed route to a miserable life is the begrudging, non-acceptance of reality. Fighting it. This is a sure-fire way to a life of emptiness, sadness, resentment and pity.

Ultimately, these options and the countless others are another way of saying, choose your own reality. Have the courage to do what you can to make your reality the best it can be.

October 6th
MY WORD

"For every word, in action, becomes beautiful in the light of its own meaning."

PROFESSOR MURRAY – THE PROFESSOR AND THE MADMAN

Words have power. If they didn't, we wouldn't speak. And like all types of power, it is innate and neutral. We direct that power to a constructive or destructive end. Think of some of your favourite words...

Peace... smile... discombobulate... meditation... custard! ☺

Some words carry latent power, some symbolise a high ideal, some conjure up happy images and feelings... and some just sound cool. Words are not everything, but as a source of power they do have the ability to build up or pull down, to elevate or denigrate. A life led with conscious intention will naturally include conscious use of language. What we say says something about us. Of course, words alone must be weighed as part of the whole observation. Sometimes kind words are delivered with harmful, ulterior motives, and just as often, hurtful words issue from people whose overall intention is loving. As when watching a magician, don't get pulled in by the words only. Keep an eye on what the hands (and feet!) are doing, too.

Let us consider if our words are in harmony with what we mean to be and convey. Let us consider if they align with our actions. Let us refine our words so that they become a natural expression of our best selves. A force for good by which we build ourselves and each other.

October 7th
RESULT: HAPPINESS

"Man, with money in your pocket, you're as free as the wind!"

TIM – THE SOUTHERNER

In Dicken's *David Copperfield*, the affable character Mr Micawber lays down a few gems for the young David, none more enduring than;

> *Annual income twenty pounds, annual expenditure nineteen [pounds] nineteen [shillings] and six [pence], result: happiness. Annual income twenty pounds, annual expenditure twenty pounds ought and six, result: misery.*

Money is power. Money is freedom. Money is the means to help and share and change and shape. But like with all elemental commodities, simply seeking more and more and more is nonsensical. Let's use time as a parallel. We all seek more time because we equate time with the ability to do and be and live and achieve, but if we're not living in this moment, spending this moment well, then what use is more time? More time to wish for more time to long for more time to consider how nice more time would be...? It's a meaningless loop. Only ever seeking more, more, more... makes of us a complete more-on! So with money. An imbalanced fixation with it is as unnatural as an imbalanced fixation with time. Instead of simply always chasing more, let us find contentment with what we have, what this moment is bringing us, and what we can do with the time and resources that lie at our disposal now.

October 8th

CHUCKLE

"Laughter is the best medicine."

DOCTOR RENDELL – DR. GIGGLES

Charlie Chaplin was quoted as saying; *life is a tragedy when seen in close-up, but a comedy in long-shot.* (From a speech by Richard Roud in 1972, referencing the legendary actor.)

As we know, working with life is a sure way to doing and feeling alright. And if we're trying to imitate life, it certainly has a better sense of humour than any of us. Slipping on ice; changing TV channels with the air-conditioner remote; starting the car with the key to the shed; learning, quite awkwardly, that when someone says in Chinese that their mother is in Shanghai, it's not just a place, the word also means *pain*… gulp… (a whole book could be written on the humour of language and its booby traps…) Laughter is not exclusive and doesn't require any subscriptions. It is a necessity, not a luxury, and there is plenty to go around for all of us. Just as the saying goes, that jest often carries a hidden truth, so serious and solemn environments and moments carry hilarity and absurdity. Laughter is the most human of foibles. It makes friends of enemies, good out of bad, sense out of the senseless. As art takes anything and beautifies it by putting a frame around it, laughter takes anything and by finding the lightness in it, makes it OK.

Best of all, laughter, except for when we laugh at someone with the intention to ridicule or demean, unites us. Ultimately, as the great artist (Chaplin) also said; *One cannot do humour without a great sympathy for one's fellow man.*

October 9th
IDEAS

"Only that which isn't in the physical realm and reaches in both directions can be eternal. Our ideas. They are what we leave behind. And only they are what can push us forward."

NIKOLA TESLA – THE CURRENT WAR

The world stands at the precipice. Technology promises to solve all our ills, individual and societal. The state seeks to nanny us, taking complete control of all aspects of human affairs. Money screams that all we need is more of it... and all will be fine. In reality, none of those are at all equipped to elevate humanity. Technology deals with matter in the physical realm. It takes something and makes it faster, stronger, further reaching, more intelligent, more convenient, but it does not elevate on the spiritual plane. Government is merely the collective term given for individual humans who should be seeking to serve, strengthen and liberate the society (also a collective term, merely indicating sovereign and sentient individuals) that they are a part of. Money suggests that it holds the key, but it is also merely an aid, a means of exchange. None of these things will take us to where we want to go. They are tools, structures, mechanisms. To get where we want to go the vehicle is ideas and ideals. Lofty, noble, kind, compassionate and spiritual ideas. Ideas that transcend space and time. Ideas that empower the most important truth:

We all matter. We are all equal. We are all free. We are all sentient and sovereign beings and no one of us has the right or the power to lay claim on that cosmic birthright of another. When we all get on this page, the glories and the places we can reach are fathomless. But remember, these glorious ideas are self-protecting, that's the point. You can't force or manipulate another to want their own freedom. Freedom and spiritual enlightenment is an entirely self-emanating and self-sustaining thing, in the most absolute and literal sense. Freedom is an entirely self-*ish* thing.

October 10th
HAPPY CLAPPERS

"I'm unhappy."
"So are millions of us."

DORIS & GEORGE – THE ARTIST (2011)

"I'm unhappy," a person says. *"Join the club,"* says another. Our happiness is not binary in the sense that it is either entirely self-determined or completely not self-determined. It is slightly more nuanced than that. A person can be as happy as they determine to be, regardless of their outer life circumstances. But in practice, a person who is enjoying feelings of abundance, health, peace and happiness in their world, who sees suffering and unhappiness in others, will feel moved with compassion toward those people. Unless they are deranged, they will feel a degree of unhappiness by proxy. This hints at our interdependence. It lays out the great paradox of happiness: the attempt to share it is only outbound. Nobody but myself can make me happy, but I can surely labour to make others happy. Is there a best way to do that, more so than lovely things like service or spending time or a smile? Perhaps to seek to share and show another that they are worthy, that they deserve happiness, and that they can claim it whenever they feel like it.

October 11th
THE HILLS ARE ALIVE WITH LOVE

"I live in Notting Hill. You live in Beverly Hills. Everyone in the world knows who you are, my mother has trouble remembering my name."
"I'm also just a girl, standing in front of a boy, asking him to love her."

WILLIAM & ANNA – NOTTING HILL

Beverly Hills in LA, Notting Hill in London or Fragrant Hills in Beijing, we all want the same thing. To be loved. To find the inexpressible joy in giving and receiving, in knowing that our candle has been the reason for another to feel a little warmth and see the light. Love has no borders, no lost in translation, no distance it cannot cover, no obstacles it cannot surmount. Be brave enough to stand and embrace the full majesty of her.

October 12th
THE RIGHT PATH

"I have come to the crossroads in my life. I always knew what the right path was. Without exception, I knew. But I never took it. You know why? It was too damn hard."

LT. COLONEL FRANK SLADE – THE SCENT OF A WOMAN

Three hours before the flight departs… plenty of time. Let's check the duty free. Two hours… no rush. Let's get a bite to eat and some drinks. One hour… still time. Just remembered, we need to get the wedding gift for Bob and Mary. 30 minutes… gate is open. We need to get the tax returns receipt. 15 minutes… final boarding call. Hang on, they've changed the gate!! It's at the opposite end of the terminal!…. Oh mercy….!!!! Take off!

Oh well… We'll get them for their golden anniversary!

Opportunities in life come and go. Choices present themselves in a never-ending sequence. Only God or a white wizard can know what the ultimate and eventual result of any given choice will be, (and perhaps more to the point, there is no singular end-result to anything… choices simply continue to mould and steer an ever-unfolding present moment.) We do the best we can. But at some point, the tough paths we avoided will seem like the easy ones. Laziness is a lie. It asks one to believe that idleness can replace activity with no loss of self-esteem. Addiction is a lie. It takes everything and gives nothing in return. Materialism without spirituality is a lie. It diverts attention from its own utter lack of ability to feed and adorn the soul.

Today, let us summon the strength to make as many good choices as possible. Let us ask the question at each crossroad, which is the right path? May we have the courage to take the hard road, the road less travelled.

October 13th
SOLO SPORT

"I do what I do best: I take scores. You do what you do best: try to stop guys like me."

NEIL MCCAULEY – HEAT

Cops and robbers, heroes and villains, there cannot be one without the other. As Gandalf said, everyone has their part to play. The bond we all share runs above and beneath those surface-level opposites. Maybe that's why Pacino held De Niro's hand. It's okay, brother. We've travelled opposite directions but the same highway. We've been on opposite teams (on the day) but the same game, same stadium. Different badges but the same thirst to feel something. A great peculiarity of life is; the more we try to differentiate ourselves from one another, the more glaring our similarities become.

October 14th
PRICELESS TREASURE

"We're meant to lose the people we love. How else would we know how important they are to us?"

GRANDMA FULLER – THE CURIOUS CASE OF BENJAMIN BUTTON

Why do we wait until our loved ones pass before we pay them a eulogy? Maybe for the same reasons we keep dessert until last and the trophy is given out at the end. It's only when a person is gone that we start to fully understand what they meant to us. This is as it should be. The living memories of the person that we cherish are the postcards they send us from heaven of the journey we took together. However! That does not stop us from appreciating all the amazing people in our life today. Let yours know what they mean to you.

珍惜身边的人
Treasure those by your side

October 15th
FRUITS OF OUR LABOURS

"I guess sometimes the past just catches up with you, whether you want it to or not."

PAUL EDGECOMB – THE GREEN MILE

We try to bury our deeds,
But wrong deeds are like weeds;
They grow and reproduce,
Ignoring them is no use;
The right way to treat our acts,
Is to view them as facts;
Like an encyclopaedia,
Or honest media;
The fruits of our labour show,
That which we already know;
When choices poorly are spent,
We surely shall lament;
Yet kindness and goodness sown,
Yield the treasures we own;
The fruits of faith, hope and love,
Fall freely from above.

October 16th
FIND THE WAY

"The way of life can be free and beautiful, but we have lost the way. Greed has poisoned men's souls, has barricaded the world with hate, has goose-stepped us into misery and bloodshed. We have developed speed, but we have shut ourselves in."

ADENOID HYNKEL – THE GREAT DICTATOR

The way of life can and will be beautiful when we start to apply the great wisdom, which is that we are spiritual beings. It is through our love and service that we must raise ourselves up. This cannot be done through coercion or force, manipulation or guilt-tripping. We are each free, sovereign and sentient beings. We have an opportunity to take a time-out and figure out what it is we as a collective are seeking. We can share our humanity at every available opportunity and build each other up to know that we each matter. Money without kindness is hollow. Power without integrity is perilous. Technology without spirituality is death. But with kindness, with integrity, with love and compassion, and a constant remembrance of who we are, *combined* with these advancements… then together these tools and our humanity can and will serve us to go to the stars and beyond.

October 17th
BET BEHIND THE EARS

"I'll bet you twenty bucks I can get you gambling before the end of the day."
"You're on."

LLOYD & HARRY – DUMB AND DUMBER

Moral of the quote: never let small things like a bet get between a good friendship. Let's believe that Harry knew exactly what has happening and thought, you know what, Lloyd could do with the 20 bucks. There are plenty of those kind of people, people who sacrifice and do little turns for others in a way that goes completely under the radar. Anonymous niceness. It's what keeps the positive vibrations buzzing and humming. Like suggesting to the cabbie a fixed amount rather than by the meter, and then offering an amount that is clearly over the going rate because you know he must have had a terrible year behind the wheel... and letting him think that despite your local accent you must be a crazy tourist!

Every day the universe bets with each of us that we can't do at least one good thing for someone else. It's a loaded bet. It knows we can, and it further knows that not only will that person feel great, we will feel great, the universe will feel great... it's a win-win-win-win-win.

October 18th
THE STATUTES OF LIBERTY

"Fre-e-e-e-e-d-o-o-o-o-o-o-o-o-m!!"

WILLIAM WALLACE – BRAVEHEART

Each and every human being is born free. All of the universal efforts throughout history at progressing humanity should have been attempts toward that overarching end, namely, to empower the self-evident truth that we are all free. To sustain the love and protection of that truth. You are endowed with the innate and inalienable freedom of self-determination, self-perpetuation, self-expression, self-manifestation and self-actualisation. This is your glory. This glory is self-evident and self-sustaining. All things exist in their own glory, and you have yours. No force on heaven or earth have the right to infringe upon that. In the absolute and final truth, no force can infringe upon your freedom. Literally. Only you can relinquish it.

People try to impose on each other's liberties and self-expression in all areas of life. Parents do it the world over. You will support this team. You will become a lawyer. You will follow the family religion. You will be quiet and let the grown-ups talk. In school, it can be the stifling of self-expression, in organisations the ability to question the status quo, and most frequently, in relationships. You will love me. You will do x because I do y. You can't speak to them, you can wear that, you're not allowed to go there, you are allowed to do that...

Freedom. Such a simple concept, so hard to get our heads around. Freedom does not mean we do not have some degree of expectations, some degree of interdependence, some degree of give and take, some degree of responsibility. Of course we do. As Viktor Frankl said, The Statue of Liberty on the east coast should have its twin, The Statue of Responsibility, on the west. But let's not conflate issues. While inextricably connected with concepts around interdependence and give and take, the issue of freedom is simple. Each and every one of us is free. Our progress as a species is inseparably connected with our ability to align with this principle.

When we come to honour the freedom in each other, then we will find real transformation in our world. Self-actualisation, true freedom and unconditional love are all one and the same thing. Ultimate freedom is the ultimate state of being. In the garden of human progress, it is the sunlight that we grow toward.

October 19th
CONSTRUCTION SITE

"Anyone who ever gave you confidence, you owe them a lot."

HOLLY GOLIGHTLY – BREAKFAST AT TIFFANY'S

There are builder-uppers and puller-downers. A builder-upper takes delight at dispensing cheer and positivity, encouraging people to feel good about themselves. They look for the good in others and revel in pointing it out when they find it (which they usually do.) They pass on the best of themselves to be used in the development of fellow humans' structures of success, and they discard their own unused and unusable waste material quietly and without fanfare. The temptation to detonate and destroy always exists, but these people-lovers stick to construction and leave destruction to others more suited to the task. We can all be a builder-upper. No hard hat or JCB is required. All it takes is pondering on what builds ourselves up, what makes us feel good, and then doing that to those around us. We remember that when we lift another, we're also lifting ourselves. Every brick we lay in building a path of happiness for another miraculously lays two in the building of our own.

October 20th
YOU ARE HERE

"You can't get so hung up on where you'd rather be that you forget to make the most of where you are."

AURORA LANE – PASSENGERS (2016)

We need to know where we are logistically before we can make the journey to a desired location. If the destination is Paris, the travel itinerary will differ greatly depending whether we're in Brussels or Bogota. That is why tourist and hiking maps usually provide a helpful YOU ARE HERE. It's all well and good knowing where the ice-cream stall is… but where are we in relation to it? As much as it is important to understand our physical location for the need of practical orientation, so we might also draw the parallel on the spiritual plane. Where we currently stand is where we're meant to be. There is a purpose for us passing this way. The place we want to get to is not going anywhere. We will arrive. But first let us honour and acknowledge where we stand. Appreciation and gratitude for our present coordinates elevates us to a level of harmony with what is, and prepares us to move forward purposefully. Step by step in the physical realm, growth by growth in the inner realm.

October 21st
DOUSE THE FLAMES OF HATE

"Every one of you hates every one of us, and we hate you right back."

BERNARDO – WEST SIDE STORY (1961)

Every one of us, at times, will be on the receiving end of aggression, abuse or wrongdoing. That is inescapable. And at times, we've all reacted in a way that tries to meet that fire with fire. And where has that got us? Did it resolve the situation? Did it harmonise the parties? Hatred and strife exist. End of story. Our perspective is not to drive it out of existence, that is flawed on lots of levels. Our task is much more modest but still plenty hard enough. It is simply to manage the anger and the hatred within ourselves, the long shadows cast by our own self-ignorance. To understand that while tea does occasionally get spilt on the carpet, we tend to avoid deliberately throwing cups of it down and revelling in the fact. Love and forgiveness are the antidotes to fear and hatred. *How* that love manifests is another matter entirely.

October 22nd
BURNING DESIRE

"I don't know how to run a newspaper, Mr Thatcher. I just try everything I can think of."

CHARLES FOSTER KANE – CITIZEN KANE

The wonderful thing about desire is it takes energy of all kinds and transmutes it toward the desired end. Let's say you feel the desire to write a book but you don't know where to start. One way is to build a burning desire. Daily affirmations: I am a successful, published author. Hold the intention and the thought of writing, of calling yourself an author. Tell yourself and others that you are an author. See the finished publication in your favourite bookstore with yourself giving book signings to your enthusiastic readers. Sooner or later that high-vibrational attachment to the desire is going to transmute to the action of writing. Another way is to just start writing. All-out scattergun. Doesn't matter what you think of the material you produce. Just write. See what comes out. The more you write, the more you give your work a chance to become defined and refined. The motion of doing, like a river cutting through the land, will naturally chart you a course. Many a successful person has begun their quest with little more than a burning desire. Many a modest, successful person would insist that far beyond accomplishing and surpassing their goal, they still had little more qualification than a burning desire. Attitude, action and desire are three essential ingredients that will always yield results. You don't need to know how, you just need to know you can and you are.

October 23rd
ACCOUNTABILITY

"There's only one person who's going to decide what I'm going to do, and that's me."

CHARLES FOSTER KANE – CITIZEN KANE

See if you can recognise any of the following statements:

- » I can't come to the party because I'm looking after mum.
- » I would have called you back but the football was starting.
- » I was drunk.
- » I didn't think anybody would notice.
- » I will go if you can give me a lift.

What is a common denominator? They all carry some degree of non-accountability. How could they be rephrased (making one of many possible presumptive translations at what the person was trying to say):

- » The party sounds amazing, thanks for the invite. I'm choosing to stay home and look after mum.
- » The football match was important to me and I decided to prioritise that over anything else.
- » I made a choice to drink alcohol to the point of inebriation…
- » I took it because I wanted to.
- » I am going to attend. Can you give me a lift please?

The infinite scenarios of life present just as many ways of dealing with them. These examples are merely an illustration toward the concept of – I am sentient and sovereign. I make choices and they have consequences. I empower through my language that I recognise, acknowledge and work with the knowledge that I chart my own course.

All things being equal, the likelihood is that a person with a high degree of self-awareness and self-honesty will make more rewarding choices than one without those qualities. Of course, we don't always express verbally our exact intentions as laid out in the second list. Tact and sensitivity ask for wisdom and decorum in aligning intentions and self-knowledge with how we outwardly communicate, but it is important from our own perspective that we understand the choices we make and use empowering language to increase self-esteem.

October 24th
UNCONDITIONAL

"You don't care about anything except you. You just want to persuade people that you love them so much that they ought to love you back. Only you want love on your own terms. Something to be played your way, according to your rules."

JEDEDIAH LELAND – CITIZEN KANE

A collocation is a series of two or more words that are habitually used in conjunction with each other. The word *unconditional* has two words that it particularly likes to form a collocation with; *love* and *surrender*. This is very interesting, as those two words are everything. To reach a place where one loves everything and surrenders to everything… what can surpass that?

Conditional love is not love. It is a trade agreement, a contract, a selfish desire masquerading as concern for another. There is only unconditional love. Love is giving with no thought or motive for any given result or return on investment. It is planting a tiny acorn knowing that the planter will never see the full majesty of the towering oak, but glorying nonetheless in the ability to give purely with no thought of recompense. Love is performing an anonymous act of service. The positivity and energy of the act rippling through the earth, spreading a vibration of kindness and consideration. Love is simply being and enjoying others being.

October 25th
VITAMIN C

"The action is the juice."

MICHAEL CHERITTO – HEAT

If you had all the money and the love you needed, what would you do for fun? What would you do for meaning? What would you do to feel fulfilled? Regardless of varying beliefs as to the purpose of life and the creation or evolution of man, what we do know is that we appear to have this thing called a physical body. A mortal shell, an earthly frame, a vehicle for our spirits... whatever we want to call it, we exist physically as well as spiritually. And the urges and desires that arise within us seek their own satisfaction. Their fulfilment can be extremely enjoyable. What can cause pain is when we forget that we are both body and soul, that both beings – flesh and spirit – need to be stimulated. The promise of a new mountain to scale, of a new challenge, is what keeps us pushing and developing. On the flip side, at any point we can decide to hang up our proverbial boots and embrace the quiet, predictable life. But at any point we feel like a dose of vitamins and minerals, all we have to do is start another round of action.

October 26th
DEAD END

"I don't know what to do anymore. Except maybe die."

JIM STARK – REBEL WITHOUT A CAUSE

Life can feel like a hedge maze at times. The riches in the middle – fulfilment and contentment – can seem to elude us at every turn. Every route we take keeps bringing us to dead ends or going around in circles. We become disoriented. At such times the best option can seem to be removed from the maze altogether. There is no definitive response to that feeling. It must be faced and journeyed through. If we can allow ourselves just a bit more time, we give ourselves the opportunity to be picked up by a new wave of hope or purpose. A question that can be useful in situations where we feel bleak is: what are my options? This puts our attention on possible solutions and simultaneously emphasises that we hold the power to make choices. It is often our feeling of lack of power and lack of choice that cause despondency. Let's strive to reignite an attitude of openness to the options available to us.

October 27th
WAIT A MINUTE

"It's not how long you wait... it's who you're waiting for."

JOE "JUNIOR" – SOME LIKE IT HOT

Some ideas on waiting:

If you're not prepared to wait... you don't deserve them/it (?).

Waiting doesn't have to be passive. It can be active.

Waiting isn't waiting when it's anticipating some exhilarating connection.

Quality, active waiting, also known as patience, purifies.

Waiting and having are two sides of the same coin. The thing I'm waiting for is already mine. If it doesn't come, it is because it was never mine to begin with.

Waiting introduces self to self.

Use the wait to elevate.

October 28th

BRING IT ON

"Are you afraid to die, Spartacus?"
"No more than I was to be born."

ANTONINUS & SPARTACUS – SPARTACUS

How do we create an attitude of fearlessness? Are people born with it? Can one learn how to meet every situation in life with courage? If you knew you could cope with whatever life brings… would you still be afraid? If you knew that everything is a gift, and that those gifts are given and taken like the waves on the shore come and go… would you still be afraid? If you felt, deep down to your bones, that you are worthy of being, worthy of life, worthy of joy… and… worthy of death… would you still be afraid?

October 29th
DO DO

"Don't do anything I wouldn't do. That gives you a lot of leeway!"

Sidney Falco – Sweet Smell of Success

The only limits you have are those you impose on yourself. The more you stretch and try new things the more you learn about yourself. The more you learn about yourself the more you learn about life. The more you learn about life the more you gain in wisdom. The more you gain in wisdom the better you are able to surrender to what is. The better you are able to surrender to what is, the greater will be your ability to experience serenity. The greater your ability to experience serenity the more you will be of service to others. The more you are of service to others the more choices will present themselves to you.

Every component of life, while in some senses compartmentalised, are indeed interlinked and interwoven in to the one fabric of existence. No one part of the jigsaw is enough to enjoy the full picture. You can do lots of stuff, but without learning something you're missing some of the juice. You can do *and* learn lots of stuff, but without applying the wisdom they bring, you're missing so much. You can have action *and* learning *and* wisdom, but without love and surrender, you'll never get to bliss.

October 30th
WASH AWAY WISHING AND WIND UP THE WORK

"Wishing never got anybody anyplace."

JACK THORNTON – THE CALL OF THE WILD (1935)

"Work will win when wishy-washy wishing won't," said Thomas Monson. What an alliteration! How many of your wishes have come true? Did you reach out and grab them, or did they grab you? What wishes are you holding now? Which ones are within your power? What are you going to do today to work toward their realisation?

October 31st
ONE WONDERS

"There is no such thing as the one. It's more of a mind boggling whole hell of a lot of potential ones. That should be comforting. It's actually pretty terrifying. We would all like to kick back and wait for some magical force to show us who we should spend the rest of our lives with. But the truth is, there isn't a lightning bolt that slaps you on the ass and tells you to pick this person over all others. It's like the rain, rain falls all the time. Sometimes we are prepared for it, sometimes we're not. And depending where you are when it hits, you either get caught in it, or you don't. In fact, most of us try like hell to avoid it."

DAVID COLLINS – BUYING THE COW

This applies to a relationship. It applies to work. It applies to holiday destinations. It applies to doughnut flavours. The more you tell yourself that of all the infinite things you could choose, there is only one that is right for you, so your chances of being disappointed increase commensurately. Being too choosy is as bad as being not choosy enough. *If it works it works* is a superb epithet to encapsulate the concept of keeping what works and changing what doesn't. But, it can only be taken so far. In relationships, as in career, there will be bumps and potholes. If we ran at the first sight of trouble there would be no happy families or businesses or football teams. It's not so much about *the right one* and more about *the one that is right in front of you*.

Plot twist… but! There might be exceptions to this philosophy. What if, like JK Simmons and Miles Teller in *Whiplash*, where it's only through the abuse and the inferno of demands that teacher places on the student that eventually draws out the genius within the latter, what if there is only *the one* and it can only be *the one*?

Well, then keep holding out for that perfect one. And if you've found it? Don't let go.

November 1st
SHOWTIME

"What's the first thing an actor learns? 'The show must go on!' Come rain, come shine, come snow, come sleet, the show must go on!"

Cosmo Brown – Singin' In The Rain

There ain't no no-shows in the show of life. It's matinees and evening runs, every day, 365, every year, forever. It's live up or give up, and giving up isn't an option. Life calls us with the clearing of a trumpet – Arise! Arise! Arise! Get up. Saddle up. Make-up on. Game face on. There are no stand-ins for your part. No stunt doubles. No backups. The show *must* go on, and you're the star on your own billboard. The tape never stops spinning, the script never runs out, the director never loses their patience. The set is ready, the cameras are rolling, cue: you.

November 2nd
IF YOU SPOT IT, YOU GOT IT

"I killed him. I killed him for money – and a woman – and I didn't get the money and I didn't get the woman."

WALTER NEFF – DOUBLE INDEMNITY (1944)

Anger, jealousy, greed, lust and resentment often cause us to make unwise decisions, and they in turn then also deal out a dose of poetic justice as our actions backfire on us. We all get drawn in to the trap of judging others and finding contempt in their attributes and actions, conveniently overlooking the same tendencies and impulses that lie within ourselves, and in many instances, ignoring that we have done exactly the same (or 'worse'). When we shame and condemn one another, we attempt to do that which is wholly unnecessary and totally unachievable; mete out of some form of justice. Only the universe has the power to play Judge Dredd. *It* is The Law. And it weighs and measures us all. We don't need to worry about judging others, we've got plenty on our plate living our own best life and striving to do the right things for the right reasons.

November 3rd

ROAMER

"Back home everyone said I didn't have any talent. They might be saying the same thing over here but it sounds better in French."

JERRY MULLIGAN – AN AMERICAN IN PARIS

Most people think of Chairman Mao as the most influential Chinese person of the 20th Century, but it was a later leader, Deng XiaoPing, who was the man that spearheaded China's opening to the world and industrial transformation. In his teens and twenties, Deng lived, studied and worked in France and then Russia, and that exposure to foreign ideologies had a strong impact on how he would later lead his country. Many successful artists, actors, activists, athletes and people of all walks of life have found a better springboard to fulfilment by changing their environment. We holiday for the same reason. New scenes tantalise the senses. They show us new ways of doing things and open our mind and heart to more than we thought life had to offer.

Now, if we're pulling a geographical to get away from a problem, we ought to first determine whether it lies within or without. If it's within, we might want to consider if a change of scenery is the solution. If the issue is in our own head, wherever we go, we're going to take the same undesirable seeds and immediately plant them in the soil beneath our feet. So if you're searching for ooh la las to drown out your own cries, first deal with the issue, and once that is solved, you're free to roam with gusto. When we can learn to endear any *here*, then we can explore and dare any *there*.

November 4th

SPIRITUAL CONNECTION

"The main thing is, Tootie, that we're all going to be together, just like we've always been. That's what really counts. We could be happy anywhere as long as we're together."

ESTHER SMITH – MEET ME IN ST. LOUIS

In the film *Parasite* by Bong Joon-ho, as various motifs present themselves through the story, one undercurrent that runs throughout is that essentially both families find their joy when together. The families live at opposite ends of the social spectrum, but the same human connection triumphs every time, regardless of material circumstance.

In addiction, one of its most powerful manifestations is that as it progresses, the patient draws further in to themselves and further away from meaningful and mutually loving relationships with others. The virus of addiction feeds on all the good in a person's life until the only thing left to feed on is the person themselves. It is in such hopeless states that many of the worst tragedies occur. For our mental health, connection is vital. We are social creatures, beings that thrive on intimacy, shared visions, humour and compassion.

November 5th
SPEECHLESS SCRIPT

"I don't know how to say goodbye. I can't think of any words."
"Don't try."

PRINCESS ANN & JOE – ROMAN HOLIDAY (1953)

Some moments defy description. Some scenes overwhelm the tongue. Some feelings render the brain utterly redundant. This is being. Being is not doing, not commentating, not understanding. It is all of those and more. It is the Way, the Source, the Oneness that confounds any attempt to confine it in words, thoughts or definitions. Yoda called it the Force. When we align with *It*, we allow ourselves to fully manifest our infinite potential. We are both the tool and the wielder of the tool, the lover and the loved, the perceiver and the perceived. We are everything and nothing.

Become one with *It*.

November 6th
PHILOSOPHER'S OWN

"Hey, you wanna hear my philosophy of life? Do it to him before he does it to you."

TERRY MALLOY – ON THE WATERFRONT

Every person has a philosophy, a religion. Here we use philosophy and religion interchangeably, both words simply pointing to that mixed bag of emotions, beliefs, feelings, attitudes, behaviours, inclinations, prejudices and passions that every human, by self-evident nature of existing, holds. Their religion is the life they live, the things they believe and the things they do. There is fundamentally no difference between a diehard football fan and a zealous religious follower and a devout scientist. Each surrender their passions and perspectives to fit the narrative that their paradigms call them to hold. In other words, every human has faith. The difference only lies in what that faith is placed in. The person without faith has faith that there is nothing worth placing faith in. Herein lies another unifying truth, if we can see it.

By looking beyond the surface level of those differentiating banners we each hoist, we see the uniformity and the unity of belief. We see the disarming humour in the realisation that we, in the very act of trying to chase after our own unique truths, are really just bouncing off of and into one another, for our own individual truths must surely all be circumscribed by one whole truth, *the* truth that cradles us all and sets us free.

November 7th
SEEN AND HEARD

*"You know, when you're little, you have more endurance
than God is ever to grant you again. Children are man at
his strongest. They abide."*

RACHEL COOPER – THE NIGHT OF THE HUNTER

We are all children, the whole human race. True, limbs grow
longer and paradigms grow stronger as the clock ticks by, but
beneath the veneer of adulthood lies a child within each of us.
Many of humanity's most glorious and ghastly deeds tie back
to the inner child that lives on long after nappies and spots and
even university are far back in the rear-view mirror. Inspiration
and derring-do bubble up in the hearts and minds of those who
still believe, with child-like faith, that all things are possible;
double-crossing and betrayal occur from hearts that still smart
over childhood trauma and embarrassment (yet in most cases,
few are aware of the influence their formative years have.) We, as
children, learn from the bigger children we call teachers, doctors
and Mum and Dad, and later we pass those lessons on down the
chain to the next round of children. The inner child in us holds
the key to a lot of the good we are searching for. Faith, trust,
intuition, courage, generosity, curiosity, adaptability – they are all
there in abundance inside each of us. If we are willing to, we can
take some quiet time to revisit our childhood. As we do, we may
find there is some trauma there that needs our acknowledgement
and to be released. Pen and paper or a compassionate ear are
wonderful tools to let out pent up emotions, long overdue
release. By contemplating our upbringing, we validate our own
life. We recognise the blessings we enjoyed, and we also see the
experiences that caused pain. Reflection on childhood will in
most cases carry a little trauma, for if we are alive then we have
experienced troubling situations. We therefore give a silent nod

to the highs and the lows and the water that passed under the bridge, the water that turned the wheels of our personal fortunes. Let us use this awareness to engender more compassion for ourselves, for what each of us has endured. Let us love that child that lives strong within each of us, and be wise enough to let them be both seen and heard.

November 8th
GOOD FRUIT

"A good tree cannot bring forth evil fruit. Neither can a corrupt tree bring forth good fruit. Wherefore, by their fruits ye shall know them."

RACHEL COOPER – THE NIGHT OF THE HUNTER

While we may like to play around with concepts such as nihilism, absurdism and non-causality at the surface level – which suggest that nobody can really know anything and everything is just pure chaos – most of us most of the time believe and align with concepts of cause and effect because to a great degree what we observe usually holds to some kind of pattern. Why do we eat fruit and not mud? Because it is discernible that the former is both amenable to be eaten and, furthermore, is pleasurable, and that the latter could not willingly be consumed and certainly would not elicit enjoyment (?!) Why do we take the laundry in when it starts to rain? Why do pigeons flock around when they see someone eating a sandwich in the park, and why do some people avoid sitting under branches with pigeons on them?! One of the biggest curiosities of life is how us humans so readily understand the law of cause and effect in the material world but fail to grasp it in the unseen one. Few people purposely drive their car off a cliff or graffiti their living room wall, yet who amongst us can say we've never done the spiritual equivalent? The sooner a person learns that all things, seen and unseen, follow universal laws, the sooner will they harmonise. If one thinks something positive it can only yield something positive. If one works industriously it can only produce benefits in kind. If one spreads kindness and cheer it can only multiply after its own. We are both the tree and fruit, the chef and the diner, the actor and the audience. The fruit we produce is the very same fruit that we consume.

What fruit are you producing?

November 9th

UNDONE TO DONE

"The law has little to say on things left undone."

CORONER – VERTIGO (1958)

To reflect on the past or project to the future too much deflects focus from the most important subject – the here and now. Yet, occasional constructive pondering on decisions and consequences can profit us greatly. Potential, by definition, is that which is still *undone*. And we all have so much potential bottled up inside each of us, undones just waiting to be let out. Within that potential is a range of acts from humble helping ones to huge heroic ones. We are fruit, and all the amazing potentiality inside us is our juice. Fruit is meant to be eaten and squeezed for its nourishing flesh and refreshing juice. Imagine huge, juicy, luscious red strawberries hanging from their stalks... but nobody comes and picks them and avails themselves of the revitalising energy and lip-smacking taste packaged inside them... what a waste. And as fantastic as strawberries are, we have much more inside us.

Ponder your potential. Your *undones*. Don't make it an exercise of self-berating or self-flagellation. There is no negativity in your undones. Link the practice only with the goodness you have given and received in your life, on the happy *dones*. Think on the passions and energies you possess. Now connect those together, and start to turn some more undones in to dones.

November 10th
WINDOWS

"When the Lord closes a door, somewhere He opens a window."

MARIA VON TRAPP – THE SOUND OF MUSIC

Every setback, trial and difficulty carries with it an equal and opposite opportunity for growth or something we desire. When a door slams in your face, you have many options. You can stand and stare at the door. You can shout and scream. You can knock on it, bang on it, try to kick it down. You can slip a note under it. You can plead through the letterbox. You can try to pick the lock! Yet, if something hasn't worked, there is a reason, and back of surface level reasons there is the ultimate reason; it hasn't worked. It hasn't worked it hasn't worked. Persistence pays, but usually with some form of change included. Edison didn't figure out the lightbulb after trying the same thing 10,000 times. He got there by trying 10,000 *different* configurations. That was a lot of doors and a lot of windows he saw along that process.

There is a window somewhere near you, and that window holds views of something even better than you thought was on the other side of the door that just closed. What is for you shan't go by you. That window is your destiny. Are you willing to let go of the door and find the window?

November 11th
I FEEL GOOD

"You're so much thought and so little feeling."

TRACY LORD – THE PHILADELPHIA STORY

There is a reason love is symbolised by the heart and not the brain. A head without a heart isn't too smart. Feel about it, nobody ever sat in a hot, soothing bubble bath and moaned 'aaaah, that thinks so good.' Nobody ever fell in love and ran around telling the whole world, 'they love me, they love me. I think so good!' Nobody ever accomplished a personal goal and exclaimed 'Yesssss. Achieving this thinks so good!' (That would be quite funny, though.)

Thought is one element of what it is to be human, and an important one. But thought without feeling is a robot. The Tin Man knew this and that's why he wanted to have a heart so badly. He wanted to feel love and happiness again.

A feeling only exists inside the carrier. In and of itself it is harmless, and yet we don't always know how to deal with them. Bizarrely, sometimes it's the pleasant feelings that send one in to a tailspin more than the uncomfortable ones. Therefore, it is the responsibility of the feeler to acknowledge a feeling, accept it and allow it. Just as we need to elevate our thinking to make progress, likewise we need to get more in tune with our feelings and emotions if we wish to deepen our connections. This is easily practiced. Next time you have a meaningful conversation with someone, really try to feel the energy and emotions that your companion is exhibiting. Don't think about what they're saying, feel it.

November 12th
SURE THING

"Are you really so sure of everything you're so sure of?"

HUBBELL GARDNER – THE WAY WE WERE

Being confident and committed requires a certain amount of conviction that certain beliefs we hold to be true are indeed true, at least as applicable to ourselves. This enables us to draw strength and power from that conviction. For example, a soup kitchen worker could give selfless service helping feed people which is fuelled by their belief that every person deserves to have a full tummy every day, regardless of status, effort on the individual's part or any other factors that would cause a person not to have food. That conviction would be the motivation to want to help others. But, if that person becomes so entrenched in the belief that every person should be fed every day, independent of any other factor – social, economic or otherwise – and takes umbrage at another who suggests an alternative view, such as that it is every person's own prerogative to go out and do what they need to do to labour for their own crust, then the person giving charity work has perhaps strayed in to closed-mindedness. When we think that what we think is the only way, our options, by automatic default, start to shrink. The harder we squeeze on to those views, the more we suffocate the life out of them. What's more, it is another one of those strange peculiarities that the people with the most ardent views are often the least sure of them. When we spout dogma, usually the person we're really trying to convince is ourselves. Being open-minded allows ourselves a real luxury – not having to always be right. What a stress that is. With an open mind, we might be right, we might be wrong, but at least we're willing to learn.

P.S. Soup kitchen workers are awesome!

November 13th
PERSON-ALLY

"You perfectly foul, French upstart!"
"Belgian upstart, please, madame."

MRS VAN SCHUYLER & HERCULE POIROT – DEATH ON THE NILE (1978)

Taking things personally is totally exhausting, and in any case, we all care about ourselves way too much for everything to be personal. Dale Carnegie in *How To Win Friends and Influence People* explained powerfully that the sweetest sound in all the world is a person's own name, and astutely noted that when you look at an old school photograph, who do you look for first? (Yes, even before that first crush.) Perhaps instead of taking things personally, we can make every person an ally. There are many tools that lie at our disposal to do so; humour, patience, mindfulness. If we can allow ourselves to be so inclined, we can get to a place where very few things may perturb us (and if they do, it is because we choose to be. For example, someone vexed by the attempt of another to take away their rights might be in a state of good indignation). We can strive to be in a state where nothing that happens outside of ourselves affects the way we feel about ourselves.

November 14th
YES AND NO

"I have lived long enough to know what I like. What I dislike, I cannot abide."

HERCULE POIROT – MURDER ON THE ORIENT EXPRESS (2017)

Knowing what one likes and dislikes is wonderful. It gives one the ability to say no. No, I don't like that. No, I'd prefer not to. No, that doesn't interest me. Yes and no are about as small and as simple a pair of opposites as you can find and yet their power is so undervalued. Yes. Yes to what is. Yes to what the universe brings. Yes to what is manifesting right now. Yes to the lessons. Yes, please! And no. No to stand up for oneself. No to lack of respect. No to people-pleasing. No to time-wasting (a paradox, granted – there is no time and there is no waste.) No, thank you.

Yes and no. Powerful.

November 15th
OUT OF CONTROL

"As soon as you realise that the random events in your life are God... you will live a much better life. You spend your life believing that you have all the control over what happens. Bulls**t! The plane you're flying goes down? Out of your control. God gives you cancer? I have no control over that. Did God give me cancer? You bet your ass God gave me cancer. You think if I begged for cancer God would have given it to me? No... because I assure you I have begged for God to take it away... and guess what? I have no control over that."

GAUNT YOUNG MAN – FLIGHT (2012)

Fate and free will. How do they reconcile? Do we choose our fate, or does fate choose us? If someone is destined for something, is it going to happen regardless of any attempts by them to avoid it (or even sabotage it, if it's a *good* thing)? What are within the boundaries of one's own control? Is there a predictable relationship between the attempt to control and the outcome?

Every person alive probably has their own anecdotal evidence of an attempt to control someone, something or some situation, with calamitous results. And it's not through a lack of ability or competence that people end up with uncontrollable egg on their face. It's simply life. Nobody has the power to insulate themselves to even a fraction of a percent against the vicissitudes of life. And the thing is, who would want to? If you could order and govern everything to be exactly as you wished it... what would that even look like? And what would be the point to anything?

November 16th
ARNIE GOES TO HOLLYWOOD

"Relax. You'll live longer."

DOUGLAS QUAID – TOTAL RECALL (1990)

If you lived in Jurassic Park with dinosaurs, this advice from Arnie might not be too sage as applied to run-ins with T-Rexs and things like that. A state of high-alert would probably be a prerequisite if you wanted to have a life expectancy more than 10 minutes. But if you're not in a dinosaur park it is absolute gold. We have so many lights and noises pinging around us, we may as well be the ball within a pinball machine. Buy this lifesaver, eat that superfood, do this miracle exercise, follow that guru, watch this, vote for that, sell this, save that, download this... the demands on our brain and body, to say nothing of our nervous system, are monumental. The old-school addictions of drink, drugs, sex and gambling are being overtaken by phones, internet, shopping and video-gaming. It's not only our devices that are plugged in 24/7, so are our heads.

While we wouldn't fare too well with dinosaurs, to be fair to ourselves, they probably wouldn't be too hot in our environment. T-Rexs would definitely have problems taking selfies and pterodactyls would struggle to get to grips with this cloud thingy while soaring through real clouds. So how do we get a bit of balance? Easy. We turn FOMO from Fear Of Missing Out into a (healthy) Fear Of Mind Overload and learn to detach, switch off, calm down, chill. If you find yourself walking 100mph everywhere you go... see if you can just ease off the throttle. If you notice you can't stop staring at your phone, see if you can switch it off for a few hours (for advanced players, go out for the whole day without it). If you haven't looked out of your window and observed life, go have a look. Find three things you never noticed before.

Live life to the max. And like Arnie... relax.

November 17th
ART IS LIFE

"All human activity lies within the artist's scope."

GEOFFREY CHAUCER – A KNIGHT'S TALE

Formalised art is merely a set of mediums for reflecting daily life. A sporting contest is but a reflection of the tussle to get on an overcrowded bus. Film is nothing more than the condensed show-reel of what people are doing and imagining every day of their lives. A ballet dancer does on stage what countless people do while dusting the living room (albeit without ending up in hospital!) To turn it on its head; all art lies within the scope of what it is to be alive. A bit of conscious injection of art can be exquisite fun. Today, can you hoover like Mrs Doubtfire? Clean the windows like Daniel-san? Enter the room like Lorelei Lee? Art brings such joy, and that joy emanates naturally because art is life. Your life, your very being, is art.

November 18th
ROAD TO SOMEWHERE

"Progress has never been a bargain. You have to pay for it. Sometimes I think there's a man who sits behind a counter and says, 'All right, you can have a telephone, but you lose privacy and the charm of distance. Madam, you may vote, but at a price: you lose the right to retreat behind the powderpuff of your petticoat. Mister, you may conquer the air, but the birds will lose their wonder and the clouds will smell of gasoline."

HENRY DRUMMOND – INHERIT THE WIND (1960)

This quote is a wonderful reminder of what physics teaches us – energy is neither created nor destroyed. Robbing Peter to pay Paul isn't just bad form according to quaint old philosophy, it's a cosmic mis-calculation. The quote also begs the question, what is progress? For eons the preeminent question on mankind's lips was; *What is the purpose of life? What is the meaning to this existence? Where are we going?* But these days it doesn't seem to matter where we're going so long as we get there quicker. We've become a little like aliens arriving and re-arriving again and again on our own planet. 'What's this?' asks one. 'Can you eat it? Smoke it? Ride it?' replies the other. 'How should I know?' 'Then who cares!'

Let's make progress! is the call we keep hearing. Yet progress without a vital connection to a higher meaning is but a headlong rush to… well, who knows…?

For sure, let us make progress. Let us do so, though, with wisdom and compassion and in acknowledgement of the question, where are we going?

November 19th
MOVE TOGETHER

"Why is it, my old friend, that you've moved so far away from me?"
"All motion is relative, Matt. Maybe it's you who've moved away by standing still."

MATTHEW & HENRY – INHERIT THE WIND (1960)

Relationships are dynamic, not static. If everyone and everything is in a constant state of flux, then it's a no-brainer that a relationship – multiple units of change – is a constant evolution.

Change + Change = **CHANGE**

There's nothing wrong with watching reruns of one's favourite show. It makes sense. We do it because we've had a positive experience with it once and we seek to recreate and recapture the enjoyment of the first time. We do the same in relationships. We attempt to press pause on the good times and happy moments, hoping to preserve them and stay in *that* place, and praying that nobody picks up the remote and changes the channel. Completely understandable behaviour. But remember, today is a brand new take. Yesterday's lines won't suffice for today's scenes. If we want to keep our relationships healthy and vibrant we need to create new moments and an ever-evolving shared vision.

November 20th
LOVE TO SUFFER

"To love is to suffer. To avoid suffering one must not love.
But then one suffers from not loving. Therefore, to love
is to suffer; not to love is to suffer; to suffer is to suffer.
To be happy is to love. To be happy, then, is to suffer, but
suffering makes one unhappy."

SONJA – LOVE AND DEATH

Has loving someone caused you pain? Has opening yourself up made you vulnerable to be used or manipulated? Has your deep care for another caused deep wear on your heart? If it has, then stop. Give up on love. Forget about it. Pack it in…

The truth is, love never caused anyone pain. Yes, at surface level language we say 'I'm in such pain, I loved so and so and now they've gone and betrayed me and let me down…' But think about it for a moment. Your love for that person, is that what backfired and hurt you? Or was it what the person did that hurt you? The madness of human thinking is that in some areas we absolve ourselves of responsibility where it is undeniably ours to own, and in others we entirely seek to assume it where we have no right to be so presumptuous. *I loved this person and now look, they've gone and stabbed me in the back…* ergo, love is the villain. Er… no, we can be pretty sure it's the knife and the wielder of it that have to own that dubious claim.

Law. Eternal law. Love does not hurt anything or anyone. Love is love. Everything is what it is. What would happen if you were to love everyone and everything? (Remember, loving everyone doesn't mean you like everyone, it doesn't mean you don't have preferences, boundaries, limits and choice. It doesn't mean you gravitate towards everything. Ponder on the distinction. Don't make love into what it is not.) But just imagine, imagine you loved everyone and everything. What would that look like and feel like?

Love, be happy, and suffer? Or just suffer?

November 21st
CREATE MORE WASTE

"What you have striven for will not end in nothing. All that you have done and been will not be wasted."

VERA BRITTAIN – TESTAMENT OF YOUTH

What constitutes a waste? Waiting for a bus for thirty minutes to take you somewhere you could have walked in ten? Spending time in prison for a crime that you could have just been smart enough not to have committed in the first place? Only finishing half the steak that you paid good money for because you couldn't resist the ice-cream on the way to the restaurant? In a balanced, unbiased, cosmic sense, there is no waste. Waste is an egoic human construct which says X happened, such a shame, Y would have been so much better. But what if Y wasn't the best thing, what if Z was? What if there was something better than Z? You see where that line of reasoning takes you.

The universe is wise. Everything gets recycled. No need to sort things in to colours and bins for it. It knows what it's doing, and we are invited to trust that it ensures what we may view as waste is actually the very stuff that will bring us joy. As the bite of winter prepares nature for the kiss of spring, so our waste of today is the fertiliser for our flowers of tomorrow.

November 22nd
TRUTH OF THE MATTER

"I shall never be afraid to confront the real. The imagined holds far greater terror for me."

VERA BRITTAIN – TESTAMENT OF YOUTH

If everything that we perceive outside of ourselves is only a reflection of our inner selves, then to flip it around, in order to see the real world, we need to first know our real selves. Facing oneself honestly takes vast courage. Like a neglected old shed with its cobwebs and leaky roof gets less and less appealing to salvage and more and more attractive to just write off and leave be, so the derelict and abandoned parts of ourselves become harder to face the longer we ignore them. Those unexamined parts of ourselves do hold webs of pain, but also the potential for renewal and a way of life better than any we have known previously. Then there are the choices we are making here and now, and likely behaviours and habits we wish to change. To be able to live in such a way as to be able to face ourselves, both the relics of our past – trauma, some say literally stored in the body – and the current news of who we are, we must cultivate a love of the truth. And that truth then calls us to embrace what we find about ourselves and work with it.

November 23rd
LIBERATION

"Hate put me in prison. Love's gonna bust me out."

RUBIN "HURRICANE" CARTER – THE HURRICANE (1999)

Imagine the anguish and turmoil of being wrongly imprisoned for a crime you didn't commit. It's difficult enough to accept just punishment when you are culpable, but to have your life destroyed when you are completely innocent is a level of challenge hard to fathom. Regardless of the crime that puts a person in prison, and regardless of whether they are guilty or innocent, the fire of the experience asks the person some serious questions. You either become engulfed and consumed by the hate and the system, another statistic of a sad life wasted, and if and when you ever get out, you carry the anger, violence and defiance with you, or, you learn enduring lessons of the need to change, the need to refine oneself and learn higher and better ways. You learn that there is only love. What The Hurricane said holds true for all people in all times in all senses and in all contexts – hate imprisons, love liberates. We get to choose today which one we reach for.

November 24th
ZEN? OR TRAINED?

"There is no such thing as tough. There is trained and untrained. Now which are you?"

JOHN CREASY – MAN ON FIRE

A man once met the Dalai Lama and asked him, "Your Holiness, how do you maintain your Zen?" The Dalai Lama pondered the question. After some consideration, with a twinkle in his eyes, he replied: "daily practice."

"We are what we repeatedly do. Excellence, then, is not an act, but a habit."

ARISTOTLE

What are you?

What are you trying to become?

What do you need to be doing daily that will transform you in to the person that you want to be?

You already are that ideal you. You are but chipping away at the excess marble to reveal yourself. Walk the path and pay the price of self-training and discipline and reveal the full majesty of who you truly are.

November 25th
4D

"Boy, I got vision, and the rest of the world wears bifocals."

BUTCH CASSIDY – BUTCH CASSIDY AND THE SUNDANCE KID

We all get given our own pair of 4D specs at the cinema of life, and what we see is unique to us. A private screening, if you will. Immersion in the action. A big part of our joy comes in realising the unique viewpoint we hold and learning to maximise it. If a person with no legs watches football every day yearning for what might have been, they won't seek the path that leads them to discover their aptitude for say, humour, and how their life and their viewpoint powers that ability. But that person is brave and does find their ability to hit others' funny bones. And someone watching their hit show thinks, 'this guy is hilarious. Wish I had talent like that.' But that woman doesn't realise that she is tailor made for something else – politics – because she, having experienced inequality, is passionate about serving society to improve peoples' lives, and that energy she carries loosens her tongue and enables her to speak truth to power. And so she does face the fear and find her platform because she heeds her calling.

Your view is your view. Nobody can see through your eyes and nobody can see the colours you can. But vision alone isn't enough. We need to act.

November 26th
WHAT THE FUNK

"Are we done, Mr Byrd?"
"I'm afraid not, Mr Brown."
"I say, are we done?"
"I think we still got mo funk in the trunk."

JAMES BROWN & BOBBY BYRD – GET ON UP

Whatever you think you've produced so far, and you've produced some good stuff, there is more to come from you. Your race is not yet run. Your masterpiece, as yet, unleashed. We don't sit back and rest on our laurels. We keep going, keep producing, keep believing. There is more within. So much more. If only we knew what fathomless depths we have. There is much, much more funk in our trunk. Find the will. Find the strength. Subscribe to the vibe and you will discover there is much, much more glory in your story.

November 27th
WALK BY FAITH

*"Hey, pardon me for asking, but how do you get around
so good without a cane or a dog?"*
"My ears gotta be my eyes, man."

JEFF BROWN & RAY CHARLES – RAY

Are you a victim or a human being? Are you a loser or a human being? Are you a pessimist or a human being?

Whether you are a victim of abuse or a sufferer of an illness or disability, none of those things define you. For sure, acknowledge the real conditions and situations of life. Talk about them. Share your feelings. Use constructive outlets and healthy ways to deal with your trauma. But never forget you are a human being. If you've lost, lost in business, sport, a pursuit, a relationship, acknowledge that stuff. Get it out. Process it. But never forget, you are a human being. Does life look tough? Bleak? All seems lost? By all means, rant, rave, get it out of your system. But never forget… you are a human being!!!

One of the chief qualities of humankind is our ability to adapt. To acclimatise to the setting we find ourselves in. This is both our genius and our Achilles heel. Genius, when like Ray, we simply refuse to let a hardship dictate to us how things will be; Achilles heel when we succumb to despondency and inaction to a status quo we're not happy about.

You are a human being. Do you know what that means? Do you know what power you possess? Do you understand the potential inside you? Can you fathom the light you are able to shine?

November 28th
SOBER FLIGHT

"Would you like a glass of wine?"
"Uh, no, no thanks. I never drink when I fly."

LOIS LANE & SUPERMAN – SUPERMAN (1978)

To be the best and reach the top certain sacrifices are necessary. A life without some measure of discipline will never yield the maximum return on what a person can achieve. We all make sacrifices, it's a question of sacrificing what. The successful person sacrifices excessive drinking and partying to read, learn, develop talents, build their empire, chase dreams, get up early to hit the gym and so forth. The party animal sacrifices all the things they could see and learn and be when not handicapped every Saturday and Sunday morning with an almighty hangover. Discipline and drive are necessary for achievement of any kind; spiritual, educational or financial. We all face the age-old decision: am I willing to sacrifice short-term pleasure and hedonism for long-term satisfaction and joy? No worthwhile achievement comes without effort. A beautiful life is the result of deliberate, disciplined living. Let's toil well today so we can enjoy the harvest.

November 29th
TRY AND STOP ME

"Guys, I'm eating junk and watching rubbish! You better come out and stop me!"

KEVIN McCALLISTER – HOME ALONE

We're all a little bit like Kevin at times. We test the boundaries of our freedoms. *You mean to tell me the office canteen has fizzy drinks on tap?! I'm finally at uni, far away from parents, and I can stay out all night?! My local pizzeria have somehow put a permanent 90% discount on my account?!* A big part of the transition from childhood to adulthood is dealing with freedom. The irony is, in the real world, nobody is going to stop you from stuffing yourself to death on ice-cream and pizza. Nobody is going to stop you from partying and missing lectures. Nobody is going to hold your hand and make healthy decisions for you. We rise and fall based on our own choices and the level of accountability we place upon ourselves. One of the best feelings in the world is learning what is genuinely good for oneself and choosing those things – self-care. Self-care honours the practical ethos that we can only pass on what we possess. Before helping and serving others, we look after ourselves so that we are filled to the brim with good stuff that we can then share and give to others, thereby avoiding the attempt to give from an empty vessel. A cookie jar with no cookies in it is not a cookie jar. A battery with no juice in it is not a battery. A human with no self-care is not a human, they are a slave. Slave to serving others, slave to a meaningless job, slave to whatever things that come along exacting upon them. Self-care gives ourselves the platform to approach life from a position of strength, vibrancy, choice and enthusiasm. Self-care is not a luxury, it's an absolute necessity.

November 30th
SPEAK NO EVIL

"You write your snide bulls**t from a dark room because that's what the angry do nowadays."

ERICA ALBRIGHT – THE SOCIAL NETWORK

Cowardice has been given a weapons upgrade in our times. Now it's easy for any of us to condemn, ridicule or abuse another behind the distance and anonymity of our screens. Perhaps an attitude that would stand us in good stead is to maintain the same integrity across all platforms – real life and virtual. Anything we wouldn't say to a person's face, we don't say via technology. Anything we wouldn't want to have our name against, we don't say it. Anything that isn't true, we don't say it. The world evolves, but old-school values don't change... do they?

December 1st
FOLLOWERS

"Private behaviour is a relic of a time gone by, and if somehow, some way, you've managed to live your life like the Dalai Lama, they'll make shit up. Because they don't want you, they want your idea."

SEAN PARKER – THE SOCIAL NETWORK

The journey of the human condition is quite funny. For millions of years the only people who knew you existed were the people immediately in your physical presence. The handful of people in your village. Within a few generations, we've gone from that to social media. Everything we say, do, eat, think, watch, wear, buy, try, all laid bare... (If. We. Choose. To. Lay. It. Bare!) Our occasional high moments and the more plentiful inanities, catalogued. The beautiful people post endless selfies, the rich post their trinkets, and the rest of us post... whatever nonsense we can get away with. To be fair, knowing what type of cling film a person uses is quite fascinating.

Will we continue down this path of becoming more and more transparent whilst, paradoxically, becoming more and more selective and deceptive at what we show and how we feel?

December 2nd
HOLY ROLLER

"It's easy to be a holy man on top of a mountain."

LARRY DARRELL – THE RAZOR'S EDGE (1984)

Most people can be a good sport when winning, Zen when all is calm, honourable in situations where it benefits them. A greater challenge is in being our best selves under pressure. Cycling through a busy city. Dealing with unfair treatment. Working from home with restless young kids. The friction of life is a good thing. It provides the opportunity for us to grow and develop. It sorts out those who are holy when the sailing is smooth from those who are holy when the going gets tough (holy = being loving and self-possessed.) We have an opportunity to front up to the unpleasant, unloving and unjust and respond with pleasantness, love and justice. Paradoxically, we can even learn to alchemise the chaos and carnage that happens around us to promote calm and kindness. If we are meditating, we don't go looking for noise and distraction, but if that is the environment we find ourselves in in the moment, then we energise our deep state of meditative being with that noise. The paradox continues as we reach a stage where our externals are irrelevant to our being. Granted, some circumstances are more conducive to us exhibiting our coolest impression of a cucumber, yet regardless of our situation, atop a literal mountain or under a figurative mountain of madness, we can choose to be our best selves.

December 3rd
CONNECTED

"That's what life is all about; connecting. In fact, that's the only time you're ever alive, really, is when you're connecting."

G – HOLY MAN

Connection is the invisible thread that runs through everything. Everything meets. Just because air cannot be seen or smelt (not always true in a bathroom) does not mean it is not something. Which means that everything is something, and even though everything is filled with a lot of nothing (atoms have a lot of space, which isn't really space, but kind of is, but more like waves and energy fields) the fact remains… everything is connected. We are each beautiful, sentient, stand-alone, sovereign, bundles of being. And we are also a one, unified, collected, connected bundle that we call the known universe. Isn't that a happy thought? Peter could definitely fly powered on that.

December 4th

LET ME ENTERTAIN YOU

"Holy Smokes! 99 channels and there's nothing on!"

Rusty Duritz – The Kid (2000)

When you look to *be* entertained you may find nothing has the power to keep your attention. Let us be the entertainment ourselves. That is the difference between receptive entertainment and active learning and adventure. The more we look to be a passive receiver; of learning, of wealth, of entertainment, the more we are likely to see no opportunities and find our senses dulled. 99… 999… 9,999 channels… and they're all rubbish! How's that even possible? Are we pressing the remote, or is it pressing us?

Let us be active seekers. Seekers of wisdom, opportunity, fun and enlightenment. We have too much to do, see and be, to be flicking through endless channels foraging for distractions. Let's make the switch inside our own heads to the discovery channel and be alive to all the abundance of life.

December 5th
HUGS AND CUDDLES ARE THE BEST

"Human touch. Our first form of communication. Safety, security, comfort, all in the gentle caress of a finger. Or the brush of lips on a soft cheek. It connects us when we're happy, bolsters us in times of fear, excites us in times of passion and love. We need that touch from the one we love, almost as much as we need air to breathe. But I never understood the importance of touch. His touch. Until I couldn't have it. So, if you're watching this, and you're able, touch him. Touch her. Life's too short to waste a second."

STELLA – FIVE FEET APART

Within our bodies there are certain chemicals which when released from the brain into the bloodstream make us feel a million bucks. Some of these are serotonin, dopamine and oxytocin. Oxytocin is the chemical agent that we secrete when we hug, touch and get intimate with someone. Our thirst for meaningful and loving interaction with fellow humans is not confined to purely biological needs (the desire to reproduce and preserve the species,) physical needs (the pleasurable stimulus of nerve endings,) or even spiritual needs (the bond of what it is to be, to harmonise.) It encompasses all of these needs and the chemical one mentioned. It is every need. That's why shaking hands is a natural phenomenon in business or with a stranger – it acknowledges that even in a formal or new connection it's important to create a physical bond. It is why we gently touch a person on the arm or shoulder to acknowledge or reassure them – the physical touch combines with the emotional care to provide dualistic support. It's why doing the conga at parties is so enjoyable – coming in to contact with others in a fun, wholesome way reminds us of the joy it is simply to have a body and move it. When we touch hearts and touch hands, we touch heaven.

December 6th
MAKE PROMISES REDUNDANT

"Don't make promises... 'cause you know you can't keep 'em."

Jordan Turner – The Call (2013)

Some people always promise and never deliver, some people never promise and always deliver. What's more important; saying the words? Or performing the action? If we live in alignment with honour, truth and accountability, there is no requirement for promises, contracts and attempts to convince. We don't promise our kids we definitely definitely definitely will be there for the next school play... we are there. We don't say sorry over and over and over again until the words have become mush... we simply don't do (or do do) the thing we've been saying sorry about.

In this context, words retroactively affirm previously provided proof of the fact. As a promise or prediction looking forward they are close to worthless. We say *I love you* at the end of the day after we've put the time and energy in to making the wedding anniversary a celebration of our love and adoration for our partner. We don't say it as a substitute when we sneak through the door coming back from the pub realising we completely forgot.

When we're about to say something grand, flourishing and promising... maybe we'd do well to stop and consider, is there a way that what I'm about to say I could show through action?

December 7th
POWER IN THE BLOOD

"You have more power than you realise. Don't think, and don't worry. If the time comes, you'll know what to do. It's in your blood."

HELEN PARR – THE INCREDIBLES

Healthy pride is not arrogance. Confidence is not ego. Trust in the universe is not foolishness. The seed which becomes the mighty tree contains within it the genetic code to instruct and advance its growth. The caterpillar which becomes the butterfly has the potentiality of the transformation stored within. You have power within. The power to transform. You are the only factor in the equation of your own destiny. You decide if and how you will manifest and align with the pure potentiality that fills your being.

December 8th
ONE FOR YOU, ONE FOR ME

"You can't just sit there and put everybody's lives ahead of yours and think that counts as love."

SAM BUTTON – THE PERKS OF BEING A WALLFLOWER

Putting others ahead of oneself without refuelling on self-care is like driving a car without refuelling on petrol or electricity. It's only a matter of time before you grind to a halt. Sometimes we swing between states of selfishness and selflessness. Neither state, if indulged too long or taken to the extreme, is healthy. Doing only one side of anything isn't really doing it at all. Putting everyone ahead of oneself is not real love or service – it sounds much more like people pleasing or lack of self-worth. Life is energy, and energy is in a constant state of dynamic exchange. For giving to truly be giving, it must be balanced and beautified by receiving, and vice versa. Giving love would be rather odd and incomplete without ever receiving love. Learning without teaching, or vice versa, speaking without listening, working without resting… they all become very lopsided when not in a pair. They say the rule of actors is to do two for the studios and one for yourself. That ain't bad wisdom for all of us.

December 9th
ALL THE DIMENSIONS

"Love isn't something that we invented. It's observable. Powerful. It has to mean something. Maybe it means something more, something we can't yet understand. Maybe it's some evidence, some artefact of a higher dimension that we can't consciously perceive. I'm drawn across the universe to someone I haven't seen in a decade who I know is probably dead. Love is the one thing that we're capable of perceiving that transcends dimensions of time and space. Maybe we should trust that, even if we can't understand it."

DR AMELIA BRAND – INTERSTELLAR

If you are ever in doubt how powerful love is, watch or re-watch this film. When it comes to love, don't mention dimensions... love cannot be put in a box in 3D, it cannot be clocked in linear time in 4D, it cannot be contained or explained through wormholes, black holes, gravitational poles or cosmic rabbit holes in 5, 7 or 10D. Love is. It reigns supreme over all things known and unknown, seen and unseen, material and immaterial, through all space, all time, all dimensions. Stop a moment and energise the love in your heart. Love of family, love of friends, love of nature, love of food, love of learning, love of sport, love of mankind, love of exploration, love of freedom... love of being. Love is the common denominator in all that is beautiful. Find one thing amazing in your life that isn't powered by love... it's impossible. Like in the film, every one of us alive today realise that as an earth and as a species, we're facing some defining questions. All kinds of ideas are being suggested as the answers to our problems. Who is talking about love as the solution? Who is inviting love to the table to share its views? Who is voting for love?!

We cannot forget our heritage. We cannot forget the power that has nurtured and nourished us and given us everything. Policies and programmes, science and spaceships are wonderful, but they haven't saved us thus far and they won't in the future. Let's give love its chance.

December 10th
GREEN MAN

"The best sacrifice is the one made by others."

SKIPPER – MADAGASCAR

A strange phenomenon has taken place in London in recent years. At designated pedestrian road crossings it has become increasingly common for vast swarms of people to congregate, waiting for a little green man to appear so that they may safely pass from one side to another. Only, the green man doesn't appear. Why not? Where's he gone? Well, he's not appeared because nobody has pressed the button that makes him appear and stops the traffic. This scene plays out daily on roads throughout the great city. It is a classic example of the growing culture: *someone else will do it*. It is highly comical to observe a dozen strangers looking around confused as to why the cars won't stop. To the keen student, however, it is another reminder that one must always take responsibility to the degree that they can. Don't wait for another to make your onward journey possible – press the button yourself and get moving. Or not. Stay right there and enjoy watching traffic.

December 11th
EYES ON THE ROAD

"It's called scotoma. The mind sees what it chooses to see."

SIR LEIGH TEABING – THE DA VINCI CODE

The scotomas (blind spots) that we all literally have in our field of vision are matched by the blind spots we have in our perceptions and judgements of life. An easy analogy is driving a vehicle. Within a car, our blind spots are represented by the areas that aren't covered by any of our forward sight, the wing mirrors or the rear-view mirror (the blind spots lying roughly at bearings of 120 and 240 degrees.) What's interesting is that a driver behind us can clearly see the points that to us are blind spots. And yet they cannot see what we can see ahead, for our car obstructs that view. They see potential dangers that may overtake us, but they don't have the perspective of the road that lies before us. They don't understand the visions we have.

The analogy becomes more complete when we consider the car in front of us. They, too, can see both the blind spots on our flanks, as well as the path before us. They, in a sense, lead the way for us. Yet the perspective they lack is what sits behind us. They know not the things of our past.

From this we learn that none of us have complete perspective of ourselves or others. We work with what we are aware of, but ought to remain willing and open-minded to learn and be teachable by others. We are each given a car and a key and the task of navigating a journey through all types of terrain. If we are open to alternative perspectives our journeying will be more fun and fulfilling, and by maintaining humility and a spirit of cooperation, even blind spots can be alchemised for our good along the highway of joy.

December 12th
LIVING IN THE MOVIES

"Life isn't like the movies. Life… is much harder."

ALFREDO – CINEMA PARADISO

The validity of Alfredo's words hinge greatly on the movie in question. *Shawshank Redemption? Hhhmmm, I'll pass, thank you. Baywatch? Sign me up! Sign me up!* The beauty of film is that nothing that happens in it hasn't happened in real life and nothing that happens in real life hasn't been put on film. When we sit down and watch a film, we are watching ourselves projected on to the screen. When we say, everything we see is but a reflection of ourselves… is film the exception to that?

To use another angle; movies are tough, life is tough, everything is tough. Movies are also beautiful and redemptive, and so is life. We love movies because, while thrilling, fantastical and usually fictional, they resonate. We see in the characters all the same traits we see in ourselves. The stereotypical hero versus villain theme in film is nothing more than a dramatisation of what goes on inside every single one of us every day of our lives. The battle between "good" and "evil" that is an inescapable part of the journey of life. The never-ending cycle of losing and finding and losing again and finding again. The angels and demons we see on screen capture our hearts and imaginations because we know them better than we think.

Sorry (not sorry) to disagree, Alfredo, but life very much *is* like the movies.

December 13th
KISS MA LUCKY EGG

"Feel the rhythm! Feel the rhyme! Get on up, it's bobsled time!"

JAMAICAN TEAM – COOL RUNNINGS

On their first bobsleigh run the team imitated the ritual of the Swiss team with less than satisfactory results. The Swiss team were the best. Top dogs. It made sense to copy them. But the Jamaicans weren't Swiss, they were Jamaican. And in the same way that the sun or a squirrel or a tulip can only be what it is, they could only be what they are. The energy, the enthusiasm, the chilled vibes, the dreadlocks. The lucky egg.

The team wanted to win alright. They wanted to compete and perform to the best of their abilities, but they quickly realised that to do that it had to emanate from their authentic selves, a pure expression of their culture and characters.

Some of the happiest people do things the most unorthodox and unconventional way. They don't say, it's my way *or* the highway, they say, my way is the highway. Not for anyone else, just themselves. Perhaps these people intuitively know that at the core of individual *and* collective success and happiness lies the requirement to live true to self.

Whatever you're doing, do it being you, on your highway (or bobsled track).

December 14th
STAIRWAY TO HEAVEN

"So, Hades, you finally made it. How are things in the Underworld?"
"Well, they're just fine. You know, a little dark, a little gloomy. And, as always, hey, full of dead people. What are you gonna do?"

ZEUS & HADES – HERCULES (1997)

Libraries are where people go to read and study, and pubs are where people go to drink (copious amounts of?) alcohol and go a little bonkers. While some libraries will have undoubtedly witnessed drunken escapades and some pubs are rather studious in feel, each environment is usually conducive to and elicits the kind of behaviour that might conventionally be associated with it. The point? Choose wisely your environment. Environment will help or hinder you in the pursuit of whatever it is that you desire. You can attend positivity seminars and read uplifting material all you want, if you then frequent places of negativity and anger and whining… they will sap your energy and make it incredibly hard to be that best version of yourself that you are striving toward. Hades environment was death… and surprise-surprise, how did he view things?

What are you seeking? Which environments align with those desires?

December 15th
BELONGING

"I never knew where I came from. But I always knew where I belonged."

MOWGLI – THE JUNGLE BOOK 2

In mortal life, some of us have a heritage and a starting point that means a lot to us. Parents, a birthplace, a story, a crest. And some of us feel a bit like Dumbo delivered by Mr Stork. A nomad with no origin story and amnesia to where we came from and how we got to where we are. If we're blessed with a past, wonderful. If not, or one we don't want to remember, that's fine too. We belong somewhere, every one of us. Like a piece of jigsaw puzzle, we're designed to slot in neatly somewhere and complete that picture. The flip side to belonging in some places is that there are many places we don't belong. A cause of much sorrow is in trying to force ourselves to situations that don't match up to who and what we are. And if we do end up somewhere we don't belong, that's okay, we're not bound to stay. We each get the chance to figure out for ourselves where we belong and successfully locate those places of belonging where we find wholeness.

December 16th
DETACH

"You've chosen a magnificent prison, but it is a prison nonetheless."

CLAUDE FROLLO – THE HUNCHBACK OF NOTRE DAME (1996)

In *Heat*, Robert De Niro utters the classic line; "Don't let yourself get attached to anything you are not willing to walk out on in 30 seconds flat if you feel the heat coming around the corner." While he said this within the context of being a high-end thief (!), the concept kind of holds up. If we liken, for a moment, attachment with enslavement, then what he said rings true. We usually think of prison as the physical place that people go to which removes their liberty to move about freely. But in a spiritual sense, anything and everything does this to the degree to which we are anchored or dictated to by it. Are you free of your mobile phone? Could you discard it for a day, a week, a month? Get rid of it altogether? What about your car? Your belongings? Your beliefs? Fears? Superstitions? Achievements? Failures?

The only thing we can ever own is nothing, because the instant we try to own something, it owns us. Perhaps you are thinking, 'Ooh I like this – liberation through detachment... hang on! What about my children?! My spouse? Pure spiritual things? Surely they're the exception to all this?' Yes and no. Yes, in the limited surface-level sense, but no in the infinite realm. The few things we might reasonably label as inseparable – such as children, that rightfully need and want loving parents – don't dictate or enslave any more than the truly separable things. Natural and inherent responsibilities come in to being the same moment a child does, but they don't enslave the parent. Children are a beautiful gift bestowed by life to those blessed to have them, but one can still find detachment from their kids even as they in the practical sense continue to care for and nurture them.

Nothing enslaves but with permission. Nothing liberates but through detachment.

December 17th
PASS THE BATON

"Let it go, let it go! Turn away and slam the door!" (Sung)

ELSA – FROZEN (2013)

Have you ever seen pigeons debating why one hoovered up all the breadcrumbs and left the other empty-handed? Have you ever seen a squirrel sat looking at the barren earth for an hour, wondering where his nuts went? Have you ever seen sparrows dive-bombing the man cutting down the tree upon which rests their nest? If you have, this point goes out of the window! But if you haven't, could it be because nature and all her creatures are a great example of letting go? The natural world moves, morphs, moulds and changes itself to the ever-constant flow of life. We can do the same. How does the relay race work? By letting go of the baton! It's a beautifully human foible to believe that the countless batons we get passed are all meant to be held on to. Look around you... some people are lugging a double-decker bus worth of batons behind them... and no, they're not competing in World's Strongest Man!

Look in your hands. How many batons are you holding? Which ones should you have let go of long ago?

December 18th
TITLE OF DATE

"You may not have learned much French today, but I think you have learned a little patience and tolerance, and that is the same in every language."

Henriette Deluzy-Desportes – All This, and Heaven Too

Tolerance is the art of self-possession in not seeking to inhibit or control another's behaviour or viewpoint. It is inextricably linked with patience, wisdom, maturity and humility. It can be a tough one to get our head around if we forget the sovereignty and inherent okay-ness of any given behaviour or belief that a person exhibits or holds. Tolerating does not mean condoning, agreeing or supporting. Nor is it apathy or disinterest. It simply means that one acknowledges the inherent okay-ness of any given thing that is occurring or existing. And that of course does not preclude the one who is tolerating any given person or situation to not take calm, considered action in response. And that's all tolerance is. The ethos *live and let live* is tolerance in action. One cannot say, I allow (looking outward) such and such to be, exist or happen, for one has no control over anything outside of self in the first instance. Rather, tolerance is but the gentle command within oneself to allow self to be okay in the face of whatever is being presented. Like everything, tolerance is a paradox because while it seems to point outward, it is purely an internal matter.

All well and good, but what if we see something that is wholly intolerable, such as a person being hurt or abused? Do we just tolerate that?

That is not a matter of tolerance or intolerance, that is a matter of following one's conscience to act or intervene in whatever way seems good in the arising moment. No spiritual law ever contravenes another. Tolerance will never muffle or silence courage when that virtue dictates to the bearer a course of action. This all being so, tolerance is as much needed a virtue as any.

December 19th
SOMEDAYS ARE DANGEROUS

"Someday. That's a dangerous word. It's really just a code for 'never.'"

ROY MILLER – KNIGHT AND DAY

What stops you from turning your *somedays* into *todays*? If an urge or an impression to do something positive, productive or pleasing arises, don't park it in the knacker's yard called 'Someday'. Either act on it or dismiss it. There are no somedays, there is only one day; T-O-D-A-Y.

The opposite of never is now, hence the aphorism, now or never. This also ties back to being enough. You will never be enough at some future point based on some future event or action or achievement. You are either enough now, or you're not. There are no futures markets for enough.

Bin someday. Claim today.

December 20th
NEVER GIVE IN, NEVER GIVE UP

"Find the ones who haven't given up. They're the future."

FRANK WALKER – TOMORROWLAND

Gal Gadot said she was on the verge of giving up on acting at the very point she landed the role of Wonder Woman, a role that she has completely owned and supercharged with her strength, energy and integrity. That's the magic of life – we simply don't know when the miracle will happen. It's not for us to choose, *I think I'll just get my big break on screen now please… I think I'll just have my big breakthrough in the laboratory now thank you… I think I'll just meet the one today… I think I'll just have my Zen moment of enlightenment right here in the park…*

We think it would be great if we could foresee and could control things to be exactly as we please… but in our hearts, we know that doesn't make any sense. Life tests us through the unknowns, the doubts, the fears. It asks all of us: who is willing to keep the faith? Who is willing to go the distance?

Our destinies are written in the stars. The magic carpet that will get us up close enough to read them is the will to keep going. Most things we let go of, but we hold fast to faith, hope and love. We never give up on them, and we never give up on ourselves.

December 21st
THIS MOMENT

"There is no future. There is no past. I live this moment as my last."

MIMI MARQUEZ – RENT

If you woke up tomorrow with no memories at all, what would you look like? What is the original, unfiltered, unadulterated you? What does that you talk like? Act like? Would you like that pure, blank version of you more or less than the one that you see in the mirror now, with all of the accumulated identity that you have amassed?

Every. Second. Of. Our. Existence… We. Can. Choose. To. Be… Renewed. By… The. Purity. Of. The. Moment.

Countless teachers through all ages have preached the gospel of the Now. It's an inclusive message. It is not elitist, separatist, secularist, fascist, ageist, racist, eugenicist, sexist, religionist… (you get the idea.) It embraces and beckons all things. No longer need we be put on the rack and stretched by time; the past pulling on our legs and the future tugging on our arms. We can live, breathe and be in this now moment, unwrapping the gift of presence, moment by moment

---

December 22nd
RISKY BUSINESS

"You're risking your political capital. You're risking your future as our leader."
"The day I am afraid to do that is the day I am no longer fit to lead."

BRENDA MAZIBUKO & NELSON MANDELA – INVICTUS

Are you leading in a way as to merely protect your perpetual placement in that leadership position, or are you leading for the purpose to serve and make a difference?

Are you playing the game with a mind-set to attempt to avoid losing, or are you playing to exhibit the inherent joy and expression wrapped up in the art form?

Are you debating to prove a pre-fixed belief, or are you pinging out ideas and passions whilst being genuinely open to learning something you hadn't considered before?

Are you turning up at your work simply to earn a wage, or are you learning and growing at every opportunity and seeking your advancement through synergistic, mutually beneficial cooperation?

Being alive is a risk, which means if you're reading or hearing this, you're a natural risk-taker. Some of us forget this. We can find ourselves voluntarily dying a little more each day in an attempt to preserve our life one more day... essentially, dying to live and living to die... the definition of madness, if ever there was one.

December 23rd
RESIST, PERSIST, INSIST

"It's better to go too far than not far enough."

ARTHUR DENNING – MISCONDUCT

Any worthwhile accomplishment requires persistence of action, resistance of distraction and insistence of focus to achieve. Single-mindedness is the practice of charting a course and unflinchingly and unwaveringly taking step after step to walk the path. Expectation and excitement accompany the beginnings of a journey, but those feelings pale in comparison to the deep satisfaction and joyful reflection which serenade the finish. As the marathon runner lines up at the start, they know that trials, distractions and calls to quit are going to come. The road is long. After a while it seems every stride hurts. The screams to quit grow louder. They build to a crescendo. There, running in suspended animation, the athlete has the binary decision: Do I quit? Or do I see this through? Marathons and the inherent ultimatum they contain – quit or finish – come along in relationships, careers, dreams, faith, studies, and the literal ones lasting 26 and a quarter miles.

What races are you running? Will you quit or finish? Will you persist and insist to be the best version of you?

December 24th
CHOOSE YOUR DOOR

"I'm trying to free your mind, Neo. But I can only show you the door. You're the one that has to walk through it."

MORPHEUS – THE MATRIX

Your priorities and your desires determine the doors you choose to enter. Your mind is the master controller, the determiner of your truths and your realities and the decision maker of which doorways to cross and which to avoid. There is no door you cannot pass through. The doors of wealth, wisdom and self-worth stand ajar for you if you wish to pass them. Who is to say which doors are right. If the red pill takes you through the door to reality, but a reality heavy with challenges, is that better than taking the blue pill and passing through the door of comfortable ignorance?

December 25th
JOY TO THE WORLD

"Christmas isn't just a day, it's a frame of mind."

KRIS KRINGLE – MIRACLE ON 34TH STREET (1947)

Special occasions and festivals bring out the joy and lightness in our being. They are usually celebrated and honoured by a focus on light, symbols of love and the sharing of food, gifts and memory-making moments. Within these hallowed moments, we get an insight in to the human psyche. We see that deep within humans there is a youthful exuberance which just needs a little shake from time to time to get it to rise to the surface. *Peace on earth and goodwill toward men* is the call we hear, and we rejoice that such lofty ideas can and do permeate our shared consciousness. The humanity we feel is not alien to us, it is the vibrations of our higher selves, revealed and harmonising. A lovely gift we could each give ourselves is to keep the spirit of goodwill and cheer throughout the year.

December 26th
COURAGE TO SEEK

"I always thought the idea of education was to learn to think for yourself."

JOHN KEATING – DEAD POET'S SOCIETY

The true purpose of education is to imbue a positive feedback loop within the learner of seeking, finding and experimenting with their truth. There is one truth, a majestic tree, under the canopy of which sits the truths of every individual person. Our personal truths may appear not to harmonise with other peoples' truths, but as different coloured balls in a bag may assert their own unique colour, nevertheless they all must admit that they belong to the one bag and that that is the overarching truth under which their own truths exist.

One of the greatest qualities necessary to follow the path of the seeker is courage. Courage is the opposite of blind acceptance and docile conformity. A hundred, a million, a world of people moving in one direction does not make it right (or wrong). Education means to nourish and bring up, which means giving ourselves an environment of love, open-mindedness and freedom to choose our own way. Courage is needed to form our own views and follow our own path. If others walk that path, too, wonderful. If they don't, may we have the courage to stay on the course that is right for us.

December 27th
CULTURE CLUB

"The cultural environment in which one lives ought to be as important as the air he breathes, the food he eats."

MR CLEARY – SCHOOL TIES

Air is the life that fuels the blood. Food is the life that powers the body. Culture is the life that enlivens the heart and mind. Without a culture, we become generic and bland, masses off a production line rather than niche handmade people. We don't always stop to consider the cultures of our day and the messages those cultures tell us about who we are and how we're thinking. Music and architecture are two good examples. The 16 to 1800s was a period of great artistic expression in Europe. The great composers of the Baroque, Classical and Romantic eras have yet to be surpassed. True geniuses, with no technological instruments, would calculate the size and shape of cathedrals and sculpt their symphonies to harmonise perfectly. The architecture dreamed and chiselled into being during the same time still stands proud in capitals throughout the continent, while all around them modern structures are built up and pulled down again within decades. One possible message from this is: quality endures.

What is our culture? Do we have a say in keeping it alive? Or does culture have a mind of its own?

December 28th
HEARTSTRONG

"When your head says one thing and your whole life says another, your head always loses."

FRANK MCCLOUD – KEY LARGO

Why is the pull of the heart so strong? Why do we put cute images of pink hearts on the end of messages, cards, clothes and duvet covers and not little pink brains?! Could it be that while the brain serves a superb purpose of running the operating programme that keeps us functioning, the sway of life is inextricably linked with the heart? The flow of life has its own rhythm, its own language. The secret to interpreting it is not through the head but the heart. This is why it's not the smartest or even the strongest that stay the course or reach their desired end, it is the faithful, the committed, the loving, and all these guttural desires come from the heart.

December 29th
KEY AND CHAIN

"Forget everything you think you know."

BARON MORDO – DOCTOR STRANGE

Knowledge is a key but also a chain. Knowledge is power but also power-corrupting. Knowledge is a double-edged sword: it both helps and hinders.

Vacate your throne of knowledge and sit upon the stool of open-mindedness.

Abdicate the crown of know-it-all and wear the cap of learning.

Surrender the castle of certainty and cross the drawbridge over the moat to roam the plains of limitless possibility.

You are not what you know. You are not what you know you know you are not. You are much, much more than you know, are you not?

December 30ᵗʰ
BEAT THE DRUM

"A machine doesn't improvise well because you cannot program a fear of death. Our survival instinct is our greatest source of inspiration."

DR MANN – INTERSTELLAR

Place your hand on your heart. Feel the power and energy of that wondrous natural machine. With every beat, it is not only pumping blood and life throughout your being, it is getting you marching to the beat of a spiritual drum. It is the beat of life. The intrinsic, self-emanating desire to exist. It is a metronome setting perfect time for you to be. As long as there is a beat within there is hope without. There is life. Each of us have our own beat, cajoling, helping, inspiring, calling us forward.

This has been a good year. The blessings and gifts have brought us joy. The trials and suffering have brought us humility, compassion and wisdom. We've crossed mountains and valleys, and at times may have found ourselves adrift at sea or stranded in desert, but here... we... are. We seek life, liberty and happiness. We rage against the dying of the light, and when the light flickers and fades, we take it upon ourselves to become the light.

You are a survivor and a thriver. Keep marching to the beat of your drum and keep being the light.

December 31st
RENEWAL

"I didn't think it would end this way."
"End? No, the journey doesn't end here. Death is just another path, one that we all must take. The grey rain-curtain of this world rolls back, and all turns to silver glass, and then you see it."
"What? Gandalf? See what?"
"White shores and beyond, a far green country under a swift sunrise. "
"Well, that isn't so bad."
"No. No, it isn't."

PEREGRIN TOOK & GANDALF – THE LORD OF THE RINGS: THE RETURN
OF THE KING

This is not the end.

The end is but the portal to our new beginning.

The fire and the flames are the purifiers that take us to rebirth.

Defeat and disappointment are the lessons that take us to victory.

Confusion is the stepping stone to clarity.

The raging storm at surface hides the imponderable stillness below.

What was lost shall be found.

What was forsaken shall be renewed and honoured.

Rising, like a phoenix, we shall not be subdued.

Rising, boundless and glorious.

From nothingness to oneness.

This is not the end.

January 1st
CLEAN SLATE

"You've been given a chance to start over with a clean slate. How many of us get that?"

DR DYSON IDO – ALITA: BATTLE ANGEL

What is a new day? What is a new sunrise? What is a fresh beginning? Who among us cannot choose that today, this day, this moment, we shake clear the etch-a-sketch that was yesterday, that was last year, that was our life, that was us (good, bad and ugly), and here, now, stand anew? Unencumbered of the road behind us, we now make choices. We are human beings – agents of power, light and love.

Your slate is clean. What are you going to do with it?

THEMES
FILMS
ACTORS

THEMES AND THEIR DATES

Abundance – Mar 1

Acceptance – Jan 26, May 7,
Aug 6, Aug 19

Accountability – Jan 17, Apr 8,
Sep 3, Dec 10

Action – Feb 18, Mar 8, Apr 21,
Aug 19, Sep 22, Oct 25,
Nov 9, Dec 6

Adaptability – Jul 3, Nov 27

Adventure – Feb 5, Mar 13,
Jun 18, Aug 31

Adversity – Aug 10, Aug 12,
Nov 10

Affirmations – May 18

Alchemy – Dec 2

Ambition – Apr 5, Oct 22

Animals – Aug 1

Answers – Apr 1

Arriving – Mar 31

Art – Nov 17

Asking – Mar 26

Attitude – Jan 4, Sep 7

Authenticity – Jan 8, Jan 28,
Feb 21, Mar 19, Apr 6,
May 27, Dec 13

Authority – Aug 23

Awareness – Oct 20

Balance – Jan 23, Sep 18

Beauty – Feb 17

Beginnings – Jan 30, Feb 11,
Jan 1 (Alita: Battle Angel)

Being – Feb 1, Feb 10, Feb 22,
Jul 9, Jul 15, Nov 5

Belonging – Apr 13, Jun 10,
Dec 15

Blind spots – Dec 11

Books – Jul 30

Boundaries – May 26, May 30

Breathing – Apr 24

Building up – Jun 2, Jun 15,
Oct 19

Calm – Apr 24, Dec 2

Captain – Jan 22

Carefree lifestyle – May 28

Carpe Diem – Jan 10, Apr 21,
Nov 9

Cause and effect – Nov 8

Celebration – Dec 25

Challenges – Jul 21

Change – Mar 12, May 20,
Jun 24

Chaos – Feb 13

Charity – Apr 11

Chocolate – Jun 22

Choice – Jan 4, Feb 1, Feb 19,
Mar 12, Apr 5, Apr 8,
Jun 27, Aug 11, Sep 3,
Sep 15, Oct 4, Oct 31, Dec 24

Clarity – Feb 27

Comfort – Jun 3

Comfort zone – Sep 2

Commitment – Jul 23, Sep 4

Communication – Mar 11,
Aug 28

Compassion – Jan 14, May 1

Compliments – Jun 2

Connection – Jul 17, Jul 27,
Oct 14, Dec 3, Dec 5

Consequences – Jan 3, Oct 15,
Dec 24

Context – Jun 20
Control – Apr 16, Apr 19,
Nov 15
Convention – Sep 21
Conversation – Aug 28
Courage – Jan 20, Jul 18,
Aug 24, Sep 10, Sep 22,
Oct 28, Nov 27, Dec 26
Creativity – Jan 16, Jan 27,
Apr 10, Nov 26
Crossroads – Oct 11
Culture – Mar 24, Dec 27
Daring – Sep 2
Death – Feb 28, May 5
Decision – Jan 6
Dedication – May 31, Sep 19
Desire – Feb 9, Aug 22, Oct 22
Destiny – Dec 20
Detachment – Jan 25, Dec 16
Determination – Nov 26
Difficulties – Jul 21
Disappointment – Feb 20
Discernment – Sep 27
Discipline – Nov 24, Nov 28
Discovery – Mar 18, Apr 26
Divinity – Jul 6
DIY – Dec 10
Dogma – Nov 12
Double standards – Jul 7
Dreams – Mar 13, Apr 27,
Jul 16, Aug 5
Duality – Jul 12, Oct 13
Earth – Feb 26, Aug 1
Education – Mar 20, Dec 26
Empowerment – Sep 15
Endings – Feb 11
Endurance – Jan 15, Jan 17,
Nov 1, Dec 23

Energy – Jun 26
Enlightenment – Feb 27
Enough – Apr 12
Entertainment – Dec 4
Enthusiasm – Jan 18, Dec 13
Environment – Dec 14
Equanimity – Nov 13
Example – Jan 9, Feb 18
Existence – Jun 13
Experience – Jun 19, Jul 29,
Jul 31, Nov 3
Experimenting – Oct 29
Explaining – Jul 11
Exploration – Sep 24
Extremes – Jan 23
Failure – May 4
Fairness – Jul 7
Faith – Feb 14, Mar 29, Jun 14,
Nov 6, Dec 7, Dec 20, Dec 31
Fallibility – Sep 18
Family – May 16, Nov 4
Fate – Nov 15
Fear – Jul 2
Fearlessness – Oct 28
Feelings – Jun 19, Aug 30,
Nov 11
Fellowship – May 1
Festivals – Dec 25
Film – Dec 12
Focus – Jul 18, Aug 22
Forgiveness – May 26, Jun 6,
Aug 9, Oct 21, Nov 23
Freedom – Jan 25, Apr 16,
Apr 20, Jun 12, Oct 9,
Oct 18, Dec 16
Free will – Nov 15
Friendship – Aug 7
Fun – May 28

Genius – Jun 18
Give and take – Dec 8
Giving – Apr 3
Glory – Feb 24, Apr 25, Jun 17
God – Aug 17
Gold medal – Jan 1 (Cool Runnings)
Good and bad – Jun 30
Good news – Jun 20
Goodness – Jan 7
Goodwill – Dec 25
Gratitude – Jan 5, Feb 4, Jul 19, Oct 7
Growing up – Nov 29
Growth – Apr 23, May 12, Oct 29, Dec 30
Habit – Nov 24
Happiness – Apr 29, Jul 28, Aug 3, Oct 10
Hate – Oct 21, Nov 23
Heart – Dec 28
Help – Jan 29
Heritage – Jul 1
Highest-self – Apr 18
Home – Mar 4, Jun 10
Honesty – Aug 7
Hope – Oct 26, Dec 31
Human being – Jun 9
Humanity – Jan 7, Feb 26, Feb 29, Apr 15, May 1, Aug 8, Sep 11, Oct 16
Humility – Feb 2, Apr 17, Dec 29
Humour – Oct 8
Ideas – Feb 23, Oct 9
Illusion – Jun 8

Imagination – Jul 16, Jul 30
Inclusivity – May 2
Individuality – Mar 9, Aug 8, Oct 2
Infinity – Sep 9
Influence – Feb 18, Dec 14
Inner child – Nov 7
Inspiration – Feb 15, May 29, Jun 21
Integrity – May 10, May 16, Nov 30, Dec 22
Intention – Jul 23
Interconnection – Aug 19
Interdependence – Oct 10, Dec 11
Intimacy – Dec 5
Joy – Apr 29
Judgement – Aug 4, Aug 26, Nov 2
Justice – Aug 26
Karma – Jul 22, Aug 27, Nov 2
Killing – Mar 25
Kindness – Apr 11, Oct 17, Oct 19
Knowledge – Feb 2, Dec 29
Language – Mar 24, Oct 6, Nov 30
Laughter – Oct 8
Law of Attraction – Aug 27, Oct 15
Leadership – Jul 24
Learning – May 23
Legacy – Jul 17
Legend – Jun 25
Letting go – Jan 31, Apr 19, Aug 9, Dec 17

Lies – Aug 13

Life – Mar 29, Apr 3, May 23, Aug 18, Sep 1, Nov 17, Dec 12

Light – Mar 27, Dec 30

Listening – Apr 2

Live and Let Live – Oct 2

Living – Jun 1, Jul 9

Loneliness – Jul 27

Loss – Jun 16, Jul 13

Love – Jan 11, Apr 4, Apr 14, Jul 5, Aug 25, Sep 13, Sep 29, Oct 11, Oct 24, Nov 20, Nov 23, Dec 5, Dec 9

Loyalty – Jan 19

Luck – May 8

Magic – Apr 10

Masks – Sep 8

Mastery – Jul 3

Matter – May 17

Maturity – Nov 29

Meaning – Jun 7, Jun 23, Aug 2, Sep 20

Means and end – Jul 12

Memories – Mar 7

Mind – Jan 24, Apr 30

Miracles – May 3

Mirrors – Apr 9

Missing piece – Sep 16

Money – Oct 7

Morals – Jul 26

Mothers – Mar 10, Sep 17

Motivation – Jun 21, Aug 15

Motives – Jul 20

Movies – Dec 12

Needs – Sep 30

Newness – Jan 1 (Cool Runnings)

Non-necessities – Jun 4

Normality – Sep 21

Now – Apr 21, Jul 19, Dec 19, Dec 21

Observation – Apr 24

Old – Sep 6

Oneness – Oct 13, Dec 3

Open-mindedness – Nov 12, Dec 11, Dec 29

Opportunity – Sep 30, Nov 10

Opposites – Feb 29, Jun 16

Optimism – May 11

Originality – Jan 27, May 27, Dec 13

Pain – Sep 28

Paradoxes – May 24, Aug 29, Oct 1

Parenthood – Mar 10

Past – Jul 15

Paths – Oct 11, Nov 25

Patience – Jan 30, May 12, Oct 27

Peace – Mar 18

Perception – Jul 7, Aug 4

Perfection – Jan 2

Perseverance – Dec 20, Dec 23

Philosophy – Jul 10, Nov 6

Pitfalls – May 9

Pity – May 6

Plans – Mar 16

Positivity – Jan 18, May 11

Power – May 21

Practice – May 31

Presence – Jan 10, Feb 7, Jul 15, Jul 19, Sep 25, Nov 5, Dec 21

Price – Feb 3

Pride – May 19

Principles – Jul 26
Privacy – Dec 1
Problems – Jan 21
Procrastination – Mar 8
Progress – Nov 18
Promises – Dec 6
Proof – Apr 22
Psychology – Mar 28
Purity – Apr 18
Purpose – Feb 27, Aug 16, Sep 20
Quality – Sep 5
Questions – Feb 22, Apr 1
Reality – Oct 5, Nov 22
Rebirth – Jan 1 (Alita: Battle Angel)
Reflection – Feb 16, Nov 18
Rejection – Nov 10
Relationships – Feb 20, Apr 4, May 14, Jun 22, Nov 19
Relaxation – Nov 16
Religion – Nov 6
Remembrance – Jan 8
Renewal – Dec 31
Repetition – May 18
Resilience – Aug 10
Resources – Feb 8, Mar 6
Responsibility – May 7
Risk – Dec 22
Romance – Jul 4, Oct 11
Rules – Jan 28
Sacrifice – Mar 15, Sep 10, Nov 28
Samurai – Jan 2
Scars – Aug 20
Science – Jun 26, Dec 3, Dec 5
Script – Apr 28

Secrets – Jul 8, Sep 12
Seeking – Dec 4
Self-acceptance – Oct 3
Self-accountability – Aug 14, Oct 23
Self-actualisation – Mar 5
Self-care – Nov 29, Dec 8
Self-confidence – Jun 29, Dec 7
Self-deception – Oct 23
Self-development – Jul 14
Self-discovery – Jan 12, Feb 5, Jun 28, Jul 2, Sep 14
Self-knowledge – Jun 28, Sep 14, Sep 24, Oct 20, Nov 14
Self-love – Sep 29, Oct 3
Self-possession – Oct 27
Self-responsibility – Sep 26
Self-worth – Jan 1 (Cool Runnings), Feb 6, Feb 16, Mar 22, Apr 12
Sensitivity – Sep 23
Service – Apr 11, Jul 24
Setbacks – Aug 10, Aug 12, Nov 10
Showbiz – Sep 11
Showing up – Nov 1
Signs – Jun 17
Silence – Jun 5, Aug 28
Similarities – Mar 14
Solitude – Jan 12
Solutions – Mar 30
Soul – Mar 17, Mar 22, Sep 23
Sovereignty – Apr 8, Sep 26
Space – Dec 9
Spirituality – Sep 23, Oct 16
Sport – Feb 24, Feb 25, Jul 25, Dec 13

Stamina – Nov 26
Stillness – Jun 5, Sep 25
Stoicism – Aug 6, Nov 13
Stories – Jun 23
Substance – Feb 17
Success – Feb 24, Mar 23
Suffering – Nov 20
Superstition – Jun 25
Surprises – Mar 2
Surrender – Jan 26, Dec 17
Survival – Dec 30
Synchronicity – Aug 2
Teamwork – Jun 15, Jul 25
Temptation – Feb 12
That's Life – Aug 21
The Way – Aug 4
Thought – Jan 13, Jan 24,
    Feb 23, Mar 28, Apr 30,
    May 22
Thriving – Jun 1
Time – Feb 7, Mar 21, May 25,
    Jun 23, Aug 29
Today – Dec 19
Togetherness – Nov 4
Tolerance – May 2, Dec 18
Tools – Mar 6
Training – Nov 24
Transcendence – Jul 6
Travel – Nov 3
Trust – Feb 14, Apr 4
Truth – Mar 3, Jul 8, Nov 22
Trying – Jul 31
Uncertainty – Mar 2
Understanding – Jan 14
Uniqueness – Jun 11
Unity – Feb 24, Feb 25, Apr 15,
    Jul 25

Universal Law – May 24,
    Aug 13, Nov 8
Universe – Jan 15, Apr 13,
    Jul 1, Aug 17
Value – Jan 1 (Cool Runnings),
Apr 7
Vanity – Apr 17
Vibration – Sep 7
Viewpoint – Nov 25
Virtue – Oct 3
Vision – May 13, Nov 25
Vulnerability – Apr 4, Aug 24
Waiting – Oct 27
War – Mar 25, Jul 14, Sep 17
Warmth – Mar 27
Waste – Nov 21
Water – Sep 1
Wheel of life – Jul 13
Will – Feb 9
Winning – Jun 7
Wisdom – Feb 2, May 9, Aug 3,
    Sep 27
Words – Jul 11, Oct 6, Dec 6
Work – Sep 19, Oct 30
Yes – Nov 14

FILMS AND THEIR DATES

12 Monkeys – Jun 27
12 Years A Slave – Jun 1
1917 – Aug 14
21 Grams – Mar 17
300 – Mar 8
42nd Street – Jul 7
A Beautiful Day in the Neighbourhood – Sep 28, Sep 29
A Beautiful Mind – Jan 11
A Bug's Life – May 12
A Christmas Carol – Apr 11
A Few Good Men – Mar 3
A Knight's Tale – Nov 17
A River Runs Through It – Jan 14
A Room with a View – Apr 14
A Star is Born – Feb 14
A Tale of Two Cities – Mar 15
Accidental Hero – Mar 28
Aladdin – Apr 20
Alita: Battle Angel – Jan 1
All The King's Men – Apr 26
All the Money in the World Feb 3
All This, and Heaven Too Dec 18
Amadeus – Jul 6
Amistad – Jun 12
An American In Paris – Nov 3
Ant-Man – Jun 28
Antwone Fisher – Aug 9
Any Given Sunday – Jul 24, Jul 25

Anything Else – Oct 2
Apollo 13 – Jan 21
As Good As It Gets – May 29
Back to the Future – May 13
Barton Fink – Sep 24
Batman: The Dark Knight May 15
Before Sunrise – Mar 21
Being John Malkovich – Apr 5
Ben Hur – Mar 9
Black Hawk Down – Apr 21
Black Panther – Apr 15
Black Swan – Apr 8
Bohemian Rhapsody – Jan 9
Braveheart – Jan 10, Oct 18
Breakfast At Tiffany's – Oct 19
Butch Cassidy and the Sundance Kid – Nov 25
Buying The Cow – Oct 31
Capone – May 16
Captain Phillips – Sep 30
Casablanca – Mar 7
Casino – Apr 4
Cast Away – Jan 12
Chariots of Fire – Mar 5
Chicago – Sep 11
Chocolat – Jul 22
Cindarella – May 3
Cinema Paradiso – Dec 12
Citizen Kane – Oct 22, Oct 23, Oct 24
City of Angels – Jul 29
City of Joy – May 1
Cleopatra – Jun 25

Coach Carter – Apr 25
Cocktail – Jan 5
Contact – Jun 13, Jun 14
Cool Hand Luke – Mar 11
Cool Runnings – Jan 1, Dec 13
Crocodile Dundee – Jul 23
Crouching Tiger, Hidden Dragon – Aug 29, Aug 30
Dallas Buyers Club – Sep 20, Sep 21
Dangerous Liaisons – Apr 17
Dead Man Walking – Jul 1
Dead Poet's Society – Jan 22, Dec 26
Death on the Nile – Nov 13
Devil's Advocate – Jun 22
Doctor Strange – Feb 13, Dec 29
Dogma – Aug 3
Dolemite Is My Name – May 8
Double Indemnity – Nov 2
Dr. Giggles – Oct 8
Dumb & Dumber – Oct 17
East of Eden – Oct 4
Eat Pray Love – Apr 30
Edward Scissorhands – Jun 11
Enola Holmes – Jul 2
Enter The Dragon – Jun 17
Envy – Aug 21
Eternal Sunshine of the Spotless Mind – Feb 20
Fences – Sep 27
Ferris Bueller's Day Off Apr 24
Fight Club – Jan 25
Finding Forrester – Apr 27

Finding Neverland – Jul 16, Jul 17
Five Feet Apart – Dec 5
Flight – Nov 15
Frida – Aug 10
Frozen – Dec 17
Get On Up – Nov 26
Gladiator – Jan 3, May 5
Going My Way – Mar 14
Good Will Hunting – Mar 20
Goodbye Christopher Robin Jul 14
Goodfellas – Jan 19
Gosford Park – Aug 4
Grease – Feb 11
Great Expectations – Jun 23, Jun 24
Green Book – Jul 27
Greyhound – May 18
Groundhog Day – Jan 28
Hacksaw Ridge – Apr 6
Harry Potter and the Goblet of Fire – Feb 19
Harry Potter and the Half-Blood Prince – Aug 6
Harry Potter and the Philosopher's Stone – Aug 7
Harry Potter and the Prisoner of Azkaban – Aug 5
Harvey – Oct 5
Havana – Jun 16
Heat – Oct 13, Oct 25
Hercules – Dec 14
Hitch – Mar 1
Holy Man – Dec 3
Home Alone – Jan 24, Nov 29

Hook – Jan 16
Hostiles – Sep 23
Howards End – Sep 17
Hunt for the Wilderpeople
    Mar 23
I'm Not There – Jul 11
I'm Thinking of Ending Things
    May 27
Inception – Feb 23
Indiana Jones and the
Kingdom of the Crystal Skull
    Feb 5
Inherit the Wind – Nov 18,
    Nov 19
Interstellar – Dec 9, Dec 30
Invictus – Dec 22
Iris – Apr 18
Ishtar – May 10
It's a Wonderful Life – Jan 18
Jaws – Mar 6
Jerry Maguire – Feb 15, May 14
JFK – Mar 22
Jurassic Park – Mar 29
Key Largo – Dec 28
Kingdom of Heaven – Jan 15
Knight and Day – Dec 19
La Dolce Vita – Aug 31
La La Land – Sep 4
La Vita E Bella – Jun 4, Jun 5
Le Petit Soldat – Feb 22
Legally Blonde – Apr 12
Limitless – Feb 27
Lock, Stock and Two Smoking
Barrels – Jun 21
Lord of War – Mar 31
Lost In Translation – Aug 22
Love and Death – Nov 20

Madagascar – Dec 10
Made In Italy – May 26
Magnolia – Apr 2
Man On Fire – Nov 24
Man on the Moon – Jun 18
Mary Queen of Scots – Feb 29
Master and Commander: The
Far Side of the World – Aug 23
Matilda – Jan 20
Meet Joe Black – Jul 28
Meet Me In St. Louis – Nov 4
Men of Honor – Jul 20
Midnight Cowboy – Mar 27,
    May 30
Miracle on 34th Street
    Dec 25
Misconduct – Dec 23
Monster's Ball – Aug 8
Monty Python and the Holy
Grail – May 11
Mr. Deeds – Aug 11
Mrs Doubtfire – Jan 29
Murder on the Orient Express
    Nov 14
My Dinner With Andre – Jun 3
My Week With Marilyn
    Sep 8
National Treasure – Feb 18
Notting Hill – Oct 11
Now, Voyager – Mar 12
October Sky – Jul 18
On The Waterfront – Nov 6
One Day – Jul 19
Onward – Apr 10
Oscar – Jun 20
Out of Africa – Mar 2
Out of Sight – Mar 26

Papillon – Feb 12

Passengers – Oct 20

Patch Adams – Jun 9, Jun 10

Pay It Forward – Jul 21

Phantom Thread – Sep 12

Pi – Sep 2

Pinocchio – Aug 13

Pirates of the Caribbean: The Curse of the Black Pearl
Feb 6

Pocahontas – May 2

Point Break – Feb 2

Pollock – Jun 19

Project Power – May 21

Psycho – Mar 10

Rambling Rose – Sep 18

Ray – Nov 27

Rebel Without A Cause
Oct 26

Remember the Titans – Feb 24

Rent – Dec 21

Rocky Balboa – Jan 17

Rocky V – Aug 15

Roman Holiday – Nov 5

Rudy – Apr 22

Sabrina – Aug 18

Safe House – Sep 26

Saving Mr. Banks – Jul 15

Saving Private Ryan – Feb 10

Schindler's List – Apr 3

School Ties – Dec 27

Secondhand Lions – Oct 3

Serendipity – Aug 2

Seven Years In Tibet – Jan 26, Sep 25

Shakespeare in Love – Sep 13

Shirley Valentine – Sep 19

Silver Linings Playbook
Sep 7

Silverado – Jul 3

Singin' In The Rain – Nov 1

Sliding Doors – Jul 31

Some Like It Hot – Oct 27

Spartacus – Oct 28

Star Wars: Episode V – The Empire Strikes Backs – Jan 6

Star Wars: Episode VIII – The Last Jedi – May 4

Stepmom – Jul 26

Still Alice – Sep 5

Superman – Nov 28

Sweet Smell of Success
Oct 29

Talladega Nights: The Ballad of Ricky Bobby – Jun 29

Tenet – May 24

Testament of Youth – Nov 21, Nov 22

The A-Team – Mar 16

The Artist – Oct 10

The Best Exotic Marigold Hotel – Apr 19

The Big Lebowski – Jun 26

The Book of Eli – Jul 12

The Bridges of Madison County – Sep 14, Sep 15

The Bucket List – Apr 29

The Call – Dec 6

The Call of the Wild – Oct 30

The Color Purple – Jul 5

The Curious Case of Benjamin Button – Feb 1, Aug 16, Oct 14

The Current War – Oct 9

The Da Vinci Code – Dec 11

The English Patient – Aug 28

The Fault In Our Stars – Jul 4

The Favourite – Aug 20, Sep 9

The Final Countdown – Oct 1

The Godfather – Apr 23

The Great Dictator – Oct 16

The Green Mile – Oct 15

The Half of It – May 17

The Hateful Eight – Aug 26

The Help – Jun 2

The Horse Whisperer – Aug 1

The Hours – Mar 18

The Hunchback of Notre Dame – Dec 16

The Hurricane – Nov 23

The Illusionist – Jul 10

The Imitation Game – Apr 7

The Incredibles – Dec 7

The Iron Lady – Sep 10

The Jungle Book 2 – Dec 15

The Karate Kid – May 31

The Kid – Dec 4

The Last of the Mohicans Apr 13

The Last Samurai – Jan 2, Apr 1

The Legend of 1900 – Jan 30

The Life of Pi – Jan 31

The Lion King – Jan 8, May 28

The Lord of the Rings: The Fellowship of the Ring May 6, May 7

The Lord of the Rings: The Return of the King – Dec 31

The Lord of the Rings: The Two Towers – Jan 7

The Magnificent Seven – Jul 13

The Matrix – Mar 30, Dec 24

The Mighty Ducks – Feb 25

The Night of the Hunter Nov 7, Nov 8

The Old Guard – May 25

The One and Only Ivan May 19, May 20

The Passion of the Christ Aug 27

The Perfect Man – Aug 12

The Perks of Being a Wallflower – Dec 8

The Philadelphia Story Nov 11

The Pianist – Jan 27

The Player – Jun 15

The Post – Sep 3

The Prestige – Jul 8, Jul 9

The Professor and the Madman – Oct 6

The Razor's Edge – Dec 2

The Revenant – Feb 28

The Scent of a Woman Oct 12

The Secret: Dare to Dream May 22, May 23

The Shawshank Redemption Jan 4

The Social Network – Nov 30, Dec 1

The Sound of Music – Nov 10

The Southerner – Oct 7

The Talented Mr Ripley Mar 19

The Theory of Everything Feb 26

The Treasure of the Sierra Madre – Sep 1
The Truman Show – Apr 16
The Untouchables – Feb 9
The Usual Suspects – Feb 21
The Village – Aug 24, Aug 25
The Way We Were – Nov 12
The Wizard of Oz – Mar 4
The Wolf of Wall Street
    Sep 22
Thelma & Louise – Feb 16,
    Sep 16
Tin Cup – Apr 28
Titanic – Feb 4
Tomorrow Never Dies
    Mar 24
Tomorrowland – Dec 20
Top Gun – Jan 23
Total Recall – Nov 16
Toy Story – Jan 13
Trading Places – May 9
Unforgiven – Mar 25
Venom – Jun 30
Vertigo – Nov 9
Vice – Aug 19
Wall Street – Feb 8
West Side Story – Oct 21
What Dreams May Come
    Jun 6, Jun 7, Jun 8
Wild Strawberries – Sep 6
Willy Wonka and the Chocolate Factory – Feb 7
Wish I Was Here – Aug 17
You Can't Take It With You
    Mar 13
You Should Have Left – Apr 9

You've Got Mail – Jul 30
Zoolander – Feb 17

ACTORS AND THEIR DATES

Abdi, Barkhad – Sep 30
Abraham, Murray – Jul 6
Allen, Tim – Jan 13
Allen, Woody – Oct 2
Andersson, Bibi – Sep 6
Andoh, Adjoa – Dec 22
Andrews, Julie – Nov 10
Arnold, Edward – Mar 13
Astin, Sean – Jan 7
Avery, Margaret – Jul 5
Bacon, Kevin – Apr 9
Bale, Christian – Jul 8, Sep 23
Barrymore, Lionel – Mar 13
Beatty, Warren – May 10
Bedard, Irene – May 2
Bellamy, Ralph – May 9
Berry, Halle – Aug 8, Dec 6
Bettany, Paul – Aug 23, Nov 17
Black, Jack – Aug 21
Bogart, Humphrey – Mar 7,
  Dec 28
Boseman, Chadwick – Apr 15,
  Nov 26
Boyd, Billy – Dec 31
Boyd, Stephen – Mar 9
Branagh, Kenneth – Nov 14
Brando, Marlon – Apr 23,
  Nov 6
Breslin, Spencer – Dec 4
Bridges, Jeff – Jun 26
Broadbent, Jim – Aug 6
Broderick, Matthew – Apr 24
Brody, Adrien – Jan 27

Brosnan, Pierce – Mar 24
Brown, Bryan – Jan 5
Buchholz, Horst – Jun 5
Buckley, Jessie – May 27
Butler, Gerard – Mar 8
Cage, Nicolas – Feb 18, Mar 31
Caine, Michael – Jul 9
Candy, John – Jan 1
  (Cool Runnings)
Carrey, Jim – Feb 20, Oct 17
Cassel, Vincent – Apr 8
Caviezel, Jim – Aug 27
Chakiris, George – Oct 21
Chaplin, Alexander – Aug 17
Chaplin, Charlie – Oct 16
Charleson, Ian – Mar 5
Chow, Yun-Fat – Aug 29
Cleese, John – May 11
Clooney, George – Mar 26,
  Dec 20
Close, Glenn – Apr 17
Cochrane, Rory – Sep 23
Collins, Pauline – Sep 19
Colman, Olivia – Aug 20
Colman, Ronald – Mar 15
Connery, Sean – Feb 9, Apr 27
Cooper, Bradley – Feb 14,
  Feb 27, Sep 7
Costner, Kevin – Mar 22,
  Apr 28
Cotton, Joseph – Oct 24
Crosby, Bing – Mar 14
Crowe, Russell – Jan 3, Jan 11,
  May 5

Cruise, Tom – Jan 5, Jan 23, Mar 3, Apr 1, Dec 19

Culkin, Macaulay – Jan 24, Nov 29

Cumberbatch, Benedict – Feb 13

Cuny, Alain – Aug 31

Curtis, Tony – Oct 27, Oct 28, Oct 29

Dale, James Badge – Nov 15

Damon, Matt – Mar 19, Mar 20, Dec 30

Dampf, Sarah – Jul 29

Daniels, Jeff – Oct 17

Davidtz, Embeth – Jan 20

Davis, Bette – Mar 12, Nov 13, Dec 18

Davis, Viola – Jun 2

Dawson, Rosario – Dec 21

Day-Lewis, Daniel – Apr 13, Sep 12

De Niro, Robert – Jan 19, Apr 4, Oct 13

Dean, James – Oct 4, Oct 26

Dench, Judi – Apr 18, Apr 19

Dennison, Julian – Mar 23

Depp, Johnny – Feb 6, Jul 16, Jul 17

Dern, Laura – Jul 18

DeVito, Danny – Jun 18

DiCaprio, Leonardo – Feb 4, Feb 23, Feb 28, Sep 22

Dillon, Matt – May 16

Doug, Doug E. – Dec 13

Douglas, Kirk – Oct 28

Douglas, Michael – Feb 8

Drake, Larry – Oct 8

Dujardin, Jean – Oct 10

Durano, Giustino – Jun 4

Dutton, Charles S. – Apr 22

Duvall, Robert – Oct 3

Eastwood, Clint – Mar 25

Ejiofor, Chiwetel – Jun 1, Dec 29

Elgort, Ansel – Jul 4

Elliot, Denholm – Apr 14

Ellis, Aunjanue – Jul 20

Ellis, Nelsan – Nov 26

Estevez, Emilio – Feb 25

Feldman, Bob – Aug 12

Felton, Verna – May 3

Ferrell, Will – Jun 29

Fiennes, Joseph – Sep 13

Fiennes, Ralph – Aug 28

Firth, Colin – Aug 14

Fishburne, Laurence – Dec 24

Foley, Dave – May 12

Ford, Harrison – Feb 5

Foster, Jodie – Jun 14

Fox, Emilia – Jan 27

Foxx, Jamie – May 21, Nov 27

Freeman, Morgan – Apr 29, Dec 22

Gable, Clark – Oct 30

Gambon, Michael – Feb 19, Aug 5

Garfield, Andrew – Apr 6

Garland, Judy – Mar 4, Nov 4

Garner, Jennifer – Sep 21

Gibson, Mel – Jan 10, Oct 6, Oct 18

Gish, Lillian – Nov 7, Nov 8

Goldblum, Jeff – Mar 29

Gonzalez, Rick – Apr 25

Gooding Jr., Cuba – Jul 20
Gosling, Ryan – Sep 4
Grant, Hugh – Oct 11
Greer, Dabbs – Oct 15
Gregory, Andre – Jun 3
Gullette, Sean – Sep 2
Gurira, Danai – Apr 15
Gwenn, Edmund – Dec 25
Haas, Lucas – Sep 18
Hall, Rebecca – Jul 8
Hanks, Tom – Jan 12, Jan 21,
    Feb 10, May 18, Jul 15,
    Sep 28, Sep 29, Sep 30
Hannah, John – Jul 31
Hardy, Tom – Jun 30
Harris, Ed – Apr 16, Jun 19
Harris, Richard – Aug 7
Harrison, Rex – Jun 25
Hathaway, Anne – Jul 19, Dec 9
Hawke, Ethan – Mar 21,
    Jun 23, Jul 13
Hayek, Salma – Aug 3, Aug 10
Hepburn, Audrey – Aug 18,
Oct 19, Nov 5
Hepburn, Katherine – Nov 11
Hoffman, Dustin – Feb 12,
    Mar 27, Mar 28, May 10,
    May 30
Hogan, Paul – Jul 23
Holland, Tom – Apr 10
Hopkins, Anthony – Jun 12,
    Jul 28, Dec 23
Hordern, Michael – Apr 11
Hoskins, Bob – Jan 16
Hoult, Nicholas – Oct 9
Howard, Bryce Dallas – Aug 24
Hunt, Linda – Jul 3

Hunter, Holly – Dec 7
Huston, Walter – Sep 1
Ivanek, Željko – Dec 27
Jay, Tony – Dec 16
Jenkins, Richard – Apr 30
Jones, Henry – Nov 9
Jones, James Earl – Jan 8
Keaton, Diane – Nov 20
Keener, Catherine – Apr 5
Keitel, Harvey – Sep 16
Kelly, Gene – Nov 3
Kemper, Charles – Oct 7
Kidder, Margot – Nov 28
Kidman, Nicole – Mar 18
Kingsley, Ben – Apr 3
Knightley, Kiera – Apr 7
Kozlowski, Linda – Jul 23
Kunis, Mila – Jul 12
Lane, Charles – Jul 7
Lane, Nathan – May 28
Law, Jude – Apr 26
Lawrence, Jennifer – Oct 20
Ledger, Heath – May 15
Lee, Bruce – Jun 17
Leno, Jay – Jun 13
Lewis, Leah – May 17
Lewis, Rawle D. – Dec 13
Lloyd, Christopher – May 13
Lucas, Josh – May 22, May 23
Luke, Derek – Aug 9
MacMurray, Fred – Nov 2
Malek, Rami – Jan 9
Mara, Rooney – Nov 30
March, Fredric – Nov 19
Martin, Strother – Mar 11
McConaughey, Matthew –
    Jun 14, Sep 20

McDowell, Malcom – Jun 15
McGinley, John C. – Feb 2
McGrath, Tom – Dec 10
McKellen, Ian – May 6, May 7,
    Dec 11, Dec 31
Menzel, Idina – Dec 17
Meredith, Burgess – Aug 15
Miller, Penelope Ann – Oct 10
Moore, Julianne – Sep 5
Moran, Nick – Jun 21
Morita, Noriyuki – May 31
Mortensen, Viggo – Jul 27
Murphy, Eddie – May 8,
    May 9, Dec 3
Murray, Bill – Jan 28, Aug 22,
    Dec 2
Neeson, Liam – Mar 16,
    May 26
Newman, Paul – Nov 25
Newton-John, Olivia – Feb 11
Nicholson, Jack – Mar 3,
    May 29
Noiret, Philippe – Dec 12
Norton, Edward – Jul 10
O'Connell, Jerry – Oct 31
O'Connor, Donald – Nov 1
O'Conor, Hugh – Jul 22
Olin, Lena – Jun 16
Osment, Haley Joel – Jul 21,
    Dec 15
Oz, Frank – Jan 6, May 4
Pacino, Al – Jun 22, Jul 24,
    Jul 25, Oct 12
Paltrow, Gwyneth – Jun 24
Pattinson, Robert – May 24
Peck, Gregory – Nov 5
Penn, Sean – Mar 17, Jul 1

Perkins, Anthony – Mar 10
Phoenix, Joaquin – Aug 25
Pitt, Brad – Jan 25, Feb 1,
    Jul 28, Aug 16, Sep 25
Piven, Jeremy – Aug 2
Plemons, Jesse – Aug 19
Plummer, Christopher – Feb 3
Powell, Clifton – Nov 27
Puri, Om – May 1
Rains, Claude – Mar 12
Ralls, Lee – Jun 11
Redford, Robert – Aug 1,
    Nov 12
Redgrave, Vanessa – Sep 17
Redmayne, Eddie – Feb 26
Reeve, Christopher – Nov 28
Reeves, Keanu – Mar 30
Reilly, John C. – Apr 2
Reynolds, Ryan – Sep 26
Rhys, Matthew – Sep 3
Richardson, Haley Lu – Dec 5
Riegert, Peter – Jun 20
Robbie, Margot – Feb 29, Jul 14
Robbins, Tim – Jan 4
Roberts, Julia – Oct 11
Robinson, Leon – Dec 13
Rockwell, Sam – May 19,
    May 20
Roth, Tim – Jan 30, Aug 26
Ryan, Meg – Jul 30
Sabella, Ernie – May 28
Sandler, Adam – Aug 11
Sarandon, Susan – Feb 16,
    Jul 1, Jul 26
Scheider, Roy – Mar 6
Schwarzenegger, Arnold
    Nov 16

Sciorra, Annabella – Jun 7

Sharma, Suraj – Jan 31

Sheen, Martin – Oct 1

Sheffer, Craig – Jan 14

Siddig, Alexander – Jan 15

Sizemore, Tom – Oct 25

Smith, Maggie – Apr 19, Aug 4

Smith, Will – Mar 1

Smoove, J.B. – Aug 11

Somerville, Phyllis – Oct 14

Spacey, Kevin – Feb 21

Spano, Vincent – Jun 20

Stallone, Sylvester – Jan 17, Jun 20

Stewart, James – Jan 18, Oct 5

Stiller, Ben – Feb 17

Stoll, Corey – Jun 28

Stone, Emma – Sep 4

Stowe, Madeleine – Jun 27

Streep, Meryl – Mar 2, Sep 10, Sep 14, Sep 15

Subor, Michael – Feb 22

Swayze, Patrick – May 1

Swinton, Tilda – Feb 13

Sydow, Max von – Jun 8

Theron, Charlize – May 25

Thomas, Kristin Scott – Aug 1

Thomsen, Cecilie – Mar 24

Timberlake, Justin – Dec 1

Torn, Rip – Dec 14

Tracy, Spencer – Nov 18, Nov 19

Travolta, John – Feb 11

Turturro, John – Sep 24

Unnamed Warriors – Mar 8

Ustinov, Peter – Nov 13

Van Holt, Brian – Apr 21

Venable, Evelyn – Aug 13

Vikander, Alicia – Nov 21, Nov 22

Waltz, Christopher – Jan 1 **(Alita: Battle Angel)**

Wangchuk, Jamyang Jamtsho Jan 26, Sep 25

Washington, Denzel – Feb 24, Jul 12, Jul 13, Aug 9, Sep 26, Sep 27, Nov 23, Nov 24

Watanabe, Ken – Jan 2, Apr 1

Watson, Emma – Dec 8

Weisz, Rachel – Sep 9

Welles, Orson – Oct 22, Oct 23

Whishaw, Ben – Jul 11

Wilder, Gene – Feb 7

Williams, Michelle – Sep 8

Williams, Robin – Jan 22, Jan 29, Apr 20, Jun 6, Jun 9, Jun 10, Dec 26

Wilson, Mara – Jan 20

Wisocky, Rebecca – Jun 19

Witherspoon, Reese – Apr 12

Wokoma, Susan – Jul 2

Wood, Elijah – Jan 7, May 6, May 7

Woods, James – Dec 14

Yeoh, Michelle – Aug 30

Yoba, Malik – Dec 13

Zellweger, Reneé – Feb 15, May 14, Sep 11

GRATITUDES

The starting place for my gratitude is the film industry. Without the vast numbers of talented and dedicated people that go in to making each film, particularly those behind the camera, the philosophy and fun generated by movies simply wouldn't be possible. A huge thank you to the studios, distributors, actors, directors, producers, funders, stunt people, scriptwriters, screenplays, lighting, make-up, costume designers, editors, special effects, location scouts and all other contributors, and, of course, the cinemas. My favourite actors, naturally, take up a soft spot in my heart, and at the top of that tree are Mr Washington, Mr Hardy and Ms Theron.

Mum, thank you for always being there. The unconditional love you have poured into me has hopefully found the tiniest of expression through this book. The talent, energy, love and light in me is but a continuation of the goodness that has flown down from you, Granny and all our ancestors.

Dabrar, you are the man! I have so much admiration for you.

Bruce, thank you for your authenticity. The past few years have been a wonderful ride. I've learned a lot more from you than you realise. I love you and only ever wish for your success.

Fraser and Jack, I'm so grateful for you as brothers. Your unique characters are a source of enjoyment to me and I cherish the relationships we have.

To the young Esquire, thank you for your loyalty and belief in me. You are a true friend and a man of integrity.

Bushido Master, the abundance is just beginning and I'm grateful to be sharing it with you. Lock up the fish and get the decks spinning. It's time to stand and deliver.

Miss Wummer, thank you for indulging my wackiness and being such a positive influence on me. Your support is unwavering. The universe loves you!

To the positivity group, a part of this belongs to you. We did it. What's next?

To my dear fellowship. You promised nothing and you have given me everything. Each and every single brother and sister is precious to me and the companionship we share is the hot air that has risen me to new vistas that I could never have dreamed possible. A special thank you to the Llama for your friendship and service – our bond endures.

And to my dear old friend, thank you for your mentorship. Your essence lives on and I shall always cherish the lessons and laughs we shared. You denied and defied God, but I always found you to be one of His biggest advocates, and I fully trust that you now take abode in His halls above.

A very brief word on the influences that have shaped and moulded and given me the inspiration and insights that went into this book, of which these are only a tiny fraction…

Eckhart Tolle for the Power of Now. Your book is profoundly inspirational to me.

Alan Watts for your wisdom, pathos and love to be true to self.

Deepak Chopra for holding space to meditate and be.

Kurzgesagt for injecting fun into astronomy and physics.

Ryan Holiday for the Daily Stoic, a superb daily reader.

Bob Proctor for being such a powerful teacher and man of integrity. I have watched countless of your videos and attended a course. To the degree to which I have implemented your teachings, I have been blessed and elevated. I love you, Bob!

Michael Vazquez for a wholesome fitness energy.

Thank you to IMDB which enabled me to check quotes and film facts.

Thank you to that garish and beautiful orange sofa in Leicester Square where I was visited of my Muse on 23rd June 2020 and a new magic carpet ride began.

Thank you to Alexa at Compass-Publishing UK for your great work and to Ruth at CPI UK for making the printing process feel very natural.

And to all those whose names are not here, but hold a place in my heart, your love, support and kindness are not unnoticed and unacknowledged. Every smile, every hug, every word and prayer and giddy-up (and admonishment) has been gratefully received. The goodness you have authored shall be returned upon you a hundred-fold.

And to God the Eternal Father, and His son, Jesus Christ, all glory be Thine, forever and ever.

- Who are you? **A human being**
- What do you want? **Everything... Nothing**
- Why do you want it? **Om**
- Where are you going? **Home**
- When is the best time? **NOW!**